Rick's experiences as a pastor, a ministry c
and confidant to many pastors and min
wealth of knowledge and understanding
His ability to think and care pastorally, theologically, strategically, and practically has provided great value to those he has served. I am confident this book will provide encouragement and practical wisdom to ministry leaders.
—Eric Geiger, Senior Pastor, Mariners Church, Irvine, California

Rick is a pastor to pastors. He is the real deal—deeply godly and profoundly humble. This is a must-read book for everyone training to become a pastor or navigating their first few years.
—Daniel Im, Lead Pastor, Beulah Alliance Church, podcaster, and author of several books, including *No Silver Bullets*

Comprehensive, helpful, and *golden.* If you asked for three words that come to mind when I read this book, those would be the ones. Rick is one of the wisest and best church practitioners I know. That is because he never pretends to have all the answers. He observes, asks questions, and discerns well. This book is an example of that.
—Ron Edmondson, Lead Pastor, Immanuel Baptist Church, Lexington, Kentucky, author of *The Mythical Leader*

All too often, church-growth ideals are espoused based on polls, statistics, and theories. *The Perpetually Growing Church* is one man's lifelong study of the real-time strategies and practices of churches experiencing decades-long growth. This book not only unearths the practices of perpetually growing churches but also tells you how to do what they are doing. I am honored to endorse this book!
—Pastor Mark Batterson, Lead Pastor, National Community Church, Washington, DC

Rick has finally done it. He has taken all the church growth and healthy learnings over the last 50 years of the church and served them up in *The Perpetually Growing Church.* If you are the lead pastor or serve in leadership of your church, this book is a must! There are so many gold nuggets to help your church reach your community, you don't want to miss any of them. If Kingdom focus is the mission of your church, pick this book up.

—Steve Gladen, Elder and Pastor of Small Groups at Saddleback Church, Lake Forest, California

Rick Howerton has written the book I wish I'd had when I first started in ministry. *The Perpetually Growing Church* is your how-to manual for leading a healthy and thriving church today. Packed with insanely practical tools and recommendations, this is not a book you'll read once—it will be the resource you turn to time and time again for wisdom and guidance.

—Jenni Catron, Founder and CEO, The 4Sight Group

THE PERPETUALLY GROWING CHURCH

Best Practices of America's Most Influential Churches

RICK HOWERTON
FOREWORD BY JOSH HOWERTON

IRON
STREAM

Birmingham, Alabama

The Perpetually Growing Church

Iron Stream
An imprint of Iron Stream Media
100 Missionary Ridge
Birmingham, AL 35242
IronStreamMedia.com

Library of Congress Control Number: 2023948786

Cover design by twolineSTUDIO.com

ISBN: 978-1-56309-678-5 (paperback)
ISBN: 978-1-56309-679-2 (eBook)

1 2 3 4 5—28 27 26 25 24

This book is dedicated to Baptist Campus Ministers, unsung heroes of the faith, the church's outside-the-box Christian leaders discipling the next generation of perpetually growing church leaders.

Today's church and the future church are unknowingly indebted to you!

Contents

Foreword

This may come across as the adult version of "my dad could beat up your dad," but I think it may actually be true that no one in America is more equipped to write a book called *The Perpetually Growing Church* than my dad, Rick Howerton.

Every pastor after God's heart wants their church to grow (a) because God wants their church to grow and (b) because heaven and hell are real.

Problem: Not every strategy to facilitate church growth translates to every church, because churches are just. so. different.
Solution: The Christian Forrest Gump

The movie *Forrest Gump* was so captivating because a humble, curious man from inauspicious beginnings stumbled around the world and by chance or fate found himself a range of experiences so wide as to be absurd—from shrimping in a bayou to Olympic Ping-Pong, from being the origin of the iconic smiley face emoji to winning championships for Bear Bryant and Alabama football.

My dad is that but with churches.

From being a church janitor in rural Kentucky to the stages of Saddleback and Catalyst, God has always just floated Dad in the breeze to the right places at the right times, culminating in a life's worth of experiences for this book.

He served Waddy Baptist Church of ninety people in rural Kentucky. As a college minister, he mentored young men in their embryonic pastoral callings who would go on to plant churches that grew to thousands.

He was on the executive team for one of the first megachurches (I kind of hate that term) in Kentucky in the 1990s, when churches of two thousand or more were like unicorns.

In 2004, he planted a church (before it was cool) in his living room in the Nashville area that to this day is still one of the larger churches there.

As the national small groups consultant at Lifeway, he collaborated and cross-pollinated with churches like Saddleback, North Point, and Southeast Christian.

As a regional coach, he coached a region of more than four hundred churches, helping rural and urban pastors alike overcome obstacles and work through tradition to reach people for Christ.

And at the time of this writing, he serves as the global groups pastor for LakePoint Church, a church of more than twenty thousand with seven campuses in two languages across two countries, and unfortunately for him, his son is his boss and senior pastor. ☺

But arguably the best thing about this book and its author is that he hasn't just perpetually grown churches. His greatest life gift is that he perpetually grows *people*. I have seen this personally. When God called me to pastor at the age of sixteen, my dad saw something in me that I could not see in myself. He helped me write my first sermon, a nine-minute talk for my youth group that had an intro, a conclusion, humor, an illustration, and most important a Jesus-centered message because my dad helped me write it. Our car rides began to be conversations about church governance structures. When he was going to visit a church in which God was moving, he spent the money on an extra plane ticket so that I could come too. He bought me a copy of *The Purpose Driven Church* in 1997 and handed it to a high schooler he wanted to see perpetually grow for the kingdom of God. When he was called away from pastoring his church plant, he handed it off to me (nepotism for the win!) and coached me along the way as it began to grow into the thousands.

Sit down in a comfortable chair. Relax. Begin to dream again about what could be—what *must be*—in light of eternity. And imagine you're sitting across the table from a father (now grandfather!) in the faith who's distilling a lifetime of behind-the-scenes insight into churches that perpetually grow.

Josh Howerton
Senior Pastor
LakePointe Church, Rockwall, Texas

Acknowledgments

I want first to thank my incredible wife, Julie. Throughout the process of writing *The Perpetually Growing Church*, she has sacrificed what she values most: time with me, our family, and friends. Julie, I am indebted to you for taking a lifelong journey with me down the outrageously arduous path of pastoring, church consulting, and church leadership.

I also want to thank many influential pastors and leadership gurus whom I have given my life to learn from, some in face-to-face conversation, others by reading their works, attending their conferences, listening to their podcasts and sermons, or picking the brains of the staff they lead. Pastors like Chris Hodges, Rick Warren, John Maxwell, Ron Edmondson, Craig Groeschel, Josh Howerton, Larry Osborne, Dr. Tim Keller, Steve Stroope, Matt Chandler, and Bob Russell, to name a few.

I also want to thank some dear friends who welcomed me into their circle of friendship and gave me my first inside view of influential megachurches that were perpetually growing. They are Dr. Bill Donahue, Steve Gladen, Bill Willits, and Eddie Mosley.

I am indebted to those who allowed me to share their wise counsel in interviews sprinkled throughout this book (some of whom have already been mentioned): Ron Edmondson, Josh Howerton, Pat Hood, Jenni Catron, Steve Stroope, Chris Kuti, Dr. Bill Donahue, David Martin, Rusty Anderson, Bill Buckingham, Aldger Armstead, Mac Lake, Geoff Surratt, Carlos Erazo, and Bob Russell.

I am also so grateful to the following churches for making available their content to aid you and your church: North Point Community Church (Alpharetta, GA), The Village Church (Flower Mound, TX), Saddleback Church (Lake Forest, CA), Life.Church (Edmond, OK), The Bridge Church (Spring Hill, TN), and LakePointe Church (Rockwall, TX).

Finally, and most important, I want to thank Jesus, my Savior, and the Lord of all. He could've chosen and equipped anyone to go on this journey. But, in His grace, He made the opportunity available to me.

In deep humility,
Rick Howerton

Introduction

Outdistancing Intuition

And the Lord added to their number daily those who were being saved.

—Acts 2:47*b*

Every church was meant to be a perpetually growing church. I realize this statement is counterintuitive. There's a reason for that!

Some church-growth experts have convinced us that a local church will, at some point, become a plateaued or declining church. Many of them will die. They have researched churches across the land, produced statistics to affirm the idea, and concluded that the situation is inevitable. They then declare it in podcast interviews, promote it in blog posts, and write books on the subject. Denominational leaders and seminary professors repeat what these church-growth experts have proclaimed and promoted.

The concept of plateaued, declining, and dying churches has been deeply embedded in ecclesiastical circles. Because these influential voices have saturated the minds of church leaders with the plateaued-declining-and-dying-church concept, church leaders intuitively believe this is the way it is and that it is inevitable.

And so, intuition whispers a lie to us, that churches, like other organizations—organizations devoid of the power of the gospel, the work of the Holy Spirit, and the guidebook of the Word of God—will start strong and grow, plateau, begin a steady decline, and sometimes die.

But Jesus said, "I will build my church" (Matthew 16:18). Does Jesus accomplish what He has promised to accomplish? Of course He does. Because He's God, He's incapable of lying. He *will* build His church. When speaking of the church, Jesus also declared, "The forces of Hades will not overpower it" (Matthew 16:18 HCSB). Does God allow Satan to defeat His bride, the church, the people of God? Never! God promised that "he who is in you is greater than he who is in the world" (1 John 4:4*b* ESV). The God of the universe will always prevail when doing battle with the Enemy.

And Jesus promised that He would send the Holy Spirit, that all believers would be filled with the Holy Spirit, and that the Holy Spirit would empower the church to make the gospel known. When the church releases the Holy Spirit to speak boldly through them, unbelievers respond to the gospel, and the church continues in a consistent growth pattern.

Embrace this fact: when a local church is a unified, biblically functioning church, tuned in to the power of the Holy Spirit, culturally relevant, exercising church-growth principles and practices, and led by spiritually mature, gifted, God-honoring leaders and pastors, it has the potential to be a perpetually growing church.

By author definition, a perpetually growing church is a church that has seen numeric growth over a decade and beyond.

Much of my life has been given to studying, engaging with, and passionately pursuing the principles and practices of perpetually growing churches. Through God's providence, it has been my privilege to work as a staff pastor serving a perpetually growing church, the church planter of a perpetually growing church, a church consultant learning from and consulting perpetually growing churches, a ravenous partaker of content provided by perpetually growing church leaders, and a pursuer of paradigm-shifting conversations with church leaders leading perpetually growing churches.

These experiences brought me to an unarguable conclusion: there are consistent principles and practices at play in perpetually growing churches. This book unearths those principles and practices.

As we begin the journey of revealing how your church might become a perpetually growing church, I need to make you aware of a few important facts.

- *The Perpetually Growing Church* is for churches of all sizes. The principles and practices are effective in any setting. They may need to be scaled down or adapted for a given culture, but they are guidelines, directives, processes, and boundaries for churches of all sizes.
- Some churches are exceptions to the guidance found in this

book. I celebrate God's work in those churches! God, in His providence, sometimes blesses a church with ongoing growth despite the church's missteps or the church's decision to ignore proven church-growth principles and practices.

- Unless affirming a church leader or church, I will not use the names of church leaders or churches. Learning from the missteps of others is helpful, but damaging reputations is never God-honoring.

- While I don't condone any believer's sinful actions, what we can learn from those who have blundered is still undeniably relevant. Some of the church leaders quoted are no longer in the good graces of the church they served due to allegations of wrongful conduct or sins confirmed. But, to not give them credit and yet reveal their strategies would be plagiarism.

- This book is primarily a church-growth book. While I pray nothing unearthed contradicts Scripture, the book is more of a how-to, bringing to the surface the most effective church-growth principles and practices rather than a theological treatise on church life. With this in mind, you will not find a plethora of guidance concerning the most important church practices such as prayer, evangelism, disciple-making, and so on.

- This best-practice book focuses on methodology. Some of the churches mentioned or church leaders interviewed may be at theological odds with your interpretation of Scripture.

- There may be cringeworthy moments. When you experience an inner wince, ask yourself the following questions. (1) Am I feeling uneasy because some of the people who have influenced my ministry (pastors, mentors, church consultants, seminary professors, etc.) would disagree with what I just read? (2) Am I more devoted to my movement's ideology or my denomination's denominational expectations than to effective church practices? (3) Am I fearful of my church's response to such ideas? (4) Am I subconsciously or consciously unwilling to revisit my long-held beliefs?

All churches will not embrace the revealed principles and practices. While the methods found in *The Perpetually Growing Church* are factual, many churches are unwilling to use them. Pastor, don't lose your ministry trying to redirect a church so set in its ways that you become their adversary and thus lose the opportunity to be their pastor/leader/shepherd. If you realize your church will not join you in the journey but believe God intended you to lead a growing church, plant it or go to a church willing to do what it takes to become a perpetually growing church.

Over decades of consulting churches, patterns became evident. Whether aiding a church in embracing and exercising a church-growth practice, creating a ministry, rebuilding a struggling ministry, or resurrecting a dying ministry, (1) the essential principles were established, (2) best practices were acknowledged, and (3) step-by-step procedures were agreed to. I then asked the question, What else can I do to help you? Either the lead pastor or another church leader inevitably asked this question, Who is doing this better than anyone else you know that we can learn from? Then the questions they would have asked the practitioner were asked of me.

With this in mind, throughout *The Perpetually Growing Church*, I'll establish best practices then, when possible, you'll read interviews and excerpts from writings of various experts. Each of the personalities is or has been a lead pastor or staff member of a perpetually growing church. Others are the authorities perpetually growing churches call on to consult them. In every instance, the goal is to allow you, the reader, to hear from those doing the work better than anyone else and for them to answer the questions that you might have asked of them.

Also, when possible, you will find models that you and your church can adapt to use in your setting.

Before diving into the deep waters of church principles, practices, and models, it's imperative that you know and understand the three lanes perpetually growing churches constantly swim in.

Chapter 1

The Three-Lane Church

I have become all things to all people so that by all possible means I might save some.

—1 Corinthians 9:22

Many pastors preach Acts 2:42–46 and its four practices, proclaiming them to their congregation with the promise that if the church devotes itself to these biblical expectations, the church will experience ongoing growth.

Four Biblical Practices

> They devoted themselves to the apostles' teaching, to the fellowship, to the breaking of bread, and to prayer.
>
> Everyone was filled with awe, and many wonders and signs were being performed through the apostles. Now all the believers were together and held all things in common. They sold their possessions and property and distributed the proceeds to all, as any had need. Every day they devoted themselves to meeting together in the temple, and broke bread from house to house. They ate their food with joyful and sincere hearts. (Acts 2:42–46 CSB)

Four biblical practices are revealed in this passage:

1. learning God's Word (the apostles' teaching)
2. relational and need meeting partnerships within the church body (fellowship)
3. partaking of the Lord's Supper (the breaking of bread)
4. prayer

While these four practices are foundational and essential, today's local church cannot continue a growth trajectory clinging only to these exercises.

I know what you may be thinking—HERESY! I get it. Please read on before you throw this book in the nearest garbage can.

The Early Church and Today's Church, a Comparison

The first-century church had no staff team, no buildings, and no parking lots. The early church didn't have to purchase and stay up to date with the latest technology. The early church wasn't responsible for keeping records of a congregant's giving and sending that information to each church member for tax-deduction purposes. The early church didn't have a paid staff team and the responsibility of managing and leading them.

Let's face it. The first-century church was a simple church on steroids. Many will say that, until Christ returns, the Acts 2 church is how the church should function. They will argue that the four practices unearthed in Acts 2 are all that is needed for a church to grow continually.

I will not argue with their assumption. I will make the case that the churches reaching the most people with Jesus's gospel are churches willing to acknowledge the complexity of the church today.

The Three-Lane Church

Perpetually growing churches unapologetically embrace what I call the three-lane church—the Church Growth Lane, the Biblical Lane, and the Business/Administrative Lane. When each of these three lanes is in play, is synergistic, stays within the boundaries of their responsibility, and knows their role related to the other two lanes, a church has a high chance of being a perpetually growing church.

The Church Growth Lane includes demographics to determine the church's primary target audience. How to best market to connect with those within a wisely determined radius of the church, strategically choosing and transitioning the church's worship style for each generation, revisiting the role and responsibility of the lead pastor as the church grows, and so on. Self-proclaimed biblical purists too often demean church-growth principles and practices.

The Business/Administrative Lane places its attention on the church as organizational. Today's growing church must hire, oversee, and manage a staff team, complete and hold church leaders accountable to the agreed-upon church budget, keep the church grounds and building in meticulous order, oversee church renovation and building projects, be certain background checks on children's and student workers are completed, and so on. These are some of the functions of the Business/Administrative Lane.

The Biblical Lane is the lane unearthed in Scripture. It tells the church what it means to be the church and how to function. Scripture tells the Christian community how to take the gospel to the world, how decisions are to be made, how church members are to relate to one another and the church leadership, what is acceptable and what isn't acceptable in the church body, when and where to meet and how to act when meeting together, and so on.

The following diagram illustrates these three lanes. As you review it, take note of the following: (1) All roads lead to the ultimate goal, making disciples, which triggers numeric growth; (2) the primary, central, and most crucial lane is the Biblical Lane; (3) the arrows pointing from the outer lanes to the center lane indicate that each of the outward lanes passively influences the center lane and is responsible for supporting its work but should never eclipse the authority of the center lane; and (4) the arrows pointing from the center lane to the outward lanes indicate that the Biblical Lane is the most essential and that the outward lanes have as their responsibility to do their work based on the guidance found in the Bible.

Make Disciples, Grow the Church

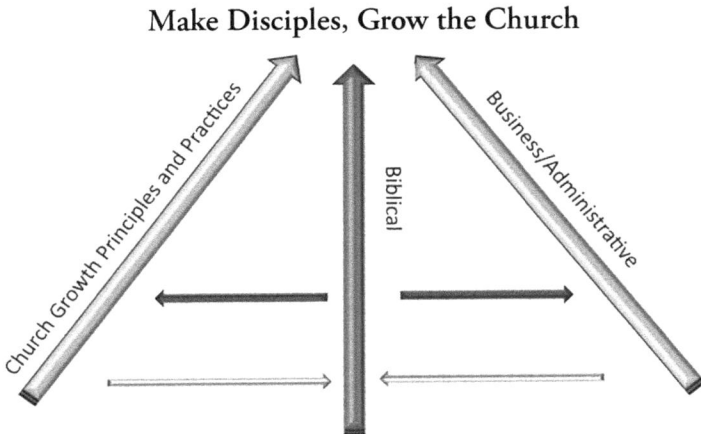

When unparalleled attention is given to the Biblical Lane, and when the other two lanes are doing their work and supporting this lane, in most instances, the church will be a growing church—the people growing spiritually and the church numerically.

Embracing All Three Is Essential?

For more than twenty years, it has been my privilege to consult hundreds of churches. For many of those churches, the mile-high barrier to becoming a perpetually growing church was an inability or unwillingness to embrace the Church Growth Lane or right-minded practices of the Business/Administrative Lane.

Three examples of this barrier are: (1) the trustees and finance team believe they have the authority to make bottom-line decisions on all matters; (2) the lead pastor, deacons, or elders deem church-growth principles and practices as unbiblical, gimmicky, or downplaying the work of the Holy Spirit; (3) the church allows the guiding documents (constitution, by-laws, and so on), influential church members' preferences, or denominational expectations to trump biblical practices.

If you and your church are unwilling to hold to the Three-Lane Church ideals, return this book and get your money back. Why do I declare this so candidly? Because perpetually growing churches live in all three of these lanes, honor each lane unapologetically, and keep each lane in its rightful role and position.

If you are reading this book so your church might become a perpetually growing church, you cannot accomplish the goal without being or becoming a Three-Lane Church.

Section 1

The Lead Pastor

Perpetually growing churches are led by extraordinarily gifted lead pastors who unapologetically and passionately pursue transformed lives at all costs. They are the human catalyst for growth and the undeniable personality driving church life. If the lead pastor isn't leading passionately, prayerfully, and purposefully, the church has no possibility of being a perpetually growing church. For this reason, the first section of this book unearths the roles and responsibilities of perpetually growing church lead pastors.

Chapter 2

A Diverse People

One day, after Moses had grown up, he went out to where his own people were and watched them at their hard labor. He saw an Egyptian beating a Hebrew, one of his own people. Looking this way and that and seeing no one, he killed the Egyptian and hid him in the sand.

—Exodus 2:11–12

God uses all breeds of lead pastors to spearhead perpetually growing churches.

From slap-a-back, hug-a-neck extrovert Rick Warren (Saddleback Church, Lake Forest, California) to more subtle Bob Russell (Southeast Christian Church, Louisville, Kentucky), the people God chooses to lead His church vary in many ways. From the off-the-scale creativity of Ed Young Jr. (Fellowship Church, Grapevine, Texas) to the carefully illustrated expository sermons of Dr. Tony Evans, God uses all kinds of pastors to lead perpetually growing churches. From the extemporaneous ardor of Steven Furtick (Elevation Church, Charlotte, North Carolina) to the measured, professorial style of Dr. Tim Keller (Redeemer Presbyterian Church, Manhattan, New York), God uses all kinds of people to lead perpetually growing churches.

Inspiring or Devitalizing Authenticity

It has been my honor to spend meaningful time with lead pastors of some perpetually growing churches. Pastors such as Bob Russell, Steve Stroope (LakePointe Church, Rockwall, Texas), Ron Edmondson (Immanuel Baptist Church, Lexington, Kentucky), and Josh Howerton, my favorite and my son (The Bridge Church, Spring Hill, Tennessee, and LakePointe Church, Rockwall, Texas). Each of these individuals welcomes others with open arms and gracious hearts. A conversation with them encourages and inspires. Although they lead or have led some of the most successful churches in the country, they give time to those many perceive to be everyday nobodies. They are men of impeccable integrity.

While it would be disingenuous to ignore the fact that some perpetually growing churches have been led by aggressive, cavalier people who were disturbingly vainglorious, I believe a church will grow better under the leadership of someone like Bob Russell.

In September 2001, my son Josh was a college student with a passion for learning from the best. His pastor told him if he wanted to learn how to do what God has called him to do, he should take someone who is the best in that area of ministry to lunch, pick their brain, and gain understanding. Somehow my son got a lunch appointment with one of the leading pastors in the country, Bob Russell: "At just twenty-two years of age, Bob Russell became the pastor of Southeast Christian Church in Louisville, Kentucky. That small congregation of 120 members became one of the largest churches in America, with 18,000 people attending the four worship services every weekend in 2006 when Bob retired."[1]

The date of their meeting was a few days after the 9/11 terrorist attacks.

My son made his way to Louisville many hours before his appointment with Bob. While he was on his way there, the phone rang at our home. (This was before ordinary people owned cell phones.) It was Pastor Bob's assistant. She informed me that Bob had had something come up and wouldn't be able to meet with Josh. I let her know that Josh was very excited and asked her to be sensitive when she gave him the bad news. Our phone rang again a few minutes later. Another call from Bob's office. Bob had decided he would meet with Josh. I asked what had happened and was informed that Bob had been asked to discuss the terrorist attacks on a nationally broadcast radio show. After considering his prior commitment, he was forgoing the interview and would be meeting with Josh.

Bob could have grown his audience and magnified his celebrity if he had been someone who cared about being a celebrity, but he chose to do something much more impressive, godly, and kingdom minded: he decided to keep a promise.

Like Pastor Bob, most people God chooses to lead perpetually growing churches are people of exemplary integrity. They are kindhearted, grace-giving, wise, welcoming leaders.

While God in His providence uses pastors of all stripes, many practices of lead pastors spearheading perpetually growing churches are consistent. Those common practices are what we will explore in the first section of this book.

Chapter 3

Visionary

Write the vision;
  make it plain on tablets,
  so he may run who reads it.
For still the vision awaits its appointed time;
  it hastens to the end—it will not lie.
If it seems slow, wait for it;
  it will surely come; it will not delay.
                                    —Habakkuk 2:2*b*–3 ESV

The understructure of a perpetually growing church (PGC) is its vision.

When constructing a building, the foundation—the understructure that everything else stands on—is put in place first. When building a PGC, the church's vision—the understructure—is the first thing put in place. The vision determines the strategy, how resources are allotted, the staff hires, and so much more.

Vision is a mental image of the final outcome, of seeing a God-inspired dream in your mind's eye and being convicted to make that dream a reality.

Pastor Rick Warren declared his vision in his first sermon at Saddleback Church, March 30, 1980. A little more than two hundred people were in attendance.

It is the dream of a place where the hurting, depressed, frustrated, and confused can find love, acceptance, help, hope, forgiveness, guidance, and encouragement.
It is the dream of sharing the Good News of Jesus Christ with the hundreds of thousands of residents in south Orange County.
It is the dream of welcoming 20,000 members into the fellowship of our church family—loving, learning, laughing, and living in harmony together.

9

It is the dream of developing people to spiritual maturity through Bible studies, small groups, seminars, retreats, and a Bible school for our members.

It is the dream of equipping every believer for a significant ministry by helping them discover the gifts and talents God gave them.

It is the dream of sending out hundreds of career missionaries and church workers all around the world and empowering every member for a personal life mission in the world. It is the dream of sending our members by the thousands on short-term mission projects to every continent. It is the dream of starting at least one new daughter church every year.

It is the dream of at least fifty acres of land, on which will be built a regional church for south Orange County—with beautiful, yet simple, facilities including a worship center seating thousands, a counseling and prayer center, classrooms for Bible studies and training lay ministers, and a recreation area. All of this will be designed to minister to the total person—spiritually, emotionally, physically, and socially—and set in a peaceful inspiring garden landscape.[1]

Pastor Rick ended with these words, "I stand before you today and state in confident assurance that these dreams will become a reality. Why? Because they are inspired by God." With this vision, the church grew to an average weekly attendance of thirty thousand in fourteen locations.[2]

PGC pastors saturate the church body with the God-inspired vision and carry the weight of three responsibilities: (1) vision creator, (2) vision caster, and (3) vision protector.

Vision Creator

Creating a compelling and clear vision is crucial. If the vision is compelling, it will imagine a future that is beyond comprehension and will bring people's hearts to life when verbalized. Believers will intuitively realize that God will have to be at work for this thing to be accomplished, leading the church to depend more on God than on its material resources, techniques, and abilities.

When creating your church's vision, five practices are essential for the vision creator:

1. praying for God's guidance
2. imagining something unimaginable
3. silencing the negative internal voice
4. surrounding yourself with dreamers and visionaries
5. including language that captures imagination

Vision Caster

PGC lead pastors are responsible for being the vision caster for the church they lead. No one else can do this effectively, and no one else can carry this burden rightfully. PGC lead pastors remind people of the vision at every opportunity—in sermons, meetings, the celebration of volunteer events, and one-on-one conversations. But the most practiced and most potent vision-casting moment is the annual vision-casting talk.

This once-a-year discourse allows the pastor to remotivate those who have grown weary, recruit those not presently serving, and elevate those who have accomplished much.

This thirty- to forty-five-minute speech is a pastor's most potent tool for unifying a church and motivating a congregation. After reviewing many vision-casting talks by PGC lead pastors, I have found nine elements that are consistently in play:

1. History. The pastor reminds the congregation of the church's humble beginnings and the sacrifices made by the early church membership.

2. Vision. The pastor must describe the vision clearly so that the church membership sees it in their mind's eye.

3. Purpose. By stating the purpose behind all the church is involved in and will be involved in, the congregation embraces the importance of all that is and what will be.

4. Truth. By telling the church where the church has fallen short, the pastor can state why some practices and ministries are being set aside and announce new opportunities and ministries that will be birthed.

5. New Strategies. Let the church know what new strategies will be put in place. This will enlighten everyone and motivate many to consider getting involved in what is to be.

6. Challenge. By raising the bar, the congregation is challenged to make sacrifices—both time-oriented sacrifices and financial sacrifices.

7. Story. Share a story of someone whose life has been transformed by the church's ministry, someone who has been in the church for many years, watched it change for the better, is still on board, and is excited about the future.

8. Goals. Share God-size goals for the upcoming year. By doing this, the pastor is making the church aware that God is still the centerpiece of church life and that the church's dependency is on Him.

9. Roles. Tell the church members how they can involve themselves in accomplishing the revealed goals. In most situations, this includes (1) trusting the church leadership, (2) giving above and beyond the tithe, (3) serving in new ministries or taking on new roles, and (4) gaining more information about new service opportunities and how to join serving teams.

Vision Protector

Even pastors of PGCs experience individuals at high levels of leadership who have their own dreams in mind. They have a vision for the church that contradicts the vision God has in mind. These individuals voice their ideas in meetings and are prone to build coalitions of like-minded cynics. Those in the coalition tell one another that the church is in trouble if it continues its current path.

PGC pastors graciously, lovingly, courageously, and unapologetically do what it takes to protect the God-inspired, God-ordained vision the church is committed to accomplishing. They graciously silence the voices contradicting or redirecting the vision God revealed.

They silence those voices by redirecting meeting discussions when necessary, meeting personally with influential church members who are questioning the direction of the church, dismissing the staff member unwilling to embrace the church's vision, and continually reminding the church body while sermonizing what the vision of the church is and how it will grow God's kingdom.

If you're going to be a PGC, it begins with a rock-solid, God-honoring, God-given, God-size vision. You will know you have that kind of vision when your heart comes to life each time you speak it and your spiritually mature dive wholeheartedly into accomplishing it.

Chapter 4

Leader

And David shepherded them with integrity of heart; with skillful hands he led them.

Psalm 78:72

A myriad of churches have the potential of being PGCs. The church building is within a ten-mile radius of tens of thousands of people. The worship service and programming are geared to the demographic surrounding the church building. The pastor is a gifted communicator and preacher. The congregation is welcoming and downright magnetic. When the church gathers to worship, there are plenty unused seats and empty parking spots. The children's and student ministries are off the charts. The elders and church body will do whatever it takes to grow the church.

Only one thing is unaccounted for: a pastor leader. The pastor preaches to, cares for, counsels, and consoles his sheep. He administers the sacraments and officiates weddings and funerals with love in his heart. He does precisely what he was taught to do in Bible school or seminary. But for his church to become a PGC he must do more than shepherd his flock. He must learn and live leadership.

Over the last nearly forty years, John Maxwell has influenced pastors and leaders with his books, speaking engagements, conferences, and podcasts. The pastors he has mentored, who have mentored other pastors, have changed the trajectory of today's church. Many PGCs would not be PGCs if it weren't for John Maxwell. Having pastored a growing church himself, John knows the importance of pastor leaders.

In John's groundbreaking book *Developing the Leader Within You*, he establishes a truth that mustn't be ignored, "The key to success in an endeavor is the ability to lead others successfully. Everything rises and falls on leadership."[1]

I once consulted a church frustrated that they weren't seeing numeric growth. My conversation with the lead pastor revealed why the church was stuck. When I told the pastor the importance of leadership and how he could become a strong leader, he heroically declared, "I preach, pray, console people in the hospital, visit the widows, and counsel the brethren. That's what a shepherd does, and that's what I'm going to do!"

His declaration concreted the trajectory of his church. The church would never be a growing one, much less a perpetually growing one, due to his lack of leadership.

A leader leads the pack on a journey to fulfill a pre-determined vision. A leader builds infrastructure to accommodate the organization that will accomplish the work. A leader is responsible for being certain those following him are placed in the right seats and are equipped to do the work they are made to do. And a leader carries the daily load of overseeing the moving parts.

Leaders are proactive, passionate out-fronters leading the pack. Leaders lead!

Pastor, the growth of your church rises and falls on your passion for leadership, your knowledge of leadership, your ability to lead, and your willingness to lead. No church will ever be a PGC without a pastor who leads!

Ron Edmondson is a leader's leader. He served as the CEO of Leadership Network, planted two churches, and successfully revitalized three churches. The churches Ron pastored appeared on *Outreach* 100's fastest-growing churches list a total of six years. He has a master's degree in organizational leadership and is the author of multiple books, including *The Mythical Leader: The Seven Myths of Leadership*. The Ron Edmondson Leadership Blog was ranked #6 Top Leadership Blog in 2021. Ron also coaches leaders and consults churches. He currently serves as senior pastor of Immanuel Baptist Church in Lexington, Kentucky.

A recent interview I had with Ron will educate, challenge, and most of all, inspire you to be the best leader you can be.

Author: On a scale of 1 to 10, how important is it that a lead pastor acquire knowledge of and exercise leadership in order for

the church they lead to experience growth? Why do you say so?
Pastor Ron: A lot of this is probably determined by the church itself. In my experience, some churches are harder to lead than others. Certainly, some governing structures change the amount of leadership required by the pastor. But leadership is required for anyone desiring to do ministry. And that seems to be more important now than ever in my career.

I would suggest that the older the church and congregation, the more difficult it can be to lead sometimes. People tend to get set in their ways, and navigating change becomes more difficult the longer we have done things a certain way.

That said, I have been involved in church planting as well and that requires a certain level of leadership. We were going in new directions all the time simply for the fact the church was new.

So, I guess I've contradicted myself to the point of saying leadership is necessary in all contexts. I have certainly never interacted with a pastor who wished they didn't have more leadership expertise or training. To answer your question, let me give it a 9 in level of importance. I don't think it is "everything," but it is certainly high on the list of things that will make a pastor successful.

Author: You coach pastors. Through coaching, what have you concluded are the leadership blind spots many pastors are unaware of?
Pastor Ron: Many times I think it's the assumptions we make as leaders. If we aren't hearing anything negative, we assume everything is going okay and everyone is in agreement with our leadership. I have learned, often the hard way, that silence does not always indicate agreement. Great leaders ask great questions. They explore the pulse of people and keep their "ear to the ground" to see where people are about issues in the church—especially during seasons of change.

Another blind spot is expecting people you know and trust the most to always have your back when controversy arises. Unfortunately, this one came to me through personal experience as well. Hopefully, every pastor has a few people they can always trust, but I have experienced many times that you just have to cross someone's comfort zone before you discover they weren't as supportive as you thought they would be. And let's be honest. This one hurts when it's discovered.

Of course, there are always the so-called sacred cows in every church. You don't often identify those until you try to change them. Even churches that say you have liberty and freedom to change things will resist when one of these sacred cows is touched. And, in fairness, I'm not sure some churches have even identified them as sacred cows until someone does try to change them.

Finally, and this is a big one, many pastors fail to realize the toll ministry is having on their families until the damage is done. I've met with so many pastors who have spouses ready to quit the church long before they were, and the pastor simply didn't know it. The pastor simply didn't realize that what affects them always comes home with them and affects the family.

Author: You are one of and have relationships with some of the other most effective and influential lead pastors in the country. What qualities are consistent in pastor leaders of this caliber?
Pastor Ron: Well, I would first say many of them are more introverted than you might realize. Some of the largest churches are pastored by introverts. It has contributed to some of them being labeled as aloof when met in public when often it is simply them being naturally quiet. I have written many times about how introversion works well for me as a senior leader, but there are downsides to being introverted as well.

But I would say two things jump out to me that are consistent in some of these leaders. Either they are very big picture and strategic minded, or they are willing to delegate issues of strategy to others on the team.

There are a few, not many, very visionary leaders who are also gifted at strategy development. They know how to build the right plan to get things done. I find more of the big-vision type people who stink at the strategy part. They need people around them who can implement the vision and "make it happen." These successful leaders are willing to empower people to carry out the work without micromanaging them. They do what only they can do.

Granted, this makes it more difficult for pastors of small churches. And this is the most frequent pushback I get when I suggest delegating strategy and implementation to others. But even in a small church I think there are usually people—often high-level volunteers—who are capable of assisting the pastor carry out the vision if the pastor is willing to entrust them with it. I'm not pretending that is easy or that you won't get burned in the process, but it is necessary if you want to remain sane and help the church reach full potential.

Author: What are some of the obstacles many lead pastors must overcome if they're going to become effective leaders?

Pastor Ron: The desire to please people over the desire to achieve the mission is probably the one I would point to first. Most pastors by nature want to please others. We all like to be liked and pastors are especially called to be caring, compassionate, and cooperative. Unfortunately, when a pastor sets out to please everyone, they end up pleasing no one. Everyone is unhappy with something because no progress will be made unless change is made. And change always comes with an emotional reaction. Some will like it and some simply won't.

Along the same lines, pastors have to learn to navigate conflict in a healthy way. Again, there is no change without a certain degree of resistance to it. That's very natural. Many pastors resist making some of the changes they know need to be made because they don't want to handle the conflict that goes along with it. They have usually experienced this in the past, and it keeps them from making changes in the future.

Also, pastors must avoid the sense that they have to be in control for success to be realized. They must learn to delegate and empower people within the church. This is hard for some pastors. Often, they feel it is their assigned role. But I would suggest it might be what's holding them back from growing as leaders and growing the church.

Finally, I would say the pastors must learn to protect their calendar and their soul. The church is not going to do that for them. In fact, the church will expect the pastor to be all things to all people. There will be an expectation to be at every event, even at the expense of the pastor's family.

Author: Can every lead pastor become an effective leader? If so, why do you say so? If not, why do you say so?

Pastor Ron: I think so. With enough effort, willingness to learn, and sometimes involving a coach, leadership can be an acquired trait. You may not have the spiritual gift of leadership, but you can learn good leadership skills and lead the church in a healthy way. I say that simply because most of the leadership skills I have now I learned along the way of leading. They were taught to me by other leaders or by experience—often the experience of trying something and doing it the wrong way and learning from that to lead better in the future.

   We all know pastors who simply didn't learn good leadership skills and either bottomed out or burned out, and many of them are no longer in the ministry or they simply allowed their churches to continue to decline. Of course, God is ultimately in charge of His church. That includes numbers of attendance and baptisms. But I believe God uses the skills of good leadership to accomplish those types of things.

Author: What would you say to lead pastors like those in the illustration I gave who are unwilling to consider learning and living leadership?

Pastor Ron: I would say, first of all, I still love you, but you are doing it the hard way. It is simply to your advantage as a pastor and to the church for you to continue to grow as a leader.

   And since we are talking leadership in the church, I might add this becomes a kingdom issue.

   Failing to grow as a leader is likely keeping you from realizing all that God would have you to do in the church. There are likely ministries to be started or improved, people to be developed (discipled), and lives to be changed that will be done only when you grow your leadership skills.

Author: What plan of action would you suggest to lead pastors who want to become off-the-charts leaders?

Pastor Ron: I think this looks different for everyone. For some, this may be going back to school and getting another degree in leadership. For others, it might be reading all the leadership books you can find, and for others, it might be listening to podcasts.

I would definitely say all pastors can benefit from having a mentor and/or coach in leadership. This doesn't necessarily have to be someone who is paid; although it could be. Most of the time, for me, it has not been. I try to glean from successful leaders in our church and in the community.

I have been surprised how willing other leaders are to invest in people who want to learn and grow from their experience. I have received leadership development from my relationships with business owners, community leaders, and other pastors.

So, start there. Look around for someone you sense or know has been successful in leading others and make the ask. Ask them to meet with you once a month or once a quarter. Come prepared with questions. Don't make them come prepared. You do the preparation. Don't waste their time but glean from their answers. There is usually gold at the end of this rainbow. Certainly that's always been my experience when I've been intentional to seek mentoring.

The bottom line is pastors have to have a desire for this level of improvement in their leadership. If the desire is there, the pastor will find a way to make it happen. And again, if I might be so frank, I believe without that desire there are kingdom issues at stake.

The necessity of *a leader* to accomplish a God-size vision cannot be overlooked. The Israelites would've remained slaves to the Egyptians if not for Moses. The land God promised wouldn't have been in the ownership of God's people if it hadn't been for Joshua. The walls of Jerusalem would've never been rebuilt without Nehemiah. And the gospel wouldn't have been taken to the Gentiles if it hadn't been for Paul.

God calls leaders to accomplish His most significant undertakings. Pastor, you are that leader.

Chapter 5

Clarity Producer

For God is not a God of disorder but of peace—as in all the congregations of the Lord's people.

1 Corinthians 14:33

PGC pastors realize disharmony leads to dysfunction. Dysfunction creates sideways energy. Sideways energy keeps the church from efficiently and effectively deep-diving into the transformational work of making the gospel known and disciple-making. When there's disunity, pastors find themselves fixing what's broken rather than leading a movement. My son Josh, who is the lead pastor of LakePointe Church in Rockwall, Texas, likes to say, "Clarity produces unity, and unity produces growth."

What Is Happening

If you ask most rapidly growing churches what their three most significant weaknesses are, in almost every instance, communication makes the list.

Growing churches have many moving parts to capture and tame, and varying personalities to juggle. This while the whirlwind of perpetual weekly obligations swirls at the pastor like a tornado. The last thing a PGC pastor wants to give time to is clearing up misunderstandings and misrepresentations. But doing so is an essential task.

We live in a world of spin, both purposeful and accidental. A verbalized statement or a written sentence is easily misconstrued. When a misinterpreted communication begins to filter through the church staff and church body, it is often augmented. The outcome is a distorted concept of what is. If not addressed, the distortion will become a perceived reality and potentially will interrupt workflow, suspend momentum, and create mistrust.

What Needs to Happen

What needs to happen begins with predetermined, documented, stated values/convictions. The written proclamations describe the church's values, honored practices, ideals, and actions. Keeping everyone on the same page is a high-level priority for PGC lead pastors. Bringing clarity to what needs to happen and what is happening is essential.

Pastor Craig Groeschel, who leads PGC Life.Church, created an amazing and practical vision/conviction document for his church. This document tells his church who they are, what needs to happen, and what is rejected.

- **We are faith-filled, big thinking, bet-the-farm risk-takers.** We'll never insult God with small thinking and safe living.
- **We are all about the "capital C" Church!** The local church is the hope of the world and we know we can accomplish infinitely more together than apart.
- **We are spiritual contributors not spiritual consumers.** The church does not exist for us. We are the church and we exist for the world.
- **We give up things we love for things we love even more.** It's an honor to sacrifice for Christ and His church.
- **We wholeheartedly reject the label "megachurch."** We are a microchurch with a megavision.
- **We will do anything short of sin to reach people who don't know Christ.** To reach people no one is reaching, we'll have to do things no one is doing.
- **We will lead the way with irrational generosity.** We truly believe it is more blessed to give than to receive.
- **We will laugh hard, loud, and often.** Nothing is more fun than serving God with people you love!
- **We will be known for what we are for, not what we're against.** There are already enough jerks in the world.[1]

By outlining exactly what is expected, the church body can move together in unity and toward the larger goal.

If your church hasn't yet created a convictional list like the one you see here, consider biblical truth, your people's hearts, and your culture, and then create your church's conviction document. The day you do that, there will be more unity, concern for those far from Christ, generosity, and passion for the spiritual lives of the next generation.

Chapter 6

Culture Creator

Come, let us sing for joy to the Lord;
let us shout aloud to the Rock of our salvation.
Let us come before him with thanksgiving
and extol him with music and song.

—Psalm 95:1–2

A joy-filled culture is the PGC's invisible superpower. It subdues the heart and holds it captive. When a guest attends a church for the first time, whether believer or unbeliever, and is blindsided by an authentic, joy-filled community, that person is hooked. The relational warmth and thrill of the ride compel them back again and again. The unbeliever often becomes a Christ-follower, and the believer seeking their next church often dives into church membership.

Also, when pursuing an off-the-charts staff member, a PGC's most attractive selling point is a joy-filled culture. In a world full of churches exhibiting negativity and conflict, the possibility of landing in a community full of grace, joy, and laughter is a dream come true, especially when the staff hire will be working in that environment daily.

The *Merriam-Webster* dictionary defines *culture* as "the set of shared attitudes, values, goals, and practices that characterizes an institution or organization."[1]

PGCs instill shared attitudes, values, goals, and practices. They are written in stone and are expectations of the church leadership and membership. As the targeted group lives them, the coveted culture is an invisible and recognizable outcome.

As you peruse The Bridge Church (Spring Hill, Tennessee) staff values below, you'll intuitively realize how a set of pre-determined values lived out generates a magnetic, exhilarating, almost idyllic culture.

Attractive Spirituality—The undeniable quality that you can only have when you walk with God that attracts people to God.

Reject Good for Great—God gave us his very best and we should want to bring our best before the Lord, not wanting things to simply be "good enough." We should always be looking for ways to make the good things we do great.

Bleed for the Bride—Having a tangible, transferable passion and excitement for the "Bride of Christ," the church. As much as we want our people to be excited about their local church, we want them to be even more excited for what Christ is doing in the whole church.

Hone Your Craft—If one chooses to stop learning, by default they have chosen to stop leading.

Honor Up, Down, and All Around—Romans 12:10 (HCSB) says, "outdo one another in showing honor." We want a culture where it feels very normal for encouraging words and honor to happen.

Laugh Loud, Hard, and Often—Having fun and enjoying serving God because we have more reason to rejoice than anyone, the tomb is empty!

Do Whatever It Takes—The willingness to put the mission of God and the church as a whole above their own values, preferences, and desires.[2]

The lead pastor carries multiple responsibilities if an intoxicating culture is going to saturate the staff team.

- *Create the staff values.* Creating the staff values is best done with the staff team. Going through the process together gives ownership of the expectations to every team member. When a staff team has ownership of the staff values, they are more apt to live the staff values.
- *Instill the staff values.* Each time the staff meets (or at the least, monthly), remind the team of a staff value, train on a staff value, or concrete a staff value by telling the story of someone

who lived a staff value and how they practiced that staff value.

- *Model the staff values.* The pastor must model the staff values and see that his executive team does the same.
- *Celebrate those who live the staff values.* At meetings, the pastor should focus on one of the staff values, speak of someone who has practiced that staff value and how that person exhibited it, and publicly present a small gift (gift card, half-day off, and so on) to that staff member.
- *Discipline or dismiss those unwilling to practice the staff values.* The pastor must never be okay with someone ignoring or downplaying any of the staff values. A staff member who isn't living the staff values must be spoken to. Those who continue to ignore the responsibility must be disciplined. And those who have proven they aren't going to live the staff values must be dismissed. They are toxic and will ultimately destroy the culture the pastor is working diligently to create.

A word of wisdom: abilities and accomplishment never trump protecting culture. Staff members hitting home runs in their work but unwilling or unable to live the staff values will keep a church from ever exhibiting a life-transforming, joy-filled culture. Their attitude will spill over into the other staff members and the ministry they lead. Those staff members must be released.

PGCs realize an extraordinary culture must be created church-wide, not just in the staff ranks. The lead pastor makes sure preestablished values saturate the entire church.

The Bridge Church also created the following culture-establishing content. These are the values to be lived out by the congregation.

Our Culture

It is possible to deny with our culture what we declare with our message. As a church, we've decided we're going to create the following gospel culture to be a living testament to our gospel message.

The following are the who-we-are values that drive our what-we-do ministry decisions . . .

Gospel Centrality—Our symbol is a cross, not a ladder. We preach good news, not good advice. Our message to the world is "it is finished," not "get to work!"

We Breathe Grace—We will NEVER deny with our culture what we declare with our message. As we inhale grace from God, we will exhale grace toward people.

Courageous Vulnerability—We are done pretending and performing because in Christ we're already approved.

Joyful Generosity—We truly believe it's more blessed to give than receive. It is an honor to sacrifice for Jesus and his church.

Welcome Home—Our attitude toward returning sinners isn't a judgmental, "Where have you been?" It's a joyful, "Welcome home." We are a church where you can belong before you believe.

Ambitions as Big as God's Promises—We are faith-led, bet-the-farm risk-takers. We will never insult God with small thinking and safe living.

Missional Aggression—Because heaven and hell are real, the church doesn't just exist for us. WE. ARE. THE. CHURCH. AND WE EXIST FOR THE WORLD.

We Laugh Loud, Hard, and Often—We are as glad as the tomb is empty. Let us eat, drink, and be merry for yesterday we were dead!

We Do More by Doing Less—We believe we will have a greater gospel impact by doing a few things well than by doing more things poorly.[3]

My son, Pastor Josh Howerton, took over The Bridge Church when the average worship attendance was just over one hundred people. In less than ten years, the church grew to an average weekend worship attendance of more than three thousand. Presently Josh is the lead pastor of LakePointe Church in Rockwall, Texas, a church with more than twenty thousand attendees on seven campuses.

Pastor Josh believes wholeheartedly that a church's culture invigorates church members to tell their friends they need to give the church a try. The culture also engages unbelievers, so they want to come back again and again. You'll want to take a deep breath and slow down your reading rhythm before swimming in the waters of my interview with him. Because in this treasure chest, there's church-growth gold!

Author: Why are you so passionate about creating a captivating culture?

Pastor Josh: When talking with pastors, I often tell them, "The culture you create is more important than the vision you cast." Everyone told me I needed an amazing vision statement when I was a church planter. They asked if I had created a vision statement that would make people want to charge through a brick wall with me. I believe this idea is massively overrated. If we have an incredibly healthy vision but an unhealthy culture, people will either leave the church in a few months or get hurt if they stay. If a church has an incredibly life-giving culture and a weak vision, my gut is people will flock to it, and their lives will be changed. I also believe that a compelling staff culture gives you a competitive advantage. In a healthy culture, level-three inputs tend to get level-eight outcomes, and in an unhealthy culture, people put in level-eight energy and get level-three results.

Let me illustrate the importance of a captivating culture. A former elder I served alongside had invited his mother to church for years, but she would never come. One day they got a text from her on a Sunday afternoon stating how great the church service was. The elder was shocked. His mother had driven from out of town to attend. When the elder asked her what compelled her to attend, her response was "I just wanted to be in a room with a group of people who were that excited to be there."

That's the power of a captivating culture.

Author: How would you describe the culture you're striving to create?

Pastor Josh: A culture where people love and follow Jesus; where they honor up, down, and all around; where they make it fun; where they reject good for great; where they love the church they're serving; where they do whatever it takes. The list is our church leadership's expectations of every staff member.

Author: What might a lead pastor have to do away with before beginning the process of creating an exceptional culture, and what approach have you used to build the list of values that is the catalyst for an extraordinary culture?

Pastor Josh: This is an insightful question. Craig Groeschel points out that your culture is always a combination of what you create and what you allow. If you want to change the culture, change what you tolerate and what you expect. The two times I've created culture, on the front end, it required undoing and removing things. John Kotter, a well-known organizational leadership guru, says, "Behavior from important people in an organization, contrary to the vision, overwhelms all other forms of communication."[4] Your culture will not be what you teach, it will not be what you say, and it will not be what you want. Your culture will be what you are. You create what you embody. To create a specific culture, you have to remove anyone from leadership who stubbornly embodies an anti-value.

For instance, both times we set out to do culture creation, the executive team placed the names of the key leaders in front of us. We asked the question, What five people embody the best of the church? Everyone privately wrote down their list of names, and then we fought about it. This discussion took a couple of hours. We continued until we reached a consensus. Then we asked the question, What characteristics do they all have in common? We fought again until we reached a consensus. It took many meetings to create this list, days—maybe weeks. Once we concluded the specific characteristics they embodied, we had uncovered our leadership behaviors.

Defining a culture is not like building a house, creating

something that wasn't there before. Defining a culture is like an archaeological dig. You're discovering what's hidden. There is a culture that every leadership team values. Most organizations have just never unearthed it. That process is a culture-uncovering process.

Once we define the values that describe the culture we strive to create, we need to remove anyone who stubbornly embodies an anti-value. Everyone questionable isn't removed. Only those who *stubbornly* embody anti-values. Those who make statements such as "That's just not who I am" or "That's just not my personality" will most likely not make the team.

I once had a staff member who would say "Sarcasm is my love language." Each time this individual would sarcastically put someone else down, someone on the leadership team would point out the indiscretion. This individual's behavior didn't change. After many conversations, the staff member said, "The value of honoring up, down, and all around is just not who I am. It's not my personality." There was no option. The staff member was removed.

Every pastor needs to realize an important fact. When someone is disciplined to the point of dismissal, the rest of the staff realizes that the lead pastor and the rest of the leadership team are truly serious about creating a healthy, captivating culture.

A church's culture will always be a combination of what you create, what you allow. To change a culture, a pastor must change what is expected and what is tolerated.

Author: Describe a couple of hard calls you've had to make to protect the church's culture.
Pastor Josh: When you are a key leader, it's hard to admit that your behavior has to change. At one point, it was brought to the leadership team's attention that we weren't embodying one of the staff values. We had a tendency to make sarcastic put-downs. We were forced to admit to the rest of the staff that we were falling short. We had to humble ourselves and own it. We apologized and promised to change.

It's also difficult when hiring. Sometimes you're interviewing a candidate who is experienced and off-the-charts capable of doing the work you would be asking of them with excellence. But you realize they are not going to embody the staff values. You are forced to make a hard call and pass on them. When hiring, our lead team will often say "Don't get distracted by talent."

Author: How much time should a pastor give a staff member struggling to live the staff values before dismissing them?
Pastor Josh: People need time and grace. No one's going to get it perfect. Again, you remove people who *stubbornly* embody an anti-value. For me, if somebody's going to get dismissed, it should not surprise that person. I will keep people longer than they deserve to ensure their dismissal is not a surprise to them.

But, when those people are trying, I'll give them grace for a long period of time. As long as they're receiving correction and I'm seeing any level of progress, I'll keep working with them.

Author: On a scale of 1 to 10, 1 being culture is of no importance to church growth, 10 being the culture is essential for exponential growth, what number would you place on the importance of a healthy, joy-filled culture?
Pastor Josh: 10, 9.5, 11. I'm not being specific because it's evident to everyone that there have been churches that grew, and the culture at the church was toxic. But, they were like a dead plant that grew big. Some of them crumbled under the weight of their own toxicity.

A church can grow without a healthy culture. It's very rare and the growth is fleeting. There are multiple examples of prominent churches—even some of the most influential churches in the country—that fell apart when the toxic culture came to light.

Every pastor should remember this fact. I say it often. People are not on a truth quest. They're on a happiness quest. Being a joy-filled church is as important as being a doctrinally accurate church. There's almost nowhere else people can go to be loved, honored, encouraged, and injected with infectious joy than the local church. If a church can create that kind of culture, people will flock to that church, and their lives will be changed.

Culture is the net that captures everyone. Hellions, the spiritually abused, spiritual babes, and spiritually mature people alike are drawn to a joy-filled, caregiving, impassioned culture. Every pastor must do whatever it takes to create a church culture people want to return to again and again.

Chapter 7

Courageous Decision-Maker

Be strong and courageous. Do not be afraid; do not be discouraged,
for the Lord your God will be with you wherever you go.
                                                              —Joshua 1:9*b*

Many churches are one courageous decision away from being a Perpetually Growing Church.

PGC lead pastors need to be undaunted decision-makers. I know of no PGC pastor who didn't dive deep into the dangerous waters of an unpopular decision. They either decided or wisely led the elders and/or the church to a game-changing conclusion. And, at the point of the decision, the church was on its way to experiencing unparalleled growth.

Pat Hood, the lead pastor at LifePoint Church in Smyrna, Tennessee, is a perfect example. The interview below will be convincing and possibly convicting.

Author: When did you become the lead pastor of LifePoint Church?
Pastor Pat: I came to LifePoint Church in 1994 as the youth pastor. I had Associate Pastor added to my title around 1996. I became the copastor with a succession plan in place in 1998. The lead pastor retired in 2001, and that's when I became the lead pastor of LifePoint Church.

Author: How many people were attending at that time?
Pastor Pat: When I came in 1994, the church averaged around five hundred people in worship attendance.

Author: How would you describe LifePoint when you arrived? What changes did you make early on?

Pastor Pat: When I came to LifePoint, the church's title was First Baptist Church, Smyrna, Tennessee. Our worship was what you'd find in many First Baptist churches, very traditional. The only instruments we used were a piano and an organ. We had a choir that sat in the choir loft with a modesty rail and pulpit chairs sitting in front of the rail. All staff, including the youth pastor, were required to wear suits with a tie Sunday mornings. It was everything you think of when you think of a traditional First Baptist church.

Our community was growing with young families who didn't attend church. So, we strategically began to change things around slowly in 1998. At that time, we had two Sunday morning services and a Sunday evening service. We started slowly changing our worship style in our Sunday evening service. We added drums and guitars and began using choruses. Before the changes, our Sunday evening crowd was probably less than one hundred. When we made these changes, it seemed to double within months. So, we began to transition our Sunday morning services and took off the ties.

Author: How would you describe the era that followed the declaring of changes to be made and the era you were implementing change?

Pastor Pat: It was both a glorious time and a stressful time at the same time. It was stressful because our long-term members were more than a little upset with the changes. We had to decide to continue, no matter the cost. It was a difficult time, but it was also glorious because we reached so many new people. Our attendance was exploding. Our giving was increasing, and we were baptizing more people than ever in the church's history. People were still upset, but we were determined to stay the course.

It was rewarding and costly at the same time. We gained so many new people, and the attendance grew so much that we had to add a third service on Sunday morning. We had to start parking people off campus and shuttling them to the church because we were completely out of parking. I remember people walking down the hallway and literally having to turn sideways because the hallways were so jammed. We definitely broke every fire code in existence.

Author: Did you lose any people? If so, how many?
Pastor Pat: Over the next five years, we'd lose more than half the people we started with. The church almost completely turned over. So, it was rewarding but very costly at the same time. Obviously, the reward outweighed the cost.

Author: Based on the church's growth and the ongoing possible future growth, what other changes were necessary?
Pastor Pat: We had grown so much that we had to relocate the church to forty-four acres in 1998. We built a multipurpose facility (gymnatorium), with a master plan to build an auditorium in the near future.

Everything had changed except one thing: our governing structure. It hadn't changed in one hundred years. We had probably fifty committees who had to approve or recommend initiatives to the deacons who met once per month. After deacon approval, it was taken to the monthly business meeting for the church to approve. All salaries were public for anyone in the church to see and vote to raise or decrease. It was a recipe for disunity, and it couldn't support our new model.

So, in 2003, we undertook the task of changing our constitution and by-laws. We moved from a monthly business meeting to an annual business meeting. We moved from deacon control to board control. It was a drastic difference.

The long-term members didn't like our new worship style or casual atmosphere, but we grew, and baptisms and giving were amazing. So, they could express their displeasure . . . and did. But the wind was taken out of their sails by what was happening. But, changing the governing documents was the last straw. In 2004, about three hundred people decided to leave and start another church in town. They were good people. We just couldn't do church together anymore.

Around this time, people began to tell me we needed to change the church's name because we were misrepresenting ourselves. Those who were looking for a traditional First Baptist church experience were shocked when they came in. Those who didn't want a traditional experience were staying away because of our name. But, I had made so many changes and paid such a high price that I was reluctant to begin the process of changing the name.

We were growing so much that we needed more space. So, I put a building team together to determine what we needed to build. We had great plans, but God wouldn't release us to build.

Around this time, God led us into three days of prayer and fasting. During this time, God broke our heart for the nations and led us to start campuses in Brussels, Bangkok, and locally. So, rather than build to bring more people in, we were to send people out. We became a sending church.

As a result, we felt the need to change the name of our church so we could have a consistent name across all campuses. So, we started the process of changing our name from First Baptist to LifePoint. After all the changes I'd been through, I was nervous. But I was overwhelmed with how the people embraced the name change. We had zero resistance and lost no one over this major change. God had changed the church, not just the name and location, but the heart of the church.

Author: Was the decision to revise church life as it once was worth it? If so, why?

Pastor Pat: Due to more changes three hundred members left, and we dropped from about fifteen hundred in attendance to twelve hundred. But, within six months, we were over fifteen hundred again. It was bittersweet—bitter because I hated to lose those people but sweet because the tension was gone. Our pre-COVID-19 numbers were around three thousand in average worship attendance. We're probably averaging 70 percent of that total post-COVID-19.

Author: What would you say to a pastor who has to make a courageous decision that will change the trajectory of his church?

Pastor Pat: All pastors will have to make many changes if they stay in their churches for a long tenure and have a desire for their churches to continue to move forward and take ground. There is no such thing as cruise control if we do our job.

So, I'd tell pastors to make sure they pray hard for the leading of the Spirit. They need the proper balance of patience and drive. Don't try to do it all tomorrow, while at the same time, don't kick the can down the road. He needs to build a team of staff that he knows has his back. He needs to put a lot of change in his pocket with the church, lead well, serve well, love well, and preach well. He also needs to be more concerned with God's kingdom than his. Being a pastor is no job for those more concerned with their job security than leading and shepherding God's people. I would also tell every pastor to build a home in the Word because that's where he needs to live. He needs to be reminded every day who owns his church: Jesus. He needs to be reminded where his marching orders come from. He needs to be encouraged and changed by the Word. I would also tell him not to try to copy what someone else is doing. We need to be aware of what God is doing in other places, but we need to be faithful to what God wants to do in our place.

Pastor Pat Hood's church represents thousands of churches and indicated one prime thing to me—many churches that have existed for more than ten years have, at some moment in time, reached a point of decision that determined the church's trajectory.

The pivotal decisions PGC pastors have courageously made are consistently the same.

- *Deciding to lead the church to be generationally relevant.* PGC pastors realize reaching the next generation with the gospel is more critical than obliging the aging who are already convinced.
- *Deciding to dismiss a staff member.* Releasing a problem staff member who creates unnecessary tension or is incompetent has turned the tide for many churches.
- *Deciding to build.* When the PGC worship center seating

reached 80 percent seating capacity consistently, the lead pastor guided his church to invest in a larger structure. It wasn't easy, and he lost some people, but he reached hundreds more than were lost.

- *Deciding to do multiple worship services.* For many PGCs, the first step to reaching the masses was to add a second worship service. Many screamed, "We'll no longer see our longtime friends!" Others declared, "We'll become two churches!" The pastor elevated the greater calling, to reach people with the gospel, and the church continued a growth trajectory.
- *Deciding to change locations.* The First Baptist Church was located downtown. Urban sprawl had engulfed the region surrounding the church building. The church was made up of a suburban constituency. The church's worship style and practices were geared to reach suburbanites. The lead pastor decided to lead the church to move the building into suburbia. A mutiny followed. Many people left and started a church. The new location was the right decision. The church reached hundreds more than those who started their own congregation.
- *Deciding to change the church's worship style.* Almost every PGC older than fifty years revisited its worship style and now reaches a new and broader audience, the next generation and those far from Christ.
- *Deciding to transition to an elder system.* When the church body votes on all or most matters, church growth often comes to a screeching halt.
- *Deciding to do away with the church's denominational title.* Many PGC churches have removed the denomination's title from their name. They are now reaching people with the gospel who wouldn't consider their church before the decision. Removing this obstacle was key to church growth.

But before diving headlong into an unpopular decision, wise PGC pastors should:

1. Do research, formal or informal, before coming to a conclusion.
2. Consider the timing of the decision they're about to make.

Often a leader is doing the right thing but at the wrong time.

3. Confer with leaders of other churches who have done what they're considering doing. Great leaders want to see if what they're considering worked elsewhere, want to learn how to deal with issues that arise from the decision, and want to master the best way to implement it. By speaking to others who have already been down the road they're considering traveling, they can get the answers to these critical questions.

4. Consider the political overtones of the decision. Suppose the decision under consideration will cause tension in the church so divisive that the initiative might seemingly never become a reality. In that case, the wise leader will carefully and slowly bring the right people on board before publicly declaring the decision.

There is only one kind of leader, a courageous one. Leadership demands courage. Leaders are created to lead people into waters they're afraid to swim in, guide them into ideas they are hesitant to embrace, and take them to places they've never been before.

Pastor, ask yourself, "Am I a courageous leader?" If not, ask God right now to give you the heart of David; the faith of Shadrach, Meshach, and Abednego; and the resoluteness of Jesus.

Chapter 8

Catalytic Change Agent

He shepherded them with a pure heart
and guided them with his skillful hands.

—Psalm 78:72 HCSB

Perpetually growing churches are in a nearly constant state of change. They change the rooms that ministries and groups meet in to grow the ministries and groups. They change the church's décor to keep up with the times. They change the church's worship style to connect with the next generation. They change the makeup of the staff team to meet the needs of a growing church. They change the role of some staff pastors to be sure every ministry is functioning at peak performance. They change who the decision-makers are. They change the roles and responsibilities of decision-making bodies. They change service times and the number of services. They change the number of campuses that make up their church. And the list could go on. Change saturates the perpetually growing church culture.

The lead pastor is the catalyst for change. Only the lead pastor is responsible for and has the authority to spearhead change. When the lead pastor embraces this essential role and wisely exercises this duty, the church's possibility of ongoing growth increases exponentially.

When leading change, it's critical that lead pastors realize the type of church they're leading. There are two church types in play— congregation-driven and entrepreneur-led.

In a congregation-driven church, the members are the driving force behind what is considered acceptable. They see themselves as privileged and place expectations on the staff and judge staff effectiveness based on their individual preconceived notions. In a congregation-driven church, the membership will speak quickly and directly, sometimes aggressively, when change is on the table. In a congregation-driven church, the congregation votes on strategic changes in business meetings.

In an entrepreneur-led church, the congregation is thrilled to be part of a church making a difference. They judge the effectiveness of the leadership based on progress, including the numbers compared to the prior year, new leaders trained and equipped, and what they as the church membership are personally experiencing. Because the leadership has proven themselves as wise decision-makers in the past, the church membership trusts them to make right-minded decisions concerning what needs to change and when change should occur in the present and future.

PGCs are entrepreneur-led churches. But, before reaching that status, many were congregation-driven. Leading change in each of these systems differs.

Congregation-Driven

The congregation-driven church must make many mini changes and some substantial redirects on the way to becoming a PGC. When making a change, a five-phase process is effective in many churches.

Phase 1: Conclude what change must occur. Every pastor spearheading a growing church is continually asking what change or changes have to be made for the church to grow to the next level. Once the essential innovation is determined, there are three phases that pastors wisely complete before bringing the change to the church for a vote.

Phase 2: Build a biblical foundation for change and preach it. When the change is in sync with the sermon or sermon series, include the biblical foundation for the change in the sermon. Also, if the change isn't biblical but is unarguably essential for the kingdom's sake, reveal that when preaching. For instance, if the church is primarily made up of sixty-somethings and beyond and the change is being made so that the next generation is reached with the gospel, speak of the church's decline and that the next generation needs a church where they can feel comfortable, accepted, and connected. During this phase, make no mention that the change is being considered for your church. This phase aims to begin making a case for the change without creating tension around the change.

Phase 3: Get key leadership teams and influencers on board. Once the change is established as a biblical practice, the lead pastor must interact with key leadership teams and individual influencers. The pastor tells them that he sees this responsibility in Scripture and asks them to do their own study and pray about the new initiative or change. When the pastor believes they've had the time to study Scripture and pray about the transition, the pastor circles back to see if they are on board. If necessary, he takes the time to answer questions, to discuss in the meetings he attends, and to continue to pray about the change. Once the teams and individuals are on board, the pastor moves to the next phase.

Phase 4: Educate the church membership. If the change is substantial and will create intense emotion, it's wise to do a short sermon series on the topic. The series offers the membership opportunities to ask questions in one-on-one or group settings. When leading group sessions it's wise to ask individuals to write their questions on a three-by-five card. The reason for this is threefold: (1) the lead pastor and other church leaders who are answering questions can choose which questions to answer based on if the question is rhetorical with an edge or if the questionee is seeking an answer for clarification's sake; (2) this format keeps the meeting from becoming a conflictual dialogue between disgruntled church members and the church leadership, which can easily get out of hand; and (3) it keeps the tone of a questionee from creating an adversarial environment.

Phase 5: Bring the change to the church membership. Once the change is known to be biblical or essential, the church leadership and church's influencers are on board, everyone has had the opportunity to receive answers to their questions, and momentum is moving in the right direction, a motion to move forward is brought before the church body for a vote. Because key influencers and teams are already on board and are interacting with the concerned church members, in most instances, the motion passes.

This five-phase process is most effective when the lead pastor has leadership equity in their account, and no longtime influencers are building a coalition to put an end to the change under consideration.

Entrepreneur-Led

Leading change in the entrepreneur-led church demands educating or convincing a few rather than the masses. In most situations, the lead pastor determines what must be done and who must bless the decision. He also reveals the reason behind the change, gains the backing of those in authority, and sets in motion the action plans that will make the change a reality.

Who must bless the change will vary from church to church. In some churches, it will be a small group of elders. In other churches, the elders and the church's other influencers are brought into the loop. And some churches will include key staff members or the entire staff team.

A word of caution. It is never wise for a lead pastor to independently conclude the change needing to be made and then move forward alone. Without the change being blessed by influencers and key teams, you may doom the change to failure. Also, if the change you independently initiated fails, you will lose credibility with the leadership and the congregation, which will keep you from holding the leadership equity to pursue other changes for many months or years. Bringing others into the decision-making process gives ownership to key leaders and protects your reputation and your ability to lead change in the future, all essentials to building a PGC.

Four Indispensable Leadership Principles

Four indispensable leadership principles must be considered when leading change.

1. The size of the church matters. Most PGCs are large churches that were once small or midsize churches. As God ordained it, a passionate pastor with a vision for reaching the masses took the reins and guided the church to perpetually growing church status. But it wasn't easy. Leading change is one of the most challenging responsibilities any lead pastor undertakes. And the smaller the church, the more difficult leading change is.

The smaller the church, the easier it is for a few people to influence the church body to hold to the status quo, misdiagnose the pastor's motive, or purposefully mislead the congregation about what the present congregation will lose if change happens. One or two influencers or a small coalition of stubborn, immovable traditionalists can easily throw the brakes on change in a small to medium-sized church.

2. Timing matters. Great leaders realize that making the right call at the wrong time is catastrophic.

Before many PGCs became exponentially growing churches with a centralized decision-making body, they were churches practicing a democratic polity. The church whole, or at least a quorum of the membership, had to approve all key decisions through a church-wide vote. If the church was going to experience growth, the pastor had to convince the masses that the pivotal decision was the right thing to do.

Too many pastors brought an essential strategic decision to the church body too quickly. The church body voted the motion down, leaving the pastor angry and frustrated, and the church body became suspect of the pastor's motives. They began to question if the pastor had their best interest in mind. When a pastor tries to turn the ship too quickly, the outcome is devastating.

Most of us use a GPS to get from one place to the next. The GPS tells us where to turn, but it doesn't tell us when to turn. Even if we're at the correct intersection, if we turn when traffic is approaching at breakneck speed, we may accidentally commit suicide.

This has been the experience of way too many pastors. They knew where to turn, but they turned too quickly. They came to the intersection of a critical decision and darted into oncoming traffic. What they saw glaring at them in their panic-stricken eyes was a Mack truck with the words "Unprepared for Change" screaming from its grill. But it was too late. The vehicle was totaled, and the pastor's agenda and future at the church were dead. Due to poor timing, the pastor committed leadership suicide and left the church almost beyond repair.

Wise pastors take their time, no matter how long it takes. Getting an inflexible group of dyed-in-the-wool church members on board may take a week, a month, six months, a year, or beyond. But trying to take a hill too soon will most likely keep a leader from taking any hill for a long, long time. Someone once wisely declared, "Too many leaders overestimate what they can do in a year and underestimate what they can do in ten." This should be the mantra of every church leader trying to turn a ship that has sailed in the same direction for decades.

3. Establishing the why matters. When leading change, the most important question of all is, Why? The lead pastor, church staff, elders and deacons, and the church's influencers must know what the party line answer to the why question is and verbalize the agreed-upon response when necessary. If not, disgruntled church members can easily build a coalition of cynical saints who create a negative narrative that saturates the church, creating an incorrect and sinister motive behind the lead pastor's decision. They may even suggest that the lead pastor is manipulating influential teams or church members.

If the church is a small to midsize church, the narrative that cynics create will stop the change in its tracks and affect the lead pastor's reputation for decades. But, when all key leadership teams and the church's influencers are brought into the conversation early, alerted to the why behind the decision, and are willing to hold to the one agreed upon why, when the disgruntled promote their narrative, those with authority and influence can contradict the false narrative with the real why and, in doing so, silence cynics and move the essential initiative forward.

4. Owning the why matters. When leading change, the pastor must own the why, not the how. Church members who are unhappy with a change in process will often subconsciously or strategically seek a reason to slow down or kill change. They will approach the lead pastor with their reasonings, often arguing that the change under consideration isn't possible. They will ask the lead pastor *how* questions. They will ask how the change can be accomplished with so few people or without the necessary leaders or without the needed resources. They hope to back the lead pastor into the metaphorical corner, leaving him with no logical response. By doing so, they can then argue the change can't be accomplished or shouldn't be considered at this time.

For instance, if the lead pastor decides the church must revisit the church's worship music style, they may be approached by disgruntled traditionalists. The concerned church members will ask questions like, "How are you going to make this transition when the only instruments in the sanctuary are a piano and an organ?" or "How do you plan on moving to a new worship style using multiple musical instruments when our stage is too small to place the instruments and players on the stage?" or "How are you going to find the musicians needed to do this new style of worship?" The pastor will either make a wise decision and own the why, or they'll make a debilitating decision and answer that they don't know how the change is going to be accomplished.

Wise lead pastors own the why, not the how. They assign the how to staff members, lay teams, or a mixture of the two. When approached by concerned church members, pastors verbalize the why behind the decision and let them know they're not involved in the how. If pressed, lead pastors continue to voice the why behind the decision, never the how. Lead pastors tell the disgruntled or curious church members that they trust those working on the how and look forward to seeing what God accomplishes through the assigned team.

No church can be a PGC without being in a constant state of change. The culture is changing, so the church must change. Methods are changing to meet the needs of the next generation, so the church must change. Musical styles that connect with the generation to come are changing, so the church must change. The only things that should not and cannot change are the truths found in God's Word.

The change that must occur can only be spearheaded by the one God called to be the catalyst for change, the lead pastor.

Chapter 9

Strategic Risk-Taker

Ship your grain across the sea;
*   after many days you may receive a return.*
                     —Ecclesiastes 11:1

PGC pastors are strategic risk-takers and are fully aware they must take risks to see their church continue on a growth trajectory. But the risks they're willing to take aren't pulled out of thin air without definite purpose or consideration but based on proven church-growth principles and practices.

For instance, PGC pastors take the risk and dismiss the stumbling block when an ineffective staff member keeps the church from growing. The pastor risks losing the staff member's followers but knows the church will ultimately gain more than it is losing. When a PGC pastor realizes his congregation is primarily sixty-somethings and beyond, he knows he must redirect the worship style. If he doesn't transition, the church will be in death mode in less than a decade. He risks losing church members, even friends, but understands the kingdom gain will be greater than the immediate losses. When a PGC pastor is aware that keeping the denominational title in the church's name is an obstacle to unbelievers, he strategically decides to go through the painful process of removing it. His ecclesiastical peers may question his loyalty, and church members might question his integrity, but he knows deep in his being that his comfort and reputation can never trump God's kingdom agenda. He makes a strategic determination and moves forward. When the outcome pays greater dividends than the strategic risk, PGC pastors dive wisely into the pool of strategic risk-taking.

They do this because they understand the return-on-investment (ROI) principle. The ROI principle asks the question, "Will I get back more than I invested?" From a numeric perspective, it's investing $100 in a share of stock and its value rising 10 percent. At the end of the year, the stock is worth $110. The return on investment was worth the strategic risk. In church life, it's asking the question, "At the end of the day, will the church receive more than what was initially invested?" Here is a great illustration taken from an annual budgeting process.

When working on the budget, most church leaders ask, How much is available for us to spend? The question they should be asking is, What is the return on investment?

Church-growth principles demand that a church hire another staff member for about 130 church members. The staff member should be brought on board before the 130 mark is reached. If a church does this, the church will most likely grow.

But, when considering another staff hire, the church leadership will often ask, Can we afford to do that now? The question the pastor and church leaders should be asking is, What's the return on investment?

If they ask the return-on-investment question, they'll quickly realize that they can't afford not to bring the new staff member on board. Why? From a strictly financial perspective, a church grows numerically each time an effective staff member is hired. As a church grows, there are more givers than before. The staff member ultimately pays for himself and more. From a financial perspective, the church's income from tithes and offerings increases. From a spiritual perspective, the return on investment is that more people come into a relationship with Christ.

Making budgeting decisions based on how much there is to spend may make the leadership more at ease. But, asking the question, What's the return on investment? and investing ahead of the return is wise.

Craig Groeschel is the PGC lead pastor of Life.Church, whose headquarters is in Edmond, Oklahoma. The church also has dozens of other locations all over the United States. Craig also has a leadership podcast called *The Craig Groeschel Leadership Podcast*. In the episode titled "Think Investment Not Spending," he revealed the following profound truth about strategic leadership and ROI. "As leaders, when we think about resources, we have to think investing not spending. Spending is a trade. It's something fair in return for what you give. But an investment is expecting an exponential return on what you put in. The best leaders are not making an even trade. They are making an investment and expecting an exponential return."[1]

Strategic risk-taking is not the same as risk-taking. Too many churches have made the unwise decision of practicing risk-taking without concluding the risk they were taking would produce a spiritual return on investment.

Before diving into a risk-taking venture, ask the following questions:

- Will the risk being taken produce more Christians?
- Will the risk being taken produce more mature disciples of Jesus?
- Will the risk being taken produce more income that can be used for kingdom purposes?

By asking these three questions, a church can conclude whether or not the risk being taken is worthy of God's blessing.

Chapter 10

Team Builder

Choose seven men from among you who are known to be full of the Spirit and wisdom. We will turn this responsibility over to them.

—Acts 6:3b

So the word of God spread. The number of disciples in Jerusalem increased rapidly, and a large number of priests became obedient to the faith.

—Acts 6:7

Hiring off-the-chart staff members and keeping them for the long haul is spearheaded by every PGC pastor. The team a pastor builds will determine the success of the church the pastor leads. "One of the most important skills you can develop will be identifying, empowering, and developing the right people. The potential of your organization rests on the strength of its people."[1] Without an extraordinarily gifted and loyal team, a church will never be a perpetually growing church.

As the church grows, the lead pastor won't be involved in every hire but will have been deeply involved in building the process used in hiring. Most of all, those doing the hiring know the heart of the lead pastor so well they are intuitively aware of the kind of person the lead pastor would hire.

Who to Hire

Determining who to hire by using traditional church-hiring methods is incredibly challenging, so perpetually growing churches revisited the standard techniques most churches use.

When determining who to hire, five ideals are common in PGC churches: the Three Cs, Hiring from Within, Loyalty to the Lead Pastor, Hire Leaders, Hire Team Architects.

The Three Cs

When you ask most PGC leaders what their criteria for church staffing are, they begin with these three words: character, competency, and chemistry. These three descriptive words have become the intuitive standard for PGCs.

Character asks the question, Is the candidate spiritually mature? Spiritually mature team members exhibit the fruit of the Spirit: love, joy, peace, patience, kindness, goodness, gentleness, faithfulness, and self-control (Galatians 5:22–23).

Competency asks the question, Is the candidate, at an extraordinary level, capable of accomplishing the work necessary to achieve the outcomes pursued or the expectations assigned?

Chemistry asks the question, Is the candidate someone I will enjoy spending time with, doing life with, and taking the next hill with? While this may seem unnecessary, lead pastors need to be surrounded by people who energize them.

Hiring from Within

Many, maybe most, PGCs seek to hire full-time staff from within their congregation. Church members with the gifts and passion for accomplishing the work of ministry with excellence are often walking among them. These individuals believe in the church's mission, are loyal to the church's pastor, and long to see the church flourish. If these three facts weren't so, these gifted lay leaders wouldn't have chosen to be church members and would not be serving in lay ministry positions. These people have proven themselves leaders while serving in non-staff positions. Wise PGC pastors tend to look for pre-proven church members before seeking résumés from outsiders.

Loyalty to the Lead Pastor

One of the most extraordinary and honorable truths about PGC staff members is their loyalty to the lead pastor. When conversing privately or working with staff teams communally, I've noted that these staff members speak highly of their lead pastor. They talk of the pastor's preaching, leadership, passion, vision, or something else that resonates with them.

Because of their spiritual maturity and character, PGC staff members purposefully *choose* to respect and honor the lead pastor. They instinctively follow biblical guidelines, which command, "Obey your leaders and submit to them, for they are keeping watch over your souls, as those who will have to give an account. Let them do this with joy and not with groaning, for that would be of no advantage to you" (Hebrews 13:17 ESV). They will only speak disparagingly of their lead pastor if the pastor has chosen to engage in acts that disqualify them for ministry and then only to the appropriate church leadership.

PGCs strive to determine if a staff candidate shows high regard for those in authority. This is accomplished by asking probing questions during the interview process. A few possible questions are listed below.:

- What words would best describe the lead pastor at your present church?
- How would you describe your relationship with the lead pastor at your present church?
- If there was one thing you'd change about your relationship with your lead pastor, what would that be?

In most cases, one of these questions will bring to the forefront whether the candidate chooses to honor the lead pastor role.

Hire Leaders

Great staff members are leaders—visionaries, goal-setters, recruiters, equippers, empowerers, and inspiring communicators.

Leaders house a compelling vision they are passionate about accomplishing. One PGC children's minister's goal was to see every child understand the gospel fully and respond to the gospel before leaving the sixth grade. While this goal wasn't achievable as the prompting of the Holy Spirit in His timing is necessary, the vision was sincere and heart-driven. The vision was both clear and God-honoring and prompted many people to join her team.

Leaders are also recruiters. They will do whatever it takes to acquire the best people. They are so passionate about seeing their vision become a reality that they seek the best people who are passionate in pursuing the vision they're casting. They then equip and empower those they have recruited.

Once they have acquired an incredible team, they continually inspire by passionately and effectively recasting the vision. Great leaders are effective communicators.

PGCs also can discern the difference between a leader and a manager and hire leaders capable of managing, not managers incapable of leading.

My definition of "leadership" is "the ability to obtain and retain followers, organize them, unify them, and direct them to accomplish a God-given vision."[2]

My definition of "management" is "supervising an efficient workforce through which the necessary work gets completed in a timely fashion."

- Leaders bring people on board by sharing an inspiring, unimaginable, God-size dream.
- Managers recruit people by telling them there's a job that needs filling.

- Leaders invite people to go on a journey with them.
- Managers encourage people to come work for them.

- Leaders inspire the teams they lead by communicating a seemingly unattainable goal passionately.
- Managers motivate the people who work for them by reminding them they are responsible for their assigned tasks.

- Leaders equip those they lead, realizing that the people they're training will someday take on even more significant roles in the future.
- Managers get the best out of people then discard them if necessary or if someone else seems more apt to do the work more effectively and efficiently.

Called leaders are so passionate about the call God has placed on them that they:

- *Pray obsessively.* They pray for God to send the right people to the ministry, people who will sacrifice much to see the vision become a reality.
- *Inspire others purposefully.* Through the uninhibited passion that radiates from them, great leaders attract and inspire like-minded followers and leaders.
- *Build a team of leaders with intentionality.* In most ministries, coleaders or coaches inspire, educate, and keep the vision alive in every volunteer, as the key staff member cannot relate to every person in an ever-expanding ministry. Great staff members build a team of leaders who lead alongside them.
- *Retain followers enthusiastically.* By consistently declaring and unpacking the inescapable, exhilarating vision, the staff member retains those who long to be around until the vision becomes a reality.
- *Overcome all obstacles courageously.* If the leader faces excessive scrutiny—intimidation, bodily harm, even death—the work does not stop. If the needed resources are unavailable, a leader finds creative solutions to accomplish the work.

Hire Team Architects

Architects are gifted in the designing of buildings and supervising their construction. PGCs are staffed with pastors gifted in designing an extraordinary team and supervising its ongoing construction.

As seen in PGCs, the five pillars of great teams are synergy, unity, ingenuity, family, and individuality. Each staff member needs to be able to create an environment where each of these is cultivated.

Synergy—When brainstorming, strategizing, and dreaming new dreams, a great team will generate ideas and future expectations together, thoughts that no one team member could have produced on their own. As one person speaks, it leads to another realizing and voicing a great idea. Synergistic conversations will almost always lead to the best plans and strategic decisions. To create synergy, the team leader must describe meetings as safe places where any comment is essential and honored, and when someone's comment creates a new idea in your mind, always voice it. And finally, let the group know that *everyone* in the room will be given credit for a great idea or strategic decision.

Unity—Great teams never allow conflict to linger. Everyone on the team is committed to dealing with internal tension immediately and, in so doing, is protecting oneness at all costs. If a team is going to experience synergy, unity must exist. The team leader cannot be timid and must hold all team members accountable for making amends when necessary.

Ingenuity—Great teams welcome creativity, are inspired by new ways of thinking, and are honored to work with forward-thinkers who take the team to places they've never been before. A traditionalist intimidated by new methods easily hijacks ingenuity. To create a team saturated in ingenuity, the team leader must graciously silence the traditionalist and set the forward thinkers free to voice their thoughts and opinions.

Family—Great teams are more family than coworkers. They're available to one another 24/7, will never bail on one another, and share laughter and tears unapologetically and without embarrassment. The team leader will create opportunities for the team to connect outside of work. Going to lunch together, having the team to the leader's home to watch a sporting event or play a game, and so on, will turn a group of coworkers into a family.

Individuality—Great teams recognize that team members bring their unique gifts and abilities, personalities, and passions. Effective team leaders lead team members to embrace their identity and encourage everyone to be authentic. To create a mindset of individuality, great team leaders do a personality assessment and a spiritual gift assessment with their team. Then, they are purposeful in consistently reminding the team members to be the person God made them.

Hiring Processes

Knowing who to hire is critical, but utilizing the right hiring process is even more important. During the hiring process, PGCs discern if the candidate is the right fit for the team and the church. Just because someone is a three-C hire, is a hire from within, and will be loyal to the lead pastor doesn't mean that person is the right fit for the church or team.

PGCs spend much time, effort, and finances to find the right people. Why? Because it's much easier to say no to someone during the hiring process than to dismiss a bad hire. PGCs deliberately and meticulously take all steps necessary to ensure that the hiree is the right person and fit.

Personality and Leadership Assessment Tools

Personality and leadership assessment tools are essential tools in the hiring process. Some churches use more than one assessment, others only one. When consulting churches and mentioning various assessment tools, I've often been asked what each tool measures. With that in mind, here are some assessments used by some influential PGCs and what information each unearths.

1. Myers-Briggs (used by Life. Church, Edmond, Oklahoma)

Through a series of questions, the MBTI assessment identifies natural preferences in four areas of personality: how you direct and receive energy, how you take in information, how you decide and come to conclusions, and how you approach the outside world.

2. Ministry Insights (used by Brentwood Baptist Church, Brentwood, Tennessee)

Ministry Insights describes their work in the following way:

> Ministry Insights helps you discover your unique design, how to value the differences in others and learn to blend them to become and accomplish more together than you could alone. Our tools and processes help you understand biblical truth about God's divine design for differences so you can build healthy relationships.
>
> We help ministry teams put the right people in the right roles. We also help existing teams understand one another better by first measuring them with accurate, proven assessments, and then by providing materials and training to help them apply

these insights. We also help couples understand and value their differences—equipping them to use their unique strengths to unite them, not divide them.[3]

3. Strengths Finders (used by North Point Community Church, Alpharetta, Georgia, and Saddleback Church, Lake Forest, California)

Strengths Finders unearths what someone naturally does best. It also aids in helping individuals know what they might need help from others to accomplish the work asked of them. There are four categories of personal understanding: (1) strategic thinking, (2) relationship building, (3) influencing, and (4) executing.[4]

4. RightPath (used by North Point Community Church, Alpharetta, Georgia)

The RightPath Path4 and Path6 behavioral assessments assist in identifying your talents and offering an in-depth display of predictable natural behaviors. These assessments are designed for leadership development, developing emerging leaders, team building, succession planning, conflict management, and interviewing.[5]

5. Caliper (used by Saddleback Church, Lake Forest, California)

The Caliper Assessment (aka Caliper Profile) is an employment assessment test that measures your personality and cognitive skills. The results of your test are used by potential employers to screen job candidates and tell them whether you are a good candidate for a specific role.

6. Culture Index (LakePointe Church, Rockwall, Texas)

The culture index survey is not about personality types but about identifying patterns based on traits. The culture index personality types are:

1. Visionary Pattern

People with visionary patterns are "me" focused, have strong opinions, and are capable of looking at the big picture.

2. Research Pattern

People in this category tend to be detail-oriented and introverted.

3. Social Pattern

People in social patterns are extroverted and tend to deal with their feelings and make their own rules.

4. Organizational Pattern

People in the organizational pattern are naturally unselfish and corporative while focusing on details and completing the task at hand.[6]

Interviews and Group Gatherings

A church staff member must be a cultural fit. Because culture has its foundation in relationships, PGCs strategically line up multiple conversations and interviews with individuals and teams when hiring a new staff member. Each interview and conversation's goal is to determine if the candidate will be a natural fit in the church's culture.

One-on-One Interviews—In some settings, there is a one-on-one interview with the candidate's future direct overseer and the lead pastor. This interview will determine if the candidate and the overseer experience chemistry, reveal the responsibilities of the role, and in some settings unearth the salary and benefits. It's also wise to discuss the list of staff values and each staff member's responsibility to live them.

In very large churches the lead pastors don't always interview a candidate. But, when a lead pastor is transitioning staff culture or the staff member will serve alongside the lead pastor on the executive team, the lead pastor will most likely interview the candidate.

Team Gathering—Many PGCs gather the staff team that the individual will serve with for a few hours of conversation. The candidate tells the group about his or her family, shares a testimony and ministry history, and answers predetermined questions the team leader asks. Since this happens publicly in a group setting, the team leader has made the candidate aware of what is required of them at this meeting and makes sure he or she knows what questions will be asked. Some PGCs allow the staff team to ask any questions of the candidate they might have. At the end of the meeting, the team leader allows the future staff member to ask questions of the team . While the team will not determine whether or not the candidate is hired, wise team leaders ask the team members what their feelings about the candidate are and if the candidate is someone whom they feel they could work with and enjoy working alongside.

Wisdom of the Crowd—PGCs realize it's important to gain insights from those who are not part of the future staff member's team. A meeting is called of individuals from various ministries of the church. This meeting might include someone from the custodial team, tech team, worship team, groups team, HR, and an executive team member's assistant. The meeting will begin like the meeting with the future employee's team. The candidate will talk about their family, verbalizing their testimony and ministry history. Then those in the room will ask the candidate any questions they would like to ask or ask predetermined questions with one being assigned to each interviewing staff member. The goal is to see if the individual is relationally inclined, how the candidate responds under pressure, and whether the person will fit in the staff culture. The opinions of this group are significant and should be taken into serious consideration.

Three Deep References—PGCs don't depend solely on those listed as references on the candidate's résumé when checking references. The church wisely goes three deep. When speaking with a listed reference, the person doing the interview asks if there's someone else they can speak with. The person checking references then calls the second-tier reference. When speaking with the second-tier reference, the person checking reference asks if they could give them someone else's name that could provide insights into the person's history. The interviewer then calls the third-tier reference.

This practice allows the church to determine if the candidate falls into a category that would be contrary to the church's culture, which would create chaos, or a category that would render the person unsuitable to serve at the church. I've noticed six types of staff members that PGC leaders wish they hadn't hired.

Combative Staff Members

Combative staff members seem to be looking for a fight. Often in staff meetings, when disagreeing with others, combative staff members speak in a tone that creates tension or demeans the person they disagree with. Their body language says "Come on! I'm up for an argument."

Know-It-All Staff Members

Know-it-all staff members behave as if they know everything. Anytime they're in a room, they speak as though they're the genius in the room. Know-it-all staff members kill synergy.

Never-Got-a-Solution Staff Members

Great pastors tell their staff that they should never bring a concern without also bringing a solution. Never-got-a-solution staff members have a penchant for bringing up concerns in meetings and conversations but never have a solution for their unearthed problem.

Victim Staff Members

Victim staff members seldom take responsibility for wrongdoing, even when they're in the wrong. In almost every situation, they talk themselves into believing they've been victimized. They sincerely think others need to be disciplined when they are the ones who need admonishment.

Encourage-less Staff Members

Encourage-less staff members are unable or unwilling to congratulate other staff members on a job well done or an initiative accomplished. In their silence, they tear others down when the situation offers them the opportunity to build others up.

I-Want-to-Be-Pastor Staff Members

I-want-to-be-pastor staff members are often unknown to the lead pastor. Behind closed doors, they speak of what should be considered, what the lead pastor should be doing, what should have been done, or how they would do something differently. These staff members seldom do their job to their full potential. This happens because they've never given their whole hearts to the role they've been given. When they could and should be seeking God to provide them with guidance concerning the role they've been given, they're pondering what they would do if they were the lead pastor.

One of these characteristics may surface by going three deep in the interview process and interviewing staff members or pastors the candidate has previously worked with.

Essential Understandings

PGCs must hire people who are willing to evolve. When a church is in a constant state of growth, the roles and responsibilities of staff members are transitional. Two scenarios are possible.

1. Evolving Roles—In a growing church, the student pastor may begin by connecting with the students personally. The ministry is small enough that the student pastor counsels students personally, leads Bible study personally, and connects with students face-to-face. He is the ministry's hero. As the ministry grows, the student minister must be willing to equip and empower others to counsel students, lead small-group Bible study, and meet face-to-face with students. The student pastor goes from being the hero of the story to creating heroes. The student pastor spends more time organizing the ministry and equipping others than being the minister to individual students. As a church grows, every minister in every role must be willing to expand their knowledge base and work differently. When interviewing, it is wise to discuss this and be sure that every pastor candidate is willing and able to evolve.

2. Changing Roles—Many PGCs no longer hire for a particular role. The church hires to acquire the hiree's giftedness, experience, and abilities. The ministry they lead, their role, and their title may change multiple times.

An individual with the gift of leadership may begin serving as the groups pastor, but, when the church needs the staff member to shore up a struggling or dying assimilation ministry, the staff member will be required to change ministries. Or the staff member may have come to the church believing he would oversee missions for a lifetime. When the children's ministry is crumbling, he will be called upon to change teams because he has the gift of administration. During the interview process, the hiring body must ask the candidate if they are willing to change ministry areas when necessary.

A PGC Hiring Model

North Point Community Church in Alpharetta, Georgia, is one of the largest churches in America. An off-the-charts staff team serves the church. Using their approach as a starting point for creating a hiring process that is effective in your situation is a wise decision. The list below reveals the methods North Point Community Church practices when hiring each team member.

Responsibilities of the Applicant

Employee Application Form
Every potential staff person completes the Employee Application Form. This document alerts the church leadership that an individual is pursuing serving in a staff role at the church (see appendix 1).

NPM Personnel Manual Acceptance of Terms
All new hires must sign this form. By signing, the employee agrees "to abide by the policies and provisions set forth in the North Point Ministries, Inc., Personnel Policy Manual. I understand that modifications may be made in the future and that the most current copy is available anytime at www.npmstaff.org" (see appendix 2).

Multiple Personal Assessments
When applicants are in consideration for positions, they complete the following assessments: Right Path, Enneagram, and "Colors" Assessment (based on the DISC personality assessment).

Responsibilities of the Church Leadership

Job Class Worksheet
The hiring manager completes the Job Class Worksheet. This form is used to determine the position salary range based on training, education, and previous experience (see appendix 3).

Hiring Statement
The hiring manager completes the Hiring Statement. This form is used to determine if the job is part or full time, job title, supervisor, salary, what vacation is provided, and so on (see appendix 4).

Background Check
A background check is required when the church extends an offer.

Required Interviews (based on role)

Campus Staff Team Members
At least two department staff, one department/division lead, and a division and/or lead pastor interviews the candidate.

Multi-Campus Staff Team Members (Central Team)
At least two multi-campus department staff, a department/division lead, a campus department lead, and multicampus ministry (children/students/adults) lead interview the candidate.

Department Heads
Two team members, at least two other department heads, one campus department head, and one executive director of ministries, ministry services, or multisite ministries interview the candidate.

Chapter 11

Team Keeper

Remember, then, you employers, that your responsibility is to be fair and just towards those whom you employ, never forgetting that you yourselves have a heavenly employer.

—Colossians 4:1 PHILLIPS

How to Keep the Best

PGCs build unparalleled staff teams. Once a lead pastor has the right team, how does the pastor keep them? After all, they will become hot commodities, and other churches will offer higher incomes. Larger churches and more influential churches will pursue them. Keeping an off-the-charts staff team is an art form too often overlooked.

PGCs are proactive in ten practices that aid in keeping the best of the best: speaking to the love language of each staff member, celebrating wins, giving significant gifts, protecting family time, giving complimentary vacation time, creating a captivating staff culture, paying them what they deserve, resourcing their dream, hiring more staff before the present staff burns out, and dismissing a bad hire.

Speaking Love Languages

A love language is an action taken toward another individual that resonates with and encourages the heart. Love languages are personal. There are many love languages, and everyone doesn't resonate with the same love language.[1]

When a lead pastor or church leader speaks the love language of the person they have oversight of, that individual feels loved, honored, and cared for. Speaking a staff member's love language is an essential practice if a church wishes to keep its best staff members.

But one fact must be understood and embraced. Everyone doesn't speak the same love language. A leader must know each person's love language and use that love language to encourage the individual. Suppose the leader chooses to exercise a love language that isn't right for the staff member. Instead of encouraging the employee, he will embarrass the staff member and have the opposite effect of what was being pursued, which is heartfelt encouragement.

A list of some love languages is noted below:

- public recognition
- monetary gifts
- personalized gifts
- personal meetings with people at high levels of leadership
- involvement in decision-making meetings
- private words of encouragement
- hand-written cards
- time off

Knowing each staff member's love language and utilizing it is an act of kindness, great leadership, and a Christlike practice.

Celebrating Wins

Many teams do the work of ministry and immediately go to work on the next project or assignment. The staff has worked overtime, sacrificed family time, and given their best. The accomplishment is a success, and the team shows up for work again on Monday. The leader can celebrate with the team but has chosen to ignore the success the team experienced together.

Celebrating wins should always be in play. Celebrating successes is a powerful way to say thanks when the leader is grateful for the team they lead, and it bonds a team in ways few other things can. And when a team has a tight bond, the best people don't want to leave.

Celebrate by reminding one another of the goals achieved and the lives that were transformed or the next steps toward faith someone took. Take the group out for a meal together. Host a party at your home, or meet at the park on a workday for a cookout. Spend time together on a houseboat or retreat location. Go golfing or bowling or to a movie. Do something that says we are a team and we are celebrating what God is doing through us together.

Giving Significant Gifts

PGCs are often financially capable of providing a significant gift to those who deserve recognition. And, in many PGCs, almost every staff member deserves such gifts. Significant gifts might include tickets to a professional sporting event, a day at the local spa, a round of golf at an elite golf course, or a collector's item someone has always wanted.

But be sure you don't see these gifts as incentives. An incentive is something that motivates or encourages someone to do something. It is known to be attainable *if* the person works and achieves something. A gift is given after the fact, out of love, as a way of saying thank you, the receiver never knowing the gift might be given.

Protecting Family Time

PGCs are quick to protect family time and, if staff members are doing their job effectively, give them time away for their children's sporting events, school programs, doctor appointments, and other responsibilities.

Sadly, too many churches celebrate those staff members who work sixty-hour weeks, even if families suffer or marriages are on the brink of destruction.

The truth is this, if the church has effective staff members on board, those staff members will accomplish the work they are called to do whether or not they step away once in a while for family responsibilities.

Giving Complimentary Vacation Time

Many churches can't pay what an impressive staff member deserves. They can give away free vacation time. Free vacation time is time away that isn't related to the vacation time accrued by a staff member. At one PGC, the staff is given the week between Christmas and New Year's Day off. The ministry teams have been at the church many days for Christmas events and services. They've attended small-group Christmas parties and cared for those hurting deeply due to loved ones lost or relationships broken. The unique gift of a week away is in addition to the vacation time each staff member has earned.

And it's an easy gift to give as the church will have little to no programming the week between Christmas and New Year's Day.

Creating a Captivating Staff Culture

It's the team you work with that determines if you love the work you do. This statement is true. Working on a dream team of close friends will keep a staff member on board for the long haul. The environment doesn't come naturally; it is created purposefully. But when it is in place, it's an environment that staff members are more than hesitant to leave.

Paying Them What They Deserve

As mentioned, when a PGC becomes known as a PGC, other churches will come in pursuit of that church's team. The pursuing church is chasing the knowledge, expertise, and experience your team possesses. The church in the hunt will pay them what they deserve.

Pastor Larry Osborne, Lead Pastor of North Coast Church in Vista, California, reveals wise counsel related to the setting of fair salaries that should not be ignored.

1. Always Compare Apples for Apples—"Many unfair compensation packages are the result of not knowing how to accurately compare a pastoral salary with a layperson's salary. Most board members have no idea of the true cost of their salary. If asked, they will seldom include the actual cost to their employer. Most forget about medical insurance, payroll taxes, retirement, continuing education, and other benefits." Pastor Larry suggests creating "two budget categories: one for salaries and one for benefits, payroll taxes, and the like. And when you discuss staff salaries, never combine these two categories."[2]

2. Establish Replacement Value—"An obvious key question when setting salaries is, 'What can we afford?' It's what any prudent leader wants to know. But it should never be the first question asked. The first question to ask is, 'What would it cost us to replace this person with someone of equal skills and abilities.' Only after that question has been answered and duly noted is it time to ask, 'What can we afford?'"[3]

3. Benchmark Parallel Responsibilities—Ask, "What secular jobs parallel this position in responsibility, education, and the skills needed for success?" Though this is a rather subjective question, it can help avoid gross inequities."[4]

I have seen a surprising trend. Some PGCs are choosing to pay lower ministry staff-level positions less than a fair wage. While paying less than the industry standard may be a seemingly wise financial decision for the church, it may be a catalyst for the loss of the best staff members. When other churches come calling, the gifted and seasoned staff members, who know and are effective in their present church's culture, may find themselves forced to move on. If staff members stay, they may never own a sufficient home, send their children to college, or prepare adequately for retirement. They are at the crossroads of a decision, choosing between serving the church they love or caring for their family and preparing for their future. They will painfully and almost always choose the second option and move on.

Resourcing Their Dream

Staff members who accomplish the extraordinary dream big dreams. They have extravagant goals in mind. A student pastor may have the goal to reach 50 percent of the local high school students. A groups pastor might long to see a biblical small group within walking distance of every person in the county where the church exists. A children's pastor may have the goal to see 80 percent of those in their ministry respond to the gospel before leaving the ministry. But, if the resources necessary to accomplish the dream aren't available, the staff member will become frustrated and move on. When possible, resource your best staff members with the employee resources, material resources, and financial resources needed to make their dreams an achievable reality.

Hiring More Staff Before the Present Staff Burns Out

Many churches lose their best staff members because they overwork them. The old adage is true, "If you want something done, give it to a busy person." Way too often a busy person is the person who has excelled many times before when given important assignments. The church leadership believes the work can be done without spending money on more staff. They don't realize that the busy person, who is also one of their best staff members, is going to come to a point where they burn out and then pursue roles elsewhere.

The wise church will hire additional staff before losing their best.

Based on the evaluation of growing churches with multiple staff, a realistic ratio of pastoral staff to worship attendance should be no more than 1:150. That is, a church should have at least one full-time pastoral staff for every 150 in worship attendance. Actually, over the last 25+ years the ratio has been decreasing and some growing churches are finding their ratio is now closer to 1:120. While it is difficult to financially support a ratio smaller than 1:100, it is unwise to allow the ratio to go beyond 1:150.[5]

Dismissing a Bad Hire

Great staff members want to work on a team of high achievers excelling together in a unified environment.

Every staff member has the potential to bring down a great team. Staff members who are lazy will model a behavior others may emulate. If they are relationally toxic, they will create friction and kill synergy. If they are building their kingdom, their pride will slow the building of God's kingdom, and their selfish attitude will destroy staff unity. Bad hires must be coached to change. If they cannot, they must be dismissed as quickly as possible.

A mantra embraced by PGC pastors is "Hire slow, fire fast." Hire slow because a bad hire is a dangerous hire. Fire fast, so the toxic staff member doesn't kill the team, cause the best people to go elsewhere, and slow the church's growth.

Any or all of these nine practices are key to keeping a staff dream team. Putting them into effect is worth every penny of the costs and the emotional toll of every hard decision made.

Because the team a pastor builds will determine the success of the church the pastor leads, we have given much acreage to recruiting, building, and keeping an off-the-charts church staff team. Before we move on, I want you to hear from someone who served in a PGC staff position, has led multiple PGC staff teams, and now coaches and consults PGCs.

Jenni Catron is the founder and CEO of The 4Sight Group. "**The 4Sight Group** brings the culture conversation to a practical level and provides a pathway and process to help leaders and their teams succeed together."[6] She has authored several books including *Clout: Discover and Unleash Your God-Given Influence* and *The 4 Dimensions of Extraordinary Leadership* and has served on the executive leadership teams of Menlo Church in Menlo Park, California, and Cross Point Church in Nashville, Tennessee. *Outreach* magazine has recognized Jenni as one of the thirty emerging influencers reshaping church leadership.

Author: Jenni, you have a view of church staffing few have. You have led at the executive pastor level so you understand the role of the lead pastor related to staff issues. Because of your responsibility as an executive pastor, you understand the complexity of executive team decisions concerning staff members and issues. You have been a staff member, so you know the plight of the church staff member. And you have and are consulting multiple PGCs concerning staffing and staff issues, so you have a plethora of knowledge in this area. Having engaged with many churches, you've learned what is effective and what isn't effective. How would you describe a healthy staff team with these facts in mind?

Jenni Catron: A healthy staff team has clarity and understanding of these three questions:

1. What's our purpose? Meaning, every team member at every level understands the specific mission and vision of the church and knows how what they do connects to this purpose.
2. Who are we? The team is clear on what they value and what makes their team culture unique.
3. How do we work together? With an understanding of purpose and culture, the team understands how they interact with one another in pursuit of the mission. Healthy teams have clarified the values that guide them and the behaviors that reflect those values. They understand how to communicate well, how to handle conflict, how to make decisions, how to spend their time, and so on.

Author: What *traits* are consistent in lead pastors whose staff respect them so much they have the lead pastors' backs and will take the next hill with them?

Jenni Catron: Two key traits that I see in the best leaders are humility and curiosity. Humility is the acknowledgment that there is always something for me to learn. When humility is the posture of the lead pastor, he is quick to identify and celebrate the gifts, skills, and wisdom of his team. Most critically the lead pastor knows that he holds that position of leadership to help bring out the best in others.

The second trait I often see is curiosity. Curiosity builds on the acknowledgment that there is always something for me to learn and takes it a step further by asking questions. A curious leader seeks out the perspective of their team and invites it. A curious leader realizes they have blind spots and asks questions of those who will be able to give them more insight.

Author: What are the *practices* of lead pastors whose staff respect them so much they have the lead pastors' backs and will take the next hill with them?

Jenni Catron: The lead pastor is hyper-respectful of the organizational structure and the leadership he has entrusted to others, and yet he is not disconnected from or aloof with the rest of the staff. This lead pastor looks for ways to connect with staff in casual settings, such as in getting to all staff meetings a few minutes early and casually chatting with staff or walking the office space to say hello. If conversations drift to decisions or suggestions, the lead pastor is careful to not give his opinion in a way that can be perceived as a directive, but suggests the team member circle up with their manager. In being conscious of the organizational structure, the lead pastor is showing respect to the leaders they've empowered.

Additionally, the lead pastor looks for ways to connect the dots for team members from what they do to how it connects with the vision. If the lead pastor observes a team member making calls to people who signed up for a class, remind that team member that every person on that list is taking a key step in seeking to know Jesus better. It might just be a phone call for us, but it could be a key moment in that person's spiritual journey.

Author: A unified staff team is essential if a church is going to keep its best players and for the team to work synergistically with high levels of effectiveness. What is the role of the lead pastor in creating and protecting unity?

Jenni Catron: The lead pastor needs to hold the vision for what he hopes the team to be. For unity to be true among the team, it must be a value and conviction for the lead pastor. He demonstrates this value by modeling the unity that he hopes for. If unity is not observed at the most senior levels of the ministry, it won't be embraced by those throughout the team. I often see lead pastors and executive-level leaders live at odds with one another, taking a divide-and-conquer type of mentality. Team members can sense when senior leaders aren't aligned or unified. This ultimately cascades to the rest of the team.

Additionally, the lead pastor in collaboration with other team members needs to define what behaviors are essential to unity. Unity doesn't have to mean uniformity or that we can ask questions or give feedback. What does it mean to your team? What does unity look like in action? Clarifying this will help set the expectation for the rest of the team.

Author: What are the responsibilities of every staff member if a team is going to remain unified?

Jenni Catron: All staff members need to recognize that they are influencing the health (or unhealth) of the team. Team culture comprises every team member. Once unity has been defined by senior leadership, all staff persons must decide whether they can align with those behaviors.

Here's a really critical point: If as a staff member you cannot align with the values and behaviors that reflect unity within your culture, you need to move on. If you choose to stay on a team in which you can't align with the behaviors that reflect unity in that culture, you are creating disunity. I'll add this caveat, if you're in an unhealthy culture and what is defined as unity is really more about control and fear, perhaps you are there to help influence change, however this is a matter of much discernment.

Author: Related to the last question. If a staff member is unwilling or unable to do what is necessary to be a unifying factor to the staff team, what options are available to the lead pastor, and when should the chosen option be exercised?

Jenni Catron: If as the lead pastor, you have a team member who is not contributing to a unifying culture, here are things to consider:

1. Have you defined what it means to be unified? Do team members understand what unity looks like in practice? If not, bringing this clarity is your first priority. If you've done that—and not just once, but you have a process for making sure this value is clear and understood—then it's time for the second question.

2. Have you had a direct and honest conversation? Have you given the staff members the benefit of the doubt that they may not be trying to be not unified. They may need coaching and clarification. Have the conversation. Ask good questions to understand why their behavior is not aligned with the unifying culture, and coach them for improvement. If they are still unwilling to demonstrate unity, it's time for number three.

3. Make a decision to exit them from the team. As hard as it is to lose staff, keeping a staff person who is unwilling to be unified creates an unhealthy and often dysfunctional culture. If you've done the first two well, a tough decision to exit someone is usually much more clear.

Author: When hiring staff members, how important is it to involve multiple individuals and teams in the process? Why do you say so?

Jenni Catron: The best hiring practices involve having a rigorous hiring process. As the hiring manager, you are faced with the urgency of filling an open seat on an already overworked team and that urgency can often blind you to important considerations in the hiring process. This is why it's essential for multiple people to be involved in the hiring process. Engaging a hiring team of individuals who have a vested interest in protecting the staff culture while giving you objective feedback on the candidate is critical to ensuring you don't make a short-sighted decision.

Author: What red flags should never be ignored when hiring staff members?

Jenni Catron: A red flag that I often see leaders ignore is when a candidate's talent is greater than their character. Don't let talent trump character in your hiring decisions. It's tempting to hire the person with the specialized skill that you are lacking, but if their character does not match their talent, this will become problematic in other ways.

Another red flag that I would pay attention to is when the candidate's spouse is reluctant. Typically this occurs when the hire involves a relocation. If the spouse is having trouble envisioning a future for their family, this inevitably creates tension and causes your new employee to feel torn between their new job and their family who is struggling to settle in.

Author: What step-by-step process have you seen used that, in your opinion, is the most effective when hiring a staff member?

Jenni Catron: A clear, consistent process that you repeatedly follow is essential for good hiring. Personally, I've written step-by-step plans for every organization where I have given oversight to hiring. Build a process that works for you and then commit to that process.

Author: What circumstances are most prevalent in churches that lose their best staff members to other churches?

Jenni Catron: The churches with the greatest staff turnover are typically marked by poor leadership and unhealthy culture. Poor leadership might include failing to cast a strong vision that helps team members see purpose for their work. It may also mean a leader who is disconnected, inconsistent, or not providing coaching and direction.

An unhealthy culture is a product of poor leadership but has become systemically pervasive. Unhealthy cultures are marked by lack of clarity in purpose, roles, and goals. Unhealthy cultures lack trust and unity. Tension, infighting, and gossip are common, leading to disengaged and unfulfilled staff who are eager to escape.

I once served on the staff of Living Hope Baptist Church in Bowling Green, Kentucky, a perpetually growing church. Led by Pastor Brad Johnson and serving alongside Dr. Scott Kilgore, Dave Love, and Jeff and Mary Beth Carlisle, we experienced something that I long for every lead pastor to experience: doing life with a dream team.

A dream team is a church staff team who truly love one another, accomplish their ministries at extraordinary levels of achievement, honor their lead pastor, leave a debate respecting one another as much as they did before the debate began, and weep at the thought of someone leaving the team.

If your church has as its goal to have a dream team, using the principles and practices unearthed in the last two chapters will be the first steps in making your dream team a reality.

Chapter 12

Evolving Role-Player

Therefore, I urge you, brothers and sisters, in view of God's mercy, to offer your bodies as a living sacrifice, holy and pleasing to God—this is your true and proper worship. Do not conform to the pattern of this world, but be transformed by the renewing of your mind. Then you will be able to test and approve what God's will is—his good, pleasing and perfect will.

—Romans 12:1–2

As a church grows, the role and responsibilities of the lead pastor must transition. Many churches are held captive in the cell of stagnation because the lead pastor is ignorant of the need or unwilling to revisit their responsibilities. When pastors don't revisit their roles and responsibilities at each stage of church growth, they become the church-growth bottleneck. If a church is going to experience numeric growth, the lead pastor *must* be willing to take on new responsibilities at each growth stage and give some up at the same time.

Dr. Tim Keller was the founding pastor of Redeemer Presbyterian Church in Manhattan, New York. He led the diverse congregation for twenty-eight years, a church that grew to a weekly attendance of more than five thousand. Dr. Keller wrote a must-read article titled "Leadership and Church Size Dynamics, How Strategy Changes Church Growth." In it, he describes the role of the lead pastor at each stage of church growth.

House Church: Up to 40 Attendance—"The pastor is often a 'tentmaker' and does church ministry part-time, though once a church has at least ten families who tithe, it can support a full-time minister. The minister's main job is shepherding, not leading or preaching."[1]

Small Church: 40–200 Attendance—The pastor is still the primary shepherd; however, as the church grows, "the pastor of a small church will feel more and more need for administrative skills. Small churches do not require much in the way of vision casting or strategizing, but they do eventually present a need for program planning, mobilization of volunteers, and other administrative tasks."[2]

Medium-Sized Church: 200–450 Attendance—When a church grows into a medium-sized church, Keller says the senior minister would shift more into a "rancher" role—training and organizing laypeople. "He also must be adept at training, supporting, and supervising ministry and administrative staff. At the medium-church level, this requires significant administrative skills."[3]

Large Church, 400–800 Attendance—Keller suggests concentrating more on preaching, vision-casting, and strategizing. The lead pastor "must let go of many or most administrative tasks; otherwise he becomes a bottleneck."[4]

The Very Large Church—The preacher cannot be the people's pastor in a large church setting but "must move from an emphasis on doing the work of ministry (teaching, pastoring, administering) to delegating this work so that he can concentrate on vision casting and general preaching."[5]

Pastor, if you now realize your church is stuck due to your unwillingness to redesign your role, make a commitment right now. Bow your head and ask God to give you the drive to learn what you need to know, the creativity to design new daily work rhythms, and the courage to partner with the leadership of your church to rewrite your job description or the church's constitution and by-laws.

One or more of these commitments may be the game-changing action necessary for you to be fulfilled and your church to start growing.

Chapter 13

Culturally Captivating Communicator

Whatever you do, work at it with all your heart, as working for the Lord, not for human masters, since you know that you will receive an inheritance from the Lord as a reward. It is the Lord Christ you are serving.

—Colossians 3:23–24

Captivating communicators capture the hearts of their audience. Churches experiencing over a decade of numeric growth are led by pastors who are captivating communicators. They have discovered their preaching style, continue to perfect it, and exercise it with passion.

Pastor Dave Stone served as the associate teaching pastor at Southeast Christian Church in Louisville, Kentucky, prior to Senior Pastor Bob Russell's retirement. At that point, Dave took on the role of lead pastor. At Pastor Dave's retirement, he was preaching weekly to twenty-two thousand people. He is unarguably one of the most gifted communicators in the country.

Finding, Refining, and Embracing Your Style

In his book *Refining Your Style*, Pastor Dave lists thirteen styles of communication:

1. The Creative Storyteller
2. The Direct Spokesperson
3. The Scholarly Analytic
4. The Revolutionary Leader
5. The Engaging Humorist

6. The Convincing Apologist
7. The Inspiring Orator
8. The Practical Applicator
9. The Persuasive Motivator
10. The Passionate Teacher
11. The Relevant Illustrator
12. The Cultural Prophet
13. The Unorthodox Artist[1]

Tracking down your preaching style is essential. Not only will you be more effective but also you'll find greater fulfillment in preaching. Pastor Dave says:

> When you follow your natural inclination, empowered by the Holy Spirit, Satan had better watch out. God used a stuttering murderer named Moses to communicate to masses of Israelites and a powerful king. Recall an introverted, soft-spoken fisherman named Andrew who brought many people—including his brother Simon Peter—to Christ. Remember how God transformed an antagonist named Saul into an evangelist named Paul. Look at the impact Jabez, an obscure Old Testament character, has had.[2]

Marrying Style and Culture

Captivating preachers are exponentially more effective when their preaching style intersects with their region's culture. Josh Howerton's "tell it like it is" style is suitable for LakePointe Church in Dallas but wouldn't be well received in Manhattan. Tim Keller's soft-spoken intellectualism is perfect for Manhattan but wouldn't be nearly as effective in Texas.

David Landrith pastored Long Hollow Baptist Church in Hendersonville, Tennessee, for seventeen years before going home to heaven on November 18, 2014, at the age of fifty-one. In less than two decades under his leadership, this PGC grew from 300 to 7,500 and from one location to five campuses. Long Hollow Baptist was the first church in Tennessee to baptize over one thousand people in a year.[3]

I first heard Pastor David preach at LifeWay Christian Resources in Nashville, Tennessee. His content was outstanding, his theology dead-on, his humor body-slammed you, and his love for God and His word was unmistakable. Most noticeable, his Tennessee accent was extraordinarily prominent.

The stereotypical speech coach would've directed David to do the work necessary to eliminate the accent. They would've told him he would never connect with a broad audience. But a *broad* audience wasn't *his* audience. His audience was good ol' Tennessee Volunteers. I wholeheartedly believe that David reached the masses because his preaching style was meant for the culture God placed him in. His congregation bled orange (the University of Tennessee's color), and he proclaimed the transforming red blood of Jesus in their language.

When a preacher's preaching style intersects with the culture he's placed in, the church has a much greater potential of becoming a perpetually growing church.

Preaching the Effective Number of Times Per Year

PGCs require excellent sermons at every weekend service. For this reason, every pastor must conclude how many times per year they can deliver an A+ to B+ sermon. Some pastors can accomplish this inescapable requirement fifty weekends a year. Others have the ability forty times per year. Some are emotionally drained by the sermon's preparation, the sermon's saturation into the mind and heart, and the proclamation of the sermon. These pastors are effective thirty-five times per year, maybe less.

The question you're probably asking yourself is, "How do I conclude how many times a year is right for me?" While I can't give you a formula, I'll try to turn you in the right direction.

I once hosted Pastor Bob Russell (Southeast Christian Church, Louisville, Kentucky) and Pastor Steve Stroope (LakePointe Church, Rockwall, Texas). Each of them pastored a church that had grown from a few hundred in attendance to over fourteen thousand.

At one point, a discussion erupted that revealed a primary difference between the two men. The conversation focused on whether lead pastors of large churches should give their attention primarily to leadership or preaching.

Pastor Steve quickly announced, "I preach so I can lead." Pastor

Bob responded, "I lead so I can preach." Steve was signifying that he was most energized and fulfilled when leading. Bob was confiding that he was most energized and fulfilled when he was preaching.

If you're energized by and find your greatest satisfaction when leading, you'll be able to preach with excellence fewer times than those who are energized by and see their greatest satisfaction when preaching. If you're energized by and find your greatest satisfaction when preaching, you'll be able to preach with excellence many more times than those who are energized by and see their greatest satisfaction when leading.

Another way to conclude the number of times per year you're to preach is to answer this question, "Do I have the spiritual gift of teaching?"

Answering a few questions will help you conclude if you have the gift of teaching.

1. Does the study of God's Word and the time spent in commentaries and concordances while preparing for a sermon excite and energize you? Preachers with the gift of teaching look forward to study days.
2. When a new and exciting truth becomes known to you, are you on the edge of your seat to share it with others? Preachers with the gift of teaching are eager to proclaim a life-changing truth that has come to light.
3. When you finish preaching, are you energized? Those with the gift of teaching are more apt to be energized by the preparation to preach and the experience of preaching than those who don't have the gift. Pastors with the spiritual gift of teaching need to preach more times per year than those void of the gift.

Perpetually growing church pastors determine how many weekends a year they can be effective without burning out and preach that number of times. They are humble enough to welcome someone else to preach in their absence. They are secure enough not to be concerned with comparison. And they are wise enough to welcome a better communicator than themselves into their pulpit when they are not preaching.

Reducing the Preaching Load

PGC pastors find ways to relieve themselves of some of the preaching burden. Three common practices are listed below.

1. Hire a full-time staff member with the teaching gift. This person serves as the secondary preacher and preaches the weekends the lead pastor doesn't.
2. Build a teaching team. Very large PGCs with many staff members have strategically hired multiple staff members with the teaching gift. When the lead pastor isn't preaching, a member of the teaching team preaches.
3. Place a gifted preacher on a retainer, agree to the number of times per year the individual will preach, and pay accordingly. In most instances, this person is not a church member and travels to the church only on the weekends he's preaching. When using this method, the church is responsible for honorarium, travel, lodging, food, and incidentals.

LakePointe Church in Rockwall, Texas, has an arrangement with Pastor Mike Breaux. He serves as the church's secondary preacher. Before taking on that role, Mike was a teaching pastor at Willow Creek Community Church in South Barrington, Illinois. Before Willow Creek, he was the lead pastor at Southland Christian Church in Lexington, Kentucky. In the eight years Mike pastored Southland Christian, the church grew from 3,500 to more than 10,000. Mike lives in Lexington, Kentucky, and is a staff preacher at LakePointe in Dallas, Texas.

I reveal Mike's bio and the location where he lives so you can see that there are gifted available preachers that would be thrilled and honored to be on your teaching team. If you choose option 3, you needn't settle for unremarkable preaching. Contact the most gifted, affordable, unaffiliated preacher in your area and beyond. They may be available, willing, and honored to join your teaching team.

The Number of Minutes PGC Pastors Preach

It may seem absurd to bring the number of minutes a sermon should last into the perpetually growing church conversation. Actually, it isn't.

The length of a preacher's sermon significantly affects church growth. Pastor Chris Hodges pastors one of the largest and fastest-growing churches in the United States. Chris founded the church with thirty-four people on February 4, 2001. Today, the church comprises twenty-three campuses with an average weekly attendance exceeding fifty thousand.

Each year Pastor Chris hosts a conference that should not be ignored. The GROW Conference unearths undeniable, proven church practices that lead to church growth. In one of the sessions, he tells the story of a pastor who asked for Chris's guidance. The story goes like this.

A seasoned pastor was seeking counsel from Pastor Chris. He was a gifted leader and preacher, but his church wasn't growing. Pastor Chris set aside time in his busy schedule to hear his story, evaluate his ministry, and give him guidance. Like the vast majority of pastors, the church leader longed to lead a growing church, but the church remained stagnant.

As part of their conversation, Pastor Chris asked the disheartened pastor to describe the worship service. Pastor Chris asked him specifically, "How long are your sermons?" The pastor proudly stated, "Fifty-five minutes."

Pastor Chris immediately realized the unarguable reason the church wasn't growing—wearisomely long sermons. When Pastor Chris pointed this out, the seasoned pastor aggressively responded that he would not shorten the length of his sermons. The meeting ended abruptly. Pastor Chris went back to leading one of the most influential and fast-growing churches in the country. The struggling pastor went back to be the ineffective leader of a stagnant church.

About four months later, the pastor contacted Pastor Chris to say he would do whatever he suggested. Pastor Chris told him to shorten the message to thirty-five minutes. The church immediately began to grow.

The amount of time a preacher preaches does affect church growth.

Pastor Bob Russell has created a formula to aid pastors in concluding how long their sermon should be. Bob suggests the following three-step process. When determining how long a pastor should preach, first determine the pastor's giftedness as a communicator on a scale of

1 to 10 (1 being a terrible preacher and 10 being an amazing preacher). Second, subtract 2. Finally, multiply by 5.

So, if you conclude your communication skills are an 8, you've completed step one. Then subtract 2. That leaves you with the number 6. Finally, multiply by 5. Your sermon should be 30 minutes long and no longer.

If you study multiple PGCs, you'll find that the sermon length varies from preacher to preacher (although most seldom preach more than thirty minutes). If you want to lead a PGC, you must determine how long you can hold the attention of the congregation God has given you and stop short of forcing them into even thirty seconds of boredom.

Preaching is the most widely celebrated, carefully scrutinized, overly analyzed, and important of all the things a lead pastor does. It is God's plan by which the world hears the gospel. Through the inspiration of the Holy Spirit, Paul penned, "For since in the wisdom of God the world through its wisdom did not know him, God was pleased through the foolishness of what was preached to save those who believe" (1 Corinthians 1:21).

With this truth in mind, it is imperative that pastors know the culture they were called into and preach to that culture, understand their giftedness and respond accordingly, reduce the preaching load so that each time they stand before their congregation they bring their best, and embrace the sermon length that is right for them.

Chapter 14

Fund-Raiser

Then the leaders of families, the officers of the tribes of Israel, the commanders of thousands and commanders of hundreds, and the officials in charge of the king's work gave willingly. They gave toward the work on the temple of God five thousand talents and ten thousand darics of gold, ten thousand talents of silver, eighteen thousand talents of bronze and a hundred thousand talents of iron. Anyone who had precious stones gave them to the treasury of the temple of the Lord in the custody of Jehiel the Gershonite. The people rejoiced at the willing response of their leaders, for they had given freely and wholeheartedly to the Lord. David the king also rejoiced greatly.
—1 Chronicles 29:6–9

Perpetually growing churches must have capital because growth creates the need for additional resources. The need to purchase property, renovate well-worn structures, construct new buildings, resurface parking lots, add new staff members, and so on, at the optimal time is an undeniable key to church growth.

Without fund-raising, numeric growth can stall and the only person who can lead the church's fund-raising efforts is the church's lead pastor. God strategically gave the top-tier leader the authority and influence to inspire people to give sacrificially.

Without question the area where many pastors feel least prepared to lead their churches is stewardship in general and church finances in particular. This is true regardless of the size of the church. Whether it is a congregation of fifteen people or fifteen thousand people, few leaders feel more than just adequate to lead in financial aspects of their ministry. The problem, however, is that most churches expect and depend on their pastor not only to raise the finances but ensure that those finances are managed in a God-honoring way after they are collected. And if pastors don't know how or can't do it, then it won't get done, at least not well.[1]

One of the lead pastor's primary roles is to inspire people to give. This is accomplished through several means—vision-casting, storytelling, and educating people about what the Bible teaches about giving and helping people manage their money.

Vision-Casting

Pastor Steve Stroope declares:

> You must regularly cast a clear, compelling vision for the church. The key to cultivating donors for your church's ministry is vision. Our experience is that people are not interested in just paying the light bills or staff salaries, nor do they respond to guilt trips, negativism, or shortages. People give to big, dynamic visions that, in turn, produce the passion that is vital to giving. They are more willing to invest in "what could be" (future possibilities) than "what is" (present reality), especially if "what is" is floundering or in the red. To a certain degree, raising finances is a vision measure. What does that mean? People's giving response will often tell you something about the quality of your church's vision and the leader's ability to cast that vision.[2]

PGC pastors continually cast a compelling, God-sized vision. You will have to find what works for your church, but below is a list of projects that illustrate big vision dreams that might inspire a church to give.

- Build a children's ministry building through which the church's AWANA program can reach 75 percent of the households in a rural community with the gospel.
- Over the next ten years, fund one hundred pastors in third-world countries.
- Build and staff a gospel-centered pregnancy support center on the church property.
- Start a church-planting network to reach every major secularized city in the United States.

- Create a ministry training school that will send hundreds of gospel-centered, influential pastors and staff members worldwide.

Storytelling

The second practice that motivates congregants to give is the art of inspiration. People give when their hearts compel them to, not because the pastor tells them they should. Inspire through storytelling. Stories of a life changed or ministries that are changing lives are the most powerful of stories. The stories can be told in various ways: (1) sermon illustrations, (2) video, and (3) personal testimonies, to mention a few.

Most PGCs have a video team. The video team can capture church members serving the poor, a mission team leading a Bible study at a prison in a third-world country, students accepting Christ and receiving the call to ministry at student camp, and so on. Two-minute video segments shown in worship services are potent ways to tell stories and will remind congregants how their gifts are making a difference. If your video team doesn't have the bandwidth, unedited B-roll or still photos can have the same impact when combined with a story told live.

The most effective time to tell stories is prior to taking the offering. "God loves a cheerful giver" (2 Corinthians 9:7 ESV). People are joyful in their giving when they see their giving is making a difference. When telling stories of lives changed before the offering is given, congregants are joyful because they find fulfillment in realizing the effect of their past giving and fulfillment in what they are about to give. When congregants see how their giving transforms lives, they are much more apt to give generously and cheerfully.

Educating

Most of all, it is the responsibility of the lead pastor to preach to and teach the congregation what God says about money and the giving of tithes and offerings. There are multiple reasons for this essential practice.

1. It is an idol issue. When believers serve money it's impossible for them to serve and love God. Unapologetically, Jesus tells his disciples, "No one can serve two masters. Either you will hate

the one and love the other, or you will be devoted to the one and despise the other. You cannot serve both God and money (Matthew 6:24).

2. It is a priority issue. Mark 10 includes the story of a man who approaches Jesus longing to become one of Jesus's followers. He asks the question "What must I do to inherit eternal life?" (v. 17). After discussing a list of sins the man has strived to refrain from all of his life, "Jesus looked at him and loved him. 'One thing you lack,' he said. 'Go, sell everything you have and give to the poor, and you will have treasure in heaven. Then come, follow me'" (v. 21). The man's response is revealing, "At this the man's face fell. He went away sad, because he had great wealth."

3. It is a faith issue. Jesus said, "Therefore I tell you, do not worry about your life, what you will eat or drink; or about your body, what you will wear. Is not life more than food, and the body more than clothes? Look at the birds of the air; they do not sow or reap or store away in barns, and yet your heavenly Father feeds them. Are you not much more valuable than they? Can any one of you by worrying add a single hour to your life? (Matthew 6:25–27)

Each of these moments in time occurs when Jesus is speaking to his disciples. Because lead pastors are the pulpit disciple makers, only when they raise the bar to the level Jesus raised it will the disciples realize that it's impossible to serve God and money. If they serve money, they are haters of God. If they prioritize money over God's kingdom, they are not worthy of followership. And if they are captured in the cell of worry, they lack the deep faith that disciples exhibit.

The only way for a disciple of Jesus to reach full maturity is for that disciple first to sacrificially, systematically, and consistently prioritize the first tenth of their income to kingdom purposes. The knowledge of this fact falls directly onto the church's lead pulpiteer, the lead pastor.

PGCs accomplish fund-raising through three primary strategies— weekly/tithe giving, gift-based donor giving, and project giving.

Weekly/Tithe Giving

Weekly/tithe giving is the most crucial giving responsibility. Not only is most of the church's income attained through repeated and consistent offerings, but it is also through making the ongoing gift that people experience spiritual growth and learn the rhythms of giving. While many churches see this as "the moment the offering plate is passed," PGCs realize that congregants have multiple ways to give.

Lifeway Generosity unearthed four telling facts about how people give: "49% of all church giving transactions are now made with a card. 60% of churchgoers say they are willing to give online. Churches that accept tithing online grew giving 30%, and, even with 'live church,' people don't carry cash or even a checkbook like they used to."[3]

PGCs make it possible for individuals and households to give in a way that resonates with them. Consider how your church could provide such options as online, automated, or even text giving in addition to in-person giving.

Some PGC pastors aid people in learning the rhythm of weekly giving by leaning into seasons of discovery. Pastor Craig Groeschel (Life.Church, Edmond, OK) calls his church members to engage in the "Three Month Tithe Challenge." He challenges those in his church not yet tithing to tithe for three months and see what God does. Pastor Steve Stroope (LakePointe Church, Rockwall, TX) set a goal for a percentage of his church to start automated giving over a specified period of weeks. He emphasized the importance of automated giving by reminding the church weekly that the church could plan ministry most effectively if the leadership knew more precisely what the church's income would be.

As Pastor Steve suggested, when a large percentage of givers are automated givers, a church will be able to plan well and the income will increase.

One church has an unusual and effective practice. After someone gives the second time, that person receives a communication with a video. In this video, the lead pastor describes the vision of the church or offers a story of someone experiencing life-change. A request is then made for the giver to sign up for automated giving and a link is provided.

Honoring first-time givers is essential. Many PGCs send a communication of thanks after receiving an individual's or household's first gift. This is a way of thanking the giver for honoring God and showing their commitment to Him.

Gift-Based Donor Giving

The Holy Spirit gives spiritual gifts to believers, "and he distributes them to each one, just as he determines" (1 Corinthians 12:11*b*).

Some people in every church have the spiritual gift of giving. Most of them, God has blessed with an above-average income. They have been given the supernatural gift of giving and are responsible for exercising it. Their hearts resonate with causes they believe in, and they are willing to go over and above the weekly tithe. Because they have the spiritual gift of giving, they will engage in financial giving far beyond that of the average church member.

Most are honored to do so and need just three things—connection to the lead pastor, to be inspired by the lead pastor's vision, and to be offered an opportunity.

The connection to the lead pastor doesn't demand the pastor and the individual be best friends, but it does mean that the pastor is journeying with the individual as they cultivate their gift.

> Rather than ignore them, as many pastors are inclined to do, identify them and meet with them periodically to cultivate their gift along with their relationship with God, just as you might someone with the gift of leadership or evangelism. Ask how the church can minister effectively to them. Do not forget to thank them for their ministry to the church. Make sure they understand the church's core organizational values, mission, vision, and strategy. There may be times when you ask them to consider exercising their gift of giving to a particular cause, such as a mission project or new facility. That is okay. It's the same as when we expect leaders to lead and evangelists to evangelize. Why should we not expect givers to give? When you make that request, it is much better if you do so out of relationship that you have already developed with your giving champions. They may also help you network with others who have the gift of giving.[4]

Two Donor Development Practices

Informal Vision Sharing—Often PGC pastors will have a meal with people who have the gift of giving. One PGC pastor of a large church sets aside one lunch of this nature per week. Because many of these gifted givers are visionaries themselves, they long to hear what the church is doing or considering doing. If the lead pastor shares passionately and with clarity what is the next hill to climb, in many instances, without any prodding or requesting, the church receives a substantial donation.

Group Gatherings—Some PGC pastors gather five couples and a non-married adult to meet in a designated room in the church building—individuals believed to have the spiritual gift of giving. At the outset of the meeting, the pastor thanks them for coming and for the difference they're making in people's lives.

After eating a meal, each person is asked to tell what the church has meant to them. Inevitably people will share of a marriage saved, a child who followed Christ, someone they know freed from addiction, or how the church has transformed their household. The lead pastor then verbalizes the vision God has given the church to reach the community and the world. By the time this conversation is completed, the spiritually gifted givers are inspired to give to God's unparalleled purposes.

Project Giving

PGCs will stagnate numerically without building buildings, updating present facilities, purchasing land, refurbishing parking lots, upgrading sound systems, and the list could go on and on. While many of these projects are taken care of through weekly tithes and some special offerings, there are times when a capital campaign is necessary.

A capital campaign is a twelve-week emphasis to seek sacrificial commitments for capital funds. The commitments are fulfilled over a three-year period. Giving is over and above church members' regular giving. In most situations, capital campaigns raise between 1 to 1.5 times the previous year's undesignated receipts. Some churches experience much better outcomes.

A few closing thoughts on giving and fund-raising. Giving to God's kingdom work isn't an obligation. It's an opportunity. PGC pastors should approach their congregants with this mindset. They should also give them concrete direction. Many PGC pastors verbalize the 10, 10,

80 formula—give your first 10 percent to God's causes and the local church, save 10 percent, and live off the other 80 percent. But they don't stop there.

Many PGCs offer classes and workshops for those in debt who couldn't presently give 10 percent to the church or involve themselves in special offerings and projects. The church journeys with them as they get out of debt, encourages them to start giving at a workable level for them at present, and encourages them to give a full tithe and beyond when the time is right. This is God-honoring and a disciple-making opportunity.

Pastor Steve Stroope was the senior pastor of LakePointe Church in Rockwall, Texas. During his tenure, the church grew from fifty-seven to over fifteen thousand on seven campuses and planted forty-eight strategic churches in spiritually under-resourced cities such as Boston, Montreal, New York, and San Francisco. Today Steve spearheads the church's Strategic Launch Network, a network of like-minded churches, leaders, and friends working together to start strategic, high-impact churches in North America, focusing on reaching people who do not know Jesus. He also provides direct coaching to these church planters and pioneer missionaries.

Steve is the author or coauthor of multiple books including *Tribal Church, It Starts at Home: A Practical Guide to Nurturing Lifelong Faith*, and *Money Matters in the Church*. I have never met a church leader with a pastor's heart and business mind like Pastor Steve.

His interview will challenge you to lead your church to give sacrificially for kingdom causes and enlighten you on accomplishing that.

Author: Why is the senior pastor the key to effective fundraising?
Pastor Steve: The senior pastor is the trusted face. He also has a regular platform for teaching God's Word, which says a lot about the blessings that come with giving.

Author: What obstacles keep most senior pastors from leading in the area of finance, and what must those who are hesitant do to overcome their reluctance?

Pastor Steve: Pastors are afraid people will think all the church cares about is raising money. The pastor must become convinced that it's a privilege to give and then communicate that truth to his people.

Author: What would you say to senior pastors who want to assign the fund-raising role to a staff member, elder team, short-term committee, or the deacon body?

Pastor Steve: Bad choice. They have neither the platform nor the influence. Another staff member can help or organize systems that facilitate the process (such as sending letters), but the pastor must be the face.

Author: In your book *Money Matters*, you speak of lead pastors cultivating the gift of giving the Holy Spirit has instilled in some church members. In what settings do you do that, and what do the conversations in each of those settings look like?

Pastor Steve: Private one-on-ones and group settings can both be used. A regular rhythm needs to be calendared for both, or given the reluctance some pastors have for these activities, it will never take place.

Author: To find out which church members may have the gift of giving, a lead pastor must know their giving record. Many pastors believe an individual's giving information should remain unknown to the lead pastor. How would you counsel pastors with this mindset?

Pastor Steve: The pastor should look at the top 25 percent of givers every year to look for discipleship opportunities. Some fear they will be tempted to treat wealthy church members with preference. Truth is they already know who is wealthy. Giving records tell you who is generous and obedient. The only temptation is anger at discovering the loudest complainers a lot of time contribute nothing.

Author: During your forty years of pastoring LakePointe Church, how many capital campaigns did you lead the church to do?
Pastor Steve: Ten.

Author: How often can a lead pastor do an effective capital campaign?
Pastor Steve: About once every five years.

Author: What are the unarguable keys to an effective capital campaign?
Pastor Steve: Smaller advance gatherings for key donors, a four-week series on vision (not giving), a commitment month (four weekends, not just one), and a clear printed and digital communication piece telling your people what will happen if they give generously. As well as physical and online combination envelope and commitment card enclosed with the publicity piece.

Author: You are known as one of the most effective capital campaign experts in the country and have guided many very large churches in their capital campaign. With that in mind, what role must the lead pastor play, and what are the responsibilities that only he can carry out if the church is to experience an effective capital campaign?
Pastor Steve: The executive pastor or counterpart can execute the details, but once again the pastor must be the face and the voice.

Author: Indebtedness is sometimes necessary to reach more people with the gospel. But some church leaders, including pastors, elders, deacons, finance teams, budget committees, and so on, are of the mindset that a church should never go into debt. What words of wisdom would you have for these individuals and teams?
Pastor Steve: The Bible doesn't prohibit debt. It warns about excessive debt. A church's portion of their annual budget servicing debt should not exceed 20 percent There is no command in the Bible prohibiting debt, but there is one we call the Great Commission. If our carrying out the Great Commission is

hampered by a self-imposed reluctance to incur reasonable debt, we are being disobedient. Debt is one tool in our toolbox. No question, it is a "power tool" and should be used carefully (and only when wearing goggles).

Many pastors are hesitant to elevate the biblical requirement of tithing and giving above the tithe. They know there will be subtle and sometimes less-than-subtle pushback. But guiding church members to give is courageously directing people to be disciples of Jesus Christ. Jesus said, "No one can serve two masters. Either you will hate the one and love the other, or you will be devoted to the one and despise the other. You cannot serve both God and money" (Matthew 6:24).

For many, the first step to making Jesus the *Lord* of their lives is a pastor directing them to steward what is God's, the income they receive for the work they do. Then and only then will they serve Him, love Him, and be devoted to Him.

Chapter 15

Virtuous Undershepherd

This is what the Lord, the God of Israel, says: "I anointed you king over Israel, and I delivered you from the hand of Saul. I gave your master's house to you, and your master's wives into your arms. I gave you all Israel and Judah. And if all this had been too little, I would have given you even more. Why did you despise the word of the Lord by doing what is evil in his eyes? You struck down Uriah the Hittite with the sword and took his wife to be your own. You killed him with the sword of the Ammonites. Now, therefore, the sword will never depart from your house, because you despised me and took the wife of Uriah the Hittite to be your own." This is what the Lord says: "Out of your own household I am going to bring calamity on you."

—2 Samuel 12:7*a*–11*a*

Nothing brings the growth of a PGC to a grinding halt more abruptly than a lead pastor's moral failure. God calls pastors to exceptionally high standards. Through the inspiration of the Holy Spirit, Paul unpacked the character of God-honoring pastors. He was amazingly specific:

Whoever aspires to be an overseer desires a noble task. Now the overseer is to be above reproach, faithful to his wife, temperate, self-controlled, respectable, hospitable, able to teach, not given to drunkenness, not violent but gentle, not quarrelsome, not a lover of money. He must manage his own family well and see that his children obey him, and he must do so in a manner worthy of full respect. (If anyone does not know how to manage his own family, how can he take care of God's church?) He must not be a recent convert, or he may become conceited and fall under the same judgment as the devil. He must also have a good reputation with outsiders, so that he will not fall into disgrace and into the devil's trap. (1 Timothy 3:1*b*–7)

When lead pastors of PGCs engage, for instance, in sexuality outside the biblical opportunities unearthed by all-knowing God, they are no longer "above reproach," "faithful to their wives," "respectable," or "of good reputation with outsiders." They have fallen "into disgrace."

Why is it essential that these extraordinary expectations be held firmly by senior leadership? Because no one will follow an integrity-less leader, especially if the person is also God's chosen lead pastor. Even those who choose to stick by a pastor's side after an indiscretion are being benevolent. They may attempt to give grace, but they won't follow him as he goes forward to take the next hill.

When a lead pastor sins, he shouldn't be surprised that many church members instantly turn away from him and the church he pastors. They aren't making a cognitive decision. Their minds remind them that God has extended His grace to the pastor and gives grace to all people and others deserve grace. But when the story of a lead pastor who has chosen sexuality outside of marriage between a husband and wife is made public, the heart overrides the mind. No one should be surprised.

There are two reasons for this.

- Allegiance. The church members have shown their dedication to the pastor. Under his leadership, they have sacrificed their time, talents, and financial resources. The communal goal was the completion of the pastor's vision, a vision that has saturated their hearts. They have given their fidelity to him, and in return, he has given them infidelity.
- The Jesus Dilemma. When a lead pastor fails morally, the spiritually immature believer's faith is devastatingly upended. Right or wrong, congregants' hearts tell them the lead pastor is the closest representation of Jesus available to them. Because the pastor is the subconscious Jesus figure for many, they subconsciously are deceived to believe Jesus did something He is incapable of, which is betraying them. Their hearts cannot accept a betrayal so overwhelming. They often leave more than the church. They leave the faith.

Sadly, if a list were made of pastors who have fallen into the pit of salacious sexuality, it would be embarrassingly lengthy.

Every pastor would be wise to adopt and live Pastor Rick Warren's staff standards with a few additions. His Saddleback staff standards for maintaining moral integrity are wise guidance for overtaking a sin before it conquers us.

1. Thou shalt not go to lunch alone with the opposite sex.
2. Thou shalt not have the opposite sex pick you up or drive you places when it is just the two of you.
3. Thou shalt not kiss any attendee of the opposite sex or show affection that could be questioned.
4. Thou shalt not visit the opposite sex alone at home.
5. Thou shalt not counsel the opposite sex alone at the office, and thou shalt not counsel the opposite sex more than once without that person's mate. Refer them.
6. Thou shalt not discuss detailed sexual problems with the opposite sex in counseling. Refer them.
7. Thou shalt not discuss your marriage problems with an attendee of the opposite sex.
8. Thou shalt be careful in answering emails, instant messages, chatrooms, cards, or letters from the opposite sex.
9. Thou shalt make your secretary your protective ally.
10. Thou shalt pray for the integrity of other staff members.[1]

I would add these two additions:

1. Thou shalt not view any questionable images on the internet.
2. Thou shalt not engage in any conversation that could be deemed inappropriate via texts, email, Instagram, TikTok, Facebook, and any other social media platforms.

I seldom use these words, but I feel this deep in my being as I write this book section. Pastor, I BEG YOU. Guard yourself in such a way that you will not "fall into disgrace," which is "the devil's trap," and dishonor yourself, your family, your church, and your God.

Keep this fact in mind. A lead pastor's sexual sin isn't a PGC's kryptonite. Superman was weak and dying when faced with kryptonite, and it took minutes to subdue him. A lead pastor's moral failure is like dropping an atomic bomb. It instantly kills the hearts of many and throws a church into chaotic decline instantaneously. The scars it leaves may never disappear completely.

Chapter 16

Long-Timer

After Joshua had dismissed the Israelites, they went to take possession of the land, each to their own inheritance. The people served the Lord throughout the lifetime of Joshua and of the elders who outlived him and who had seen all the great things the Lord had done for Israel. Joshua son of Nun, the servant of the LORD, died at the age of a hundred and ten.

—Judges 2:6–8*b*

In 1979, Rick Warren, pastor of Saddleback Church, one of the most prominent and influential perpetually growing churches in the world, did a deep dive into the actions of healthy, growing churches. One of his earliest learnings was that churches experiencing long-term growth are led by pastors who spearhead one church over the long haul. In his groundbreaking book *The Purpose Driven Church*, Pastor Rick wrote these words:

> Healthy, large churches are led by pastors who have been there a long time. I found dozens of examples. A long pastorate does not *guarantee* a church will grow, but changing pastors every few years guarantees a church *won't* grow.
>
> . . . I prayed, "Father, I'm willing to go anyplace in the world you want to send me. But I ask for the privilege of investing my entire life in just one location. I don't care where you put me, but I'd like to stay wherever it is for the rest of my life."[1]

Saddleback Church began in 1980 with a Bible study group of seven people. In 2018, Saddleback announced it had baptized fifty thousand people. In 2020, Saddleback's weekly attendance averaged 23,494 people on fifteen campuses. All under the leadership of Pastor

Warren.

Some question the lead pastor longevity and church-growth concept. They believe that long-term pastors will wield too much power. They perceive that the pastors may grow complacent, lose the passion they once had, and do only what is necessary to receive their paychecks. They say that a church will grow stagnant and lose its momentum if one pastor leads for many years.

After peering into the PGC world for many years, I see through a different lens. After many years of serving a thriving church, PGC pastors gain outrageous amounts of honor, but they don't throw their power around. They yield their influence for kingdom purposes. They don't grow complacent and lose their passion for the work, because they live their lives working in tandem with God to see people rescued from hell and see the vision God has given them become a reality, both of which demand a lifelong commitment. And that commitment and dream bring their heart to life every day. The church doesn't grow stagnant and lose momentum because PGC pastors are off-the-charts leaders. Leaders of PGC caliber consistently seek God's guidance on the next hill that needs to be taken and lead their congregation to join them in the taking of it. Even if momentum has waned, anticipation and exhilaration are by-products of a new initiative yielding eternal dividends.

The longevity principle was true when Pastor Rick Warren declared it in 1979, was true before 1979, and remains true today.

Section 2

Principles and Practices of Perpetually Growing Churches

If you think of church attendance as gaining attenders through the front door and losing them out the back door, then perpetually growing churches have figured out how to close the church's back door and have concluded what is necessary to assimilate guests and keep church members for the long haul. No church will ever be a perpetually growing church without doggedly doing what must be done to keep people.

Pastor Larry Osborne, in his extraordinary book *Sticky Church*, compares two churches. The churches he's speaking of both grew in attendance from 250 to 500 people over a ten-year period:

> Church A is a revolving door. It loses 7 people for every 10 it adds. To reach 500, it will have to add 834 new members or attenders.
>
> Church B is a sticky church. It loses only 3 people for every 10 it adds. To reach 500, it has to add 357 new members or attenders.
>
> On the surface, both churches appear to have doubled. But the revolving door church had to reach 834 new people to get there, while the sticky church only needed to reach 357.
>
> Obviously, doubling attendance is a lot easier for a sticky church than for a revolving door church. No surprise there. But here's the kicker: *After ten years, the church with the big back door will have 500 attenders and 584 former attenders!* And every year after that, the spread between the number of ex-attenders and the number of current attenders will grow larger.
>
> No matter what the church does to expand the size of the front door, it's going to be hard to keep reaching people when the predominant word on the street is, "I *used* to go there."[1]

Perpetually growing churches have concluded, embraced, and are practicing those ministries, ideals, and initiatives that make it possible to close the church's back door. In doing so, those churches continue to be perpetually growing churches. The rest of this book unearths what perpetually growing churches do to connect with people, assimilate people, remain relevant, and continue a growth trajectory.

Chapter 17

Revolutionary Relevance

There is a time for everything, and a season for every activity under the heavens.

—Ecclesiastes 3:1

In Thom Schultz's article "The Church's Frightful Kodak Moment," he illustrates the mindset of many churches:

> Kodak dominated the photographic scene for over 100 years. It commanded an 89 percent market share of photographic film sales in the United States. Almost everyone used the brand. And the company's advertising language of a "Kodak moment" became part of the common lexicon.
>
> What happened since then has become a colossal story of failure and missed opportunities. A gigantic casualty in the wake of digital photography—a technology that Kodak invented.
>
> That's right. Kodak engineer Steve Sasson invented the first digital camera in 1975. He later said, "But it was filmless photography, so management's reaction was, 'That's cute, but don't tell anyone about it.'" And the company entered into decades of agonizing decline, unable to perceive and respond to the advancing digital revolution. In 2012 this American icon filed for bankruptcy.[1]

Schultz reveals that there were three reasons for the demise of Kodak: (1) a misunderstanding of the mission. Kodak believed they were in the film business when they were actually in the image business. (2) A failure to read the times. They thought people would never give up hard copies. They believed people might leave hard copies for a period of time but would return to hard copies. They had contempt for new technologies. (3) Fear of loss. They believed they would lose their preexisting customers.

Many churches are losing ground for the same three reasons. First, they have a misunderstanding of the mission. They believe the mission is to sustain the church's preaching ministry, programs, and practices when the mission is really to reach the world with the gospel. Second, they fail to read the times. They believe new church practices are fads that will pass. They hold firmly to what has been, waiting for people to return for what once was. Finally, they fear the loss of their present congregants. They're unwilling to revisit practices, so they can keep the already convinced in place, at ease, and paying the bills.

PGCs read the times and know that reaching the next generation with the gospel will demand meeting them where they are. They embrace that preaching, worship styles, ministries, and branding must be revised for the next generation. PGCs don't fear the loss of the presently saved congregants as much as they fear standing before their Lord having been the generation that selfishly clung to their outdated practices for the sake of comfort while the next generation spends eternity separated from God.

PGCs hold to the fact that elderly, already convinced church members are not their primary target audience. They will do what it takes to reach the lost, especially the next generation, with the gospel. Relevance is not an option. It is a necessity!

PGCs revisit their methods consistently and make the necessary changes systematically.

Preaching

In his book *Preaching: Communicating Faith in a Skeptical Age*, Pastor Tim Keller reminds pastors that relating to the culture a pastor is preaching to, and connecting to that culture, is essential:

> When Paul speaks of life-changing preaching he is not limiting himself to the listeners' inner world. He is also looking at the culture in which they live.
>
> "For since in the wisdom of God the world through its wisdom did not know him, God was pleased through the foolishness of what was preached to save those who believe. Jews demand signs and Greeks look for wisdom, but we preach Christ crucified: a

stumbling block to Jews and foolishness to Gentiles, but to those whom God has called, both Jews and Greeks, Christ the power of God and the wisdom of God" (1 Corinthians 1:21–24, NIV).

Paul here deftly summarizes the differences between Greek and Jewish cultural narrative. Each society has a worldview or "world story" or "cultural narrative" that shapes the identities and assumptions of those in that society. In general, the Greeks valued philosophy, the arts, and intellectual attainments, while the Jews valued power and practical skill over discursive thought. Paul challenges both cultural narratives with the cross of Jesus. To the Greeks, a salvation that came not through elevated thought and philosophy but through a crucified Savior was the opposite of wisdom—it was foolishness. To the Jews, a salvation that came not through power, through a deliverer who overthrew the Romans, but through a crucified Savior was the opposite of strength—it was weakness. Paul uses the gospel to confront each culture with the idolatrous nature of its trusts and values.

And yet after challenging each culture, he also discerns and affirms its core aspiration.[2]

In our ever-changing society, each generation holds to a set of cultural norms. While the gospel is always the message, PGC pastors realize and accept that they must tweak their preaching style if they're going to reach each generation with the gospel.

In the last sixty years, three methods of preaching have been practiced, each connecting with and being effective for a generation. Evangelistic preaching dominated the scene in the sixties and was prevalent into the eighties—the era of Billy Graham's crusades. The Holy Spirit chose to work through gospel-centric sermons with a call to "come forward" at the end of each service. Because of Christian culture and the gospel-saturated rural and urban societies, the evangelistic method of preaching was welcomed, accepted, and effective. It was the preaching method utilized in most evangelical churches.

The late eighties and nineties brought the seeker sermon to the forefront—a much different method of preaching. The seeker sermon focused on everyday real-life issues like having a healthy marriage, raising God-honoring children, and so on. Done right, the sermon always led to a presentation of the gospel. Because the generation was a generation of self-help individuals longing to find and live a happy and robust life, there needed to be a connecting rod between the self-absorbed, unsaved person and the gospel of Jesus Christ. When the preacher spoke of real-life issues, he built a bridge that led to a relatable proclamation of the gospel.

Presently the gospel-only sermon is a prominent practice. Whether proclaimed through expository preaching or topical preaching, the gospel-only sermon takes laser-like aim at the person of Jesus and His gospel. In an era when individuals sincerely believe their truth is truth and will verbally attack those who question their confusion, presenting the person of Christ is the effective evangelistic preaching paradigm. The present generation is much more apt to connect the dots of the gospel to a loving Father who sacrificed His Son on their behalf than accept what they believe to be the antiquated doctrine and dogma of a preacher they consider a radicalized, illogical, proselytizing zealot. The person of Jesus and His love for all people resonate in our present era.

While the message will never change, the method of preaching does. PGC pastors accept this fact and transition as necessary or bring teaching pastors on board who preach effectively to reach the next generation.

For those who cannot revisit their preaching style due to an ingrained conviction or institutional requirement, consider the following aid in connecting with the next generation.

Exhibit a demeanor of joy. In an era where everyone seems to be angry at someone or is mad at people who have an opposing viewpoint, the next generation and beyond will be drawn to a preacher exhibiting a spirit of joy.

Prioritize grace over judgment. The generations before the present generation attend church acting as though they have avoided sin. This pharisaical mindset breeds a church in judgment of those who admit to their struggle with sin. Next generations are fully aware that they are sinners and that no one, even Christians, can live sinless lives. Grace despite, not judgment because of, sin resonates with them and should be a primary theme of today's sermons.

Dress casually. Many people say that dressing up for church is appropriate and necessary. If you're in that camp, I encourage you to attend a church that's reaching a massive number of Gen Ys and older Gen Zs. Check out what the pastor, the band, and those on the stage are wearing. Younger generations consider "dressing nice" to simply mean clean and presentable. They will often be seen in jeans even at weddings and funerals. Dressing "down" is more apt to make you a magnet for the next generation than dressing for your boomer friends.

Be authentic. If there's one thing that will turn the next generations away from church, it's a lack of pastoral authenticity. When you preach, just be you. Don't use an Adrian Rogers voice, travel around the room like T. D. Jakes, or hang from the rafters for effect. That is, unless that's truly who you are.

Encourage them just as they are. I'm amazed at the number of preachers who stand in their pulpits and start sentences with the words "The next generation . . ." and end with phrases like "is sinful and needs to repent," "is ungodly and needs Jesus," "is going to bring God's judgment upon us all," and the list could go on and on. You will never reach the next generation with verbal attacks. Only by embracing them where they are and accepting them as they are will they be drawn to you and your church. Instead of judging the subsequent generations, tell them you're grateful for them and you love them. Instead of beating up on them, thank them for coming. Instead of judging them, be a loving friend and father figure for them.

Be transparent. If you want to reach the next generation, speak of your struggles with sin, mistakes you've made, and the bad decisions that led to painful consequences for you and others. Talking openly about your mishaps speaks volumes to fellow strugglers, especially the age group that is seldom hesitant to speak of their own. By the way, they already know your life isn't perfect, and they'll only connect with you more when you are honest enough to tell them you're broken, just like they are.

Make them laugh. Humor transcends all age barriers. Preachers who reach the next generation and beyond laugh at themselves, tell jokes that connect (but aren't corny), and have a natural ability to create laughter when preaching. Teens and young men and women, like everyone else, love and need to laugh! While I can't prove it biblically, I believe wholeheartedly that laughter pries the heart open so the gospel can be poured into it.

Remove visible sacred cows. Visible symbols of a bygone era are major obstacles if you're declaring "It's a new day!" The pulpit that has been in place for fifty years is a constant reminder that we are who we once were and will always be just that. A Lord's Supper table built by a charter church member one hundred years ago displayed between you and your congregation each Sunday screams "We ain't changin' for nobody!" to young adults. While removing the pulpit or the Lord's Supper table may be controversial, it may also be a key to connecting with the next generation. Check out the preachers who are reaching the next generation and beyond, and you'll find that, when preaching, some use music stands and sit on stools, some just sit on a stool (this is my practice), and some sit at a tall coffeehouse-type of table. But very, very seldom are any of these preachers standing behind a pulpit. And you will rarely, if ever, see a Lord's Supper table gracing the front of the worship center.

For many, the bottom line is this. If you choose to be a so-called model preacher as you were taught to be in Bible school or seminary many years ago, you may not reach the next generation through your preaching. If the model you were taught inhibits you from being humorous, transparent, grace-giving, accepting of sin-soaked sinners, authentic, casually dressed, or joyful when you preach, then it's probably a model for a bygone era.

Worship Services

PGCs continue to practice biblical worship while revisiting some methods. They do this to reach the next generation and those far from Christ.

Some of the practices that PGCs are practicing are listed below.

- Set the Tone Early. Set the tone in the parking lot and the church lobby. As attendees arrive in the church parking lot, they'll hear celebratory worship music echoing through loudspeakers. These sounds are also reverberating in the church lobby.

- Worship Experience for Two Audiences. Many PGCs are preparing a service for two audiences, believers and the not-yet-convinced. The worship experience is more celebration than meditation. An environment of joy and jubilation is the primary mood of the worship experience, which is captivating for both believers and unbelievers.

- Strategic Worship Leaders. Those who take the stage are strategically cast to connect with the church's primary target audience. Seventy percent of those on the stage are the people group a church is striving to reach. If the church is longing to reach Gen Ys and older Gen Zs, a choir made up of fifty-, sixty-, and seventysomethings is an ineffective choice. If the church is in a community made up of many people of color, the people group the church is striving to reach, 70 percent of those on stage should be people of color.

- Service Host. PGCs have transitioned from the lead pastor "doing announcements" to another individual hosting the worship service. The host greets the guests and requests they turn in a guest card or digitally let the church know they are in attendance, reminds those in attendance of the importance of giving, how their gifts have been used for kingdom purposes, and the multiple ways they can give (onsite via passed offering plates or buckets in the back as attendees are leaving, by mail, or digitally), and builds anticipation for the sermon to come by telling the congregation what the sermon series is and how the sermon about to be presented is vital to their own lives.

- Prerecorded Announcements. PGCs have done away with announcements that interrupt the worship experience. The only opportunities announced are activities that are available to a large percentage of the congregation. Many shoot a three-minute video that is played before the service, at the beginning of the service, or the end of the service. A vibrant voice passionately making people aware of important upcoming events and ministry opportunities is captured in a captivating setting.

- Worship Teams/Bands, Not Choirs. Except in culturally appropriate situations, PGCs have replaced choirs with worship bands. In most settings, choirs resonate with prior generations, bands with millennials and beyond.

Churches often ask, "When is it time to do away with the choir?" Each church must individually make this determination as every situation is different. Before concluding, I suggest you assess your choir and the choir's effectiveness. Answering the following five questions should help you in your assessment.

1. Can they sing? When a guest comes to a church for the first time, if the elements of worship they experience aren't done with some level of excellence, the guest will seldom return and give the church a second try.

2. Does your choir exhibit celebration and joy? People return to a church when the environment is celebratory and joyful. If your choir enters the choir loft with apathetic expressions on their faces, you can be sure they are a detriment to your church's growth. If, while singing, they're going through the motions and exhibit no emotion, you can be confident they're detrimental to your church's growth.

3. Is your choir distracted? Are they staring blankly into the sky, whispering to one another, or waving at a child seated in the congregation during the non-musical elements of worship? If so, your choir is a distraction and a detriment to your church's growth.

4. Is the choir made up of those who are your target audience? Seventy percent of those who stand before the congregation during worship services should be your primary target audience. For instance, no matter the age of your congregation, if your target audience is thirtysomethings, 70 percent of those on-stage singing should be thirtysomethings or younger. If you ignore this principle, you can ensure your church will not reach your primary or future target audience.

5. Is the only reason you still have a choir that it'd be politically painful to do away with it? Many church leaders are in a very awkward position. They know that even suggesting that their choir is no longer necessary will cost them much, maybe even their pastorate. If you decide you're going to dive into the dangerous waters of choir deletion, be sure that you do so slowly, graciously, and with the consent of your elders and, if possible, the church's influencers.

Musical Styles

The term "worship wars" is real! Older church members will go to battle over and again to win the music-style war. They'll fight the fight in personal conversations, in coalitions of their own creation, and meetings and church-wide town halls. Before judging aging saints, it's important to remember that music moves the heart and the heart is the most potent emotion producer on planet earth. Hearts are easily inspired and easily broken. They are inspired by memories of past musical moments, and they are broken when they are told they will no longer experience the songs that have been an inspiration to them their entire lives.

Heart memory is a real thing. When the church sings a song once sung the day the power of Christ transformed an alcoholic brother, the heart recalls the moment and cries in recognition of God the Father's love and grace. When the church sings a song once sung at a grandfather's funeral, the heart remembers and celebrates a precious and moving memory. When the church sings a song once sung the day a wayward child was baptized, the heart recollects and celebrates. Heart memories are subconscious, but they are real, nonetheless.

Judging those who long to experience heart recall is unhealthy and unnecessary. But clinging to past musical sounds at the expense of the next generation's salvation is a tragedy like no other.

PGCs are stylistically strategic. They strategically determine when their present musical style is no longer effective in connecting with a new generation and transition to a more relevant musical expression.

Let's face it. Each generation originates and is moved by a new combination of musical instruments, a contemporary decibel level, and lyrics that depict the heart of a next-generation worshipper. PGCs embrace this fact and revisit their worship music on an ongoing basis. They base their decision on an assumption that is a reality. People groups determine what church they will attend or if they will attend church based on musical style.

If a church wants to reach a primarily senior-adult audience, then the church will sing songs from past decades. Heart memory will kick in, and the nostalgia of the past will move the senior saints to moments of emotion. If a church wants to reach the next generation and beyond with the gospel, the church will purposefully "sing to the LORD a new song" (Psalm 96:1). The sounds, lyrics, and volume will resonate with an unbelieving generation, create an experience worth returning to, and make it possible to make the gospel known to them.

PGCs don't see transitioning the church's worship style as a sacrifice. They see it as a missional responsibility.

I've been asked by pastors how to make the decision to transform the church's worship style palatable to those who are adamant about clinging to the past. There is one question that should resonate with all church members. If it doesn't, nothing will. Ask the question, Do you want your children and grandchildren to come to Christ and continue to attend church with you? Most parents and grandparents dream of their children and grandchildren worshipping alongside them on earth and in heaven. Changing the church's musical style may be the decision that makes it possible for both to be experienced.

You may be asking, "Is there a formula that I can use to determine what musical style is best during any given era?" I once spoke with a pastor of an influential PGC. He told me that his church is strategic in watching what music is used in the student ministry and utilizing the same musical style in worship services in about seven years.

Chris Kuti is a worship artist and speaker whose passion is connecting people to God's heart through word and song. He and his wife are currently Global Worship Pastors at LakePointe Church in Rockwall, Texas. Chris has led worship across the country for more than fifteen years, including nine years with Life.Church (Edmond, Oklahoma).

Chris has written songs on major label releases like Cody Carnes's "Death of Death" and Big Daddy Weave's "We Want the World to Hear." Chris was also half of *CCM Magazine*'s 2009 Breakout Artist Chris and Conrad, whose recording career earned the duo massive Billboard-radio success including their number one song, "Lead Me to the Cross."

As you read Chris's interview, ask yourself the following question, "Has my church transitioned to meet the needs of the next generation?" If not, ask, "Am I willing to lead the necessary changes to reach the next generation?"

Author: How would you describe the role of the worship team?
Chris Kuti: First, the role of the worship team is still what it has always been. As worship is seen in Scripture, the musicians go forth in battle. They prepare the way before the battle is fought. Every day the church is in the midst of a spiritual battle. We prepare the way for that battle when we lead the people in worship as worship leaders. We prepare the congregation for the battles coming throughout their week or the days ahead.

Second, the role of the worship pastor is also to create environments that move people closer to the heart of God. Music has the power to evoke internal movement and external movement. Through praise, gratitude, understanding His goodness, and experiencing His grandness, people's hearts are moved, and so they move. When I turn on music for my two- and three-year-old kids, I don't have to teach them how to dance. Music naturally moves them to dance. I believe in God's ordained worship through song because the real power music has moves the church. We, as worship leaders, give context to the direction of the church's movement.

The third role of the worship team is to put prayers on the lips of people. We play these songs, play these melodies, and give purpose to the church's sung prayers to God. Understanding the context of the people we lead, what's going on in their lives, then purposefully putting the right prayers on their lips is a great honor and an even greater responsibility. Because of this, we don't take the theology of the song lightly. We don't take the selection of the songs lightly. These are prayers lifted to our Father in heaven, and we long to put the right prayers on the lips of our people.

Author: How is the flow of worship services different from fifteen years ago?
Chris Kuti: We're in an age where the duration of our services

really matters. We're in an age where people can watch a fifteen-second video online. They can watch hundreds of them on YouTube or their Instagram feed. The bite-sized, shorter-duration content is what our people connect with. I don't think that should fully inform how we structure our services, but we need to keep that in mind when planning worship.

Also, the flow has moved into more of a free-flowing, organic experience. Worship for today's church feels like it's happening in the moment versus "We've been planning this for weeks." That's not to diminish the production value or intentionality. People can see past the over-produced and the over-hyped. They just want to be part of a conversation in a room with other believers. So, I think the flow has transitioned from being over-produced to being more in tune with what God is doing in the moment.

Author: What is your strategy for keeping up with ever-evolving musical sounds?

Chris Kuti: It starts with the worship pastor. I have to be constantly developing, growing, evolving. I must work to be culturally in tune. I'm always listening to every genre of music, including secular music. And I'm not just listening to the top five worship leaders. I'm listening to the newest worship sounds. I'm constantly keeping my ear to the ground to see what's happening.

I hold myself responsible for not being okay with being the same worship leader I was ten years ago, even five years ago. I'm always watching tapes of myself, both current and old. I'm asking the questions, What's different in my leadership? What's grown in my leadership? What doesn't need to change in my leadership? I'm always asking what needs to change in my approach and methods.

This has a lot to do with vocal technique. I can't sound like the me of fifteen years ago because the era calls for a different sound. The new songs call for a different sound. I must be meeting people where they are today. To do that, I must be a constant learner.

Some components of our worship leadership will always be consistent. But in terms of style, technique, and the sound of our music, it's always on me, the worship leader, be in a constant state of growth.

Also, having a very intentional eye and ear to who on the worship team is stretching us is essential. Who on our team is current? I try to keep people on my worship team who are better and younger than me. That doesn't mean that everybody on the team has to be better than me (that'd be awesome, though), and it doesn't mean that everybody on the team has to be younger than me. But, you need to trust those who are younger. Trust their ear and eye when they notice something you don't. Give them permission to say "Hey, I think we're stuck. I think we're stagnant. I feel like we need to grow. I think we need to infuse some of the new songs into the life of our church." I trust the younger worship team members to keep me from becoming stagnant, and I permit them to push me.

Author: What is your system for saturating new worship songs into the hearts of your church members?

Chris Kuti: I can't have more than about twenty songs in our song bank at any one time. These are the current songs within the last few years that are familiar to our people. When I add a song to our church's song bank, I will subtract one and move it to what I call our recurrent list. Two out of three or three out of four in the worship set each week will come from the song bank. Anything from the recurrent list I pepper throughout song sets. For example, I'm not going to play "What a Beautiful Name" a couple of times in two months. I may play it once every three months. It's on the recurrent list so it gets played less than those songs in the song bank. It's an older song and is a good staple and still has the power to move people to the heart of God.

I think of the addition of new songs in that way. I'm asking, "What needs to come off a list?" "What's too overplayed that needs to be moved to a less current rotation?" Then I slave over the addition of new songs. If I'm going to add a song, I'm going to add only those songs that are relevant to move people closer to the heart of God. I'm looking for a couple of things when adding a new song—the singability of a song and the theology of a song.

When I've chosen a new song, I'm committed to that song being part of our church's experience for a long, long time. To infuse a song, we use a new song the first week then the second week. I then give the new song a break and play it the following week.

Using social media to help galvanize the songs is really effective. The 167 hours in the week that the church isn't worshipping with me, I want our worship songs to be in their lives. With that in mind, I'll put the song set on Instagram, or tell them where they can find an acoustic YouTube version of the song we played last weekend. Or I give them a Spotify link to find the songs we sang the past weekend. Sometimes, when introducing a new song, I may tease it on social media the week before we sing it for the first time.

Author: What decibel level is most effective for today's church? What is that based on?

Chris Kuti: This is scientific as well as feel. From the science perspective, on average, 96 to 98 decibels are a great number depending on your congregation. That is a safe exposure per OSHA. If you go to a football game, the decibel levels are much higher.

Also, when looking at frequencies, we're A-weighted. We're not measuring the low-end frequencies. Low-end frequencies cannot hurt, and you actually need the low-end frequencies to tame some of the high-end frequencies that can hurt someone's ears. No musical venue ever measures beyond the A-weighted frequencies.

Sometimes I'm asked, "Why is our decibel level as high as it is?" First off, feel is more important for us than science. I want to move air. I want there to be energy in the room. I don't want our worship to be anemic. I want it to move the person in the back of the room. I have to kick the low end to get that much energy, but I promise heaven's not gonna be quiet. There will be peaceful times, but our worship will be loud, powerful, and passionate. We have the most extraordinary story, and we're singing about the all-powerful God, so I feel like good energy in the room; that volume in the worship experience creates an awe-inspiring time in the presence of God.

We also choose the decibel level we utilize for those who are new and those who have been led to believe they're bad singers. Those who don't consider themselves singers are intimidated to sing if they think others can hear them singing. Others hearing them sing may be a deterrent to them singing. Being lost in the sea of musical sounds aids many people in singing. Although they can't hear themselves and others, they feel part of something powerful.

Author: You have oversight of worship on seven campuses. How do you continue to meet the standard of excellence on every campus?

Chris Kuti: Hire better people than you whom you trust to lead. I can't be in all those places at once. I've got to have amazing worship leaders with extraordinary vocal abilities on every campus. I've also got to know when I'm sending them out to lead that they are going to actually pastor people from the stage. I'm in tune with my worship leaders constantly. I know who they are, I know what they're doing, I know what they need to improve on, I continually pour gas on their strengths, and I make sure the vision about how to lead is clear.

Also, we inspect what we expect. I'm consistently checking out services on our other campuses via the recorded service and coaching worship leaders on each of our campuses.

Author: What word of wisdom do you have for lead pastors and worship pastors who are hesitant to update their church's worship experience?

Chris Kuti: What got you here won't get you there. This is an adage I constantly remind myself of. Worship must evolve as the generation we're called to reach changes. Cultural changes lead to changes in worship. Our theology will never change, but our methods must.

The fear is that our message will change if we change our methods. It may feel as though this is true, but in reality, it isn't.

If methods don't change, there won't be anyone around to hear the most excellent and most transforming message, the gospel of Jesus Christ.

Worship Practices

Next-generation worshippers are emotive. They feel profoundly and worship passionately. When worshipping, they need the freedom to express themselves.

There are at least four practices that some churches throw the brakes on, biblical and God-honoring practices that the next generation have a penchant to exhibit.

1. High-volume worship. Psalm 150:3–5 (ESV) commands,

Praise him with trumpet sound;
   praise him with lute and harp!
Praise him with tambourine and dance;
   praise him with strings and pipe!
Praise him with sounding cymbals;
   praise him with loud clashing cymbals!

Interestingly, some of the loudest instruments in today's orchestra are the trumpet and cymbals. And if you've ever been in a church when someone is pounding on a tambourine, you know it overtakes almost all other instruments. Today's young worshippers seem to be high-volume worshippers.

2. Shouting. Psalm 47:1*b* (ESV) tells worshippers to "shout to God with loud songs of joy!"

When attending a collegiate conference, student camp, or church primarily made up of transformed Gen Ys and older Gen Zs, one of the most inspiring moments is experienced when a song lyric, passage of Scripture read aloud, or testimony drives attendees to shout in agreement or out of a heart of passion.

3. Clapping. Psalm 47:1*a* (ESV) declares, "Clap your hands, all peoples!"

God said for "all peoples" to clap their hands. This is a common practice in many churches today and is commonplace for young worshippers.

4. Lifted Hands. Psalm 134:2 (ESV) orders God's people to "lift up your hands to the holy place and bless the Lord!"

While all are instructed to lift hands in praise to the Lord, the next generation of worshippers unabashedly and in praise throw their hands toward the heavens and in so doing "bless the Lord."

While all are not prone to engage in these practices, those who follow these biblical directives need to know these biblical expectations are welcomed and that the church they worship in believes them to be appropriate and acceptable.

Ministries

PGCs consider people's lifestyles, present sociological norms, and disciple-making methods, and decide what ministries will be in play.

In decades past, by hosting many ministries, the church effectively met felt needs. The church had a "mall mentality." Offer as many opportunities as possible. People will choose the ministry area that connects with them most, become engaged in it, and dive deeply into all of church life.

With this in mind, churches hosted a plethora of ministries. Some of those included opportunities such as missions-education programs, men's ministry, women's ministry, basketball teams, softball teams, choir (and many other musical ensembles), quilting groups, and so on.

It was an era when people had more discretionary time and used it to engage in church life. This is no longer true.

Today's lifestyles are very demanding. Families are overactive, overextended, and under the gun.

Church members today don't have much nonmandatory time. They are being pushed and pulled in many directions. They long to be considered good Christ followers and church members and are passionate about growing in their relationship with Christ and His people. But they are not going to come to the church building over and again weekly. Especially when they are fully aware that being in the building multiple times each week isn't a biblical requirement, nor does it necessarily grow one's relationship with Christ.

PGCs realize this fact and have streamlined church programming. Most PGCs offer five foundational ministries, do them with excellence, and praise those who engage in them.

1. **Worship.** PGCs expect church members to come together to worship their Savior weekly at a weekend worship gathering.

2. **Groups.** PGCs strive to see every believer involved in a small group. They drive people into worship and groups because these are biblical requirements. Acts 2 tells us the early church met in homes (small groups) and temple courts (large group gatherings).

3. **Student Ministry.** PGCs are passionate to see the next generation evangelized and discipled. PGCs passionately pursue young men and women with the gospel and disciple-making, knowing we are one generation away from Christianity becoming nearly non-existent.

4. **Children's Ministry.** PGCs know that most people will come to Christ as children. The church gives much of its time, resources, and people to the children's ministry.

5. **Missions.** PGCs will, at high costs, carry out the Great Commission and take the gospel to people locally, state-wide, nationally, and internationally.

Many PGCs offer other opportunities. They are seldom publicized from the pulpit and are not considered of equal value.

I would like to share one last thought related to relevance and church programs. The primary reason PGCs are offering less programming is twofold: (1) they keep church members from engaging in the weightier practices exercised by growing disciples, and (2) programs no longer resonate with next-generation church members. Present generations are longing for relationships, not programs. By doing away with many programs, the church has made time for the membership to live in meaningful relationships alongside other believers. Rather than coming to the church building for a Wednesday night prayer meeting, church members meet together in their homes for Bible study, prayer, and encouragement. Their small group is meeting a need Wednesday night worship can't. Rather than singing in the choir, church members are getting together at restaurants to hang out and are exhibiting the joy of Christ for all to see. Rather than coming to a sparsely attended Sunday night service, individuals are meeting in living rooms, discipling a few, and raising up future heroes of the faith.

Relationships have replaced programs, and spiritual growth is the fascinating and exhilarating outcome!

Evangelistic Branding

Branding is "the promoting of a product or service by identifying it with a particular brand."[3]

PGCs know that the service they are promoting is the eternal transformation of lives through the power of the gospel of Jesus Christ. The product produced is described in 2 Corinthians 5:17 (ESV), "Therefore, if anyone is in Christ, he is a new creation. The old has passed away; behold, the new has come."

PGCs unapologetically will do whatever it takes to remove any obstacle that hinders the masses from experiencing becoming "new creations" and having eternal life in heaven. While some brands were once a draw, they are presently the wall too massive for many unbelievers to claw their way over. With that in mind, many PGCs have removed the denominational title.

There was a time when denominational titles were descriptors revealing the church's theology, methodology, and ministry philosophy. That era has passed. Today, denominational titles are perceived as connecting a church to a political party, an outdated belief system, or a group of judgmental proselytizers more concerned with living life as it was five decades ago than caring for those in desperate need today. While these descriptors are not accurate of most churches, they are the perception of a vast majority of unbelievers. And, as we all know, perception is reality.

Outreach magazine's "100 Fastest-Growing Churches" list for 2022 revealed a startling and telling fact: only ten churches listed carry a denominational designation.[4]

An Easy Test

Pastor, you cannot lead a church that experiences ongoing growth if your market is diminishing. Your market is made up of those who see your product and buy into it. And, if your church is primarily made up of boomers and beyond, your market is diminishing at an unfathomable rate. You need to put yourself in the shoes of a twenty- or thirtysomething then evaluate your church's relevance. Do this by answering the following questions.

1. If a twentysomething visited my church, would he walk away saying "Their greeters looked like me"?
2. If a twentysomething visited my church, would she walk away saying "Their people dressed like me"?
3. If a twentysomething visited my church, would he walk away saying "Their people spoke my language"?
4. If a twentysomething visited my church, would she walk away saying "Their music sounds like my music"?
5. If a twentysomething visited my church, would he walk away saying "The pastor struggles with life just as I do and speaks highly of my generation"?
6. If a twentysomething visited my church, would she walk away saying "The people on stage are my people"?

If the answer to many—maybe any—of these questions is a resounding no, you will want to consider moving your church toward a relevant reality.

PGC pastors continually study the latest trends, learn the latest practices, and prayerfully integrate culturally relevant methods. Pastors need to ask themselves if their unwillingness to be teachable is a bottleneck for their church.

Pastor Teachability

The obstacle keeping many churches from becoming PGCs is a lack of pastoral teachability. Pastors who are unteachable will soon have a church that is no longer relevant. When a church is no longer relevant, it will quickly be stagnant and, before too awfully long, will be dying.

There are two undeniable reasons that all church leaders must be teachable.

1. No culture is static. Churches that fix their feet in concrete, comfortable, bygone practices will fall behind and be ineffective. The culture is constantly changing.

2. Ministry models are consistently changing. No church leader should embrace every trend that comes along. We can't ignore them either. Only when we see what's working elsewhere and adopt or adapt those relevant and effective practices will we be able to reach the next generation with the gospel.

Many pastors are hesitant to make changes because the aging, present, and diminishing congregation may mutiny. Too many believe this situation is new to church life. Not so. Catherine Marshall was Pastor Peter Marshall's partner in ministry and his wife.

In the 1930s Pastor Marshall was one of the most highly renowned preachers in the United States and was the chaplain of the United States Senate. Each Sunday, he planted himself in the pulpit of New York Avenue Presbyterian Church in Washington, DC. People longing to attend his services often stood in line and waited in the rain with hopes of entering the sanctuary. In Catherine Marshall's book *A Man Called Peter*, she recounts the church's situation in 1938.

"A group of people at New York Avenue, including a few of the officers, were intent upon resisting any changes, and Peter felt that the old church would have to change or eventually die."[5]

What was true in 1938 is true today. Churches that are unwilling to change may eventually die.

Chapter 18

Centralized Decision-Making

The elders who direct the affairs of the church well are worthy of double honor, especially those whose work is preaching and teaching.

—1 Timothy 5:17

The way decisions are made, who makes decisions, and the speed in which they are made is a key to being a PGC.

PGCs use governance that allows the right people to come to the right-minded conclusions in the right time span on behalf of the church. PGCs are elder-led churches.

Democracy and Decision-Making

I have lived my life as a Southern Baptist. My father was a Southern Baptist pastor, and I served Southern Baptist churches and entities most of my life. For more than twenty years, I've consulted churches, many of them SBC churches. Many were on the cusp of experiencing substantial growth, just one strategic decision away from reaching many more with the gospel—but a game-changing motion was voted down in a business meeting. I remember one such church where a few influential traditionalists spoke against the strategy, leading others to cast their vote against the motion too. At that moment, the church's trajectory was set. The church began a debilitating decline and continues to decline today.

Leaving those types of meetings broke my heart. Although the lead pastor was a gifted preacher and leader with the gifts and abilities to declare the gospel powerfully and grow the church numerically, and a substantial percentage of church members dreamt of a flourishing church with him, a vote determined the fate of the church and the future of many people far from Christ.

Following the vote at this particular church, forward thinkers left the church, the church's reputation in the community was tainted (due to known infighting), and the lead pastor resigned and sought a new place to serve.

When a church body votes on most or all matters, doors often slam shut. There are two logical reasons church-wide votes are the death of church growth.

- Cultural Christians, carnal Christians, unsaved church members, and spiritually immature people are self-serving. They cannot grasp the importance of looking beyond themselves to see the spiritual needs of others. They fight for their comfort while ignoring the eternal needs of people in their community. Sadly, many churches are made up of a majority of members who land in one of these four categories.
- Influencers are the key to bringing the church membership on board. More often than not, influential church members aren't educated concerning church-growth principles and practices. They often deem them unnecessary, even unbiblical. When they stand against an innovative decision, others follow their lead and vote against a game-changing motion.

Wayne Grudem, in his book *Systematic Theology*, unearths a truth that cannot be overlooked. When speaking of a church using pure democracy in decision-making, he announces, "In this system, everything must come to the congregational meeting. The result is that decisions are often argued endlessly, and, as the church grows, decision-making reaches a point of near paralysis."[1]

When a church votes on most or all matters, it seldom grows beyond the three-hundred-people mark. In the lion's share of cases, a game-changing decision will be voted down, and the church will begin an era of stagnation followed by decline.

The Elder-Led Church and Decision-Making

However, when a church is elder-led, decisions are made by spiritually mature people who have the spiritual needs of others in mind. Because the elders are the church's influencers, have been affirmed by the congregation, and are therefore trusted by the congregation, the biblical church body most often follows their lead when the elders make a decision.

The Bible points out that the church is to be subject to the elders. Hebrews 13:17 announces, "Have confidence in your leaders and submit to their authority, because they keep watch over you as those who must give an account. Do this so that their work will be a joy, not a burden, for that would be of no benefit to you." When elders "direct the affairs of the church" (1 Timothy 5:17), and the church body has "confidence in your leaders and submit to their authority" (Hebrews 13:17), the church has a much greater chance of becoming a PGC.

Two basic elder systems are common in PGCs.

1. Elder-Led—In an elder-led church, the elders are responsible for making many of the church's key decisions. The church votes only on the annual budget, the church's next lead pastor, and property purchases.

2. Elder-Ruled—In an elder-ruled church, the elders are responsible for making all key decisions independently.

An essential undeniable principle is this: the larger a church becomes, the more centralized decision-making must be. Only a small portion of the church is aware of all or most of what is taking place at any one time. Only a small part of the church is equipped and educated to make decisions for the rapidly expanding organization. And only a small portion of the church has the spiritual gifts, knowledge, and spiritual maturity to make the best decisions for a growing church. That small portion is the elders.

I am not implying that elders in PGC churches micromanage the church. Ministry teams led by staff members are responsible for accomplishing their work and making most of their own decisions. They do so while being encouraged by and cared for by the elders.

In some small to midsize church situations, committees such as the finance committee and a personnel committee are in place, and they work under the direction of the elders. Staff members are led by the lead pastor and the executive team and are free to make most of their choices. When putting together descriptors of the roles of leadership entities in megachurch PGCs, the mantra would read "protected by the elders," "led by the staff," and "gifted by the church members."

I have seen a few churches that tried to balance the tension between elder decision-making and church-wide votes by using a two-step process. First, the elders conclude a plan of action, and then, second, the church votes on that plan of action. In almost every instance, this creates nothing more than tension and roadblocks.

The church membership asks the question, "Why did you make a decision then ask us to rubberstamp it?" They're frustrated and seldom bless the elders' decision because they're in a state of discontent. And the elders are frustrated because they've prayed, studied Scripture, researched, and come to a timely and right-minded plan of action that has been rejected.

The Makeup of the Elder Team

The makeup of the elder team is essential. Elders must meet the biblical requirements revealed in 1 Timothy 3:2–7 and Titus 1:6–9. While all elders must meet these requirements, it's crucial to have a few entrepreneurs on the elder team. Entrepreneurs intuitively long to start and grow things. They are willing to take risks necessary to accomplish a God-sized vision. When others hesitate to consider a forward-thinking initiative, entrepreneurs lunge forward, ready to do whatever it takes to reach seemingly impossible goals. But it is also wise to have an elder on the same team who is prone to throw the brakes on an idea. An individual with a hesitant heart revealing the reasons the initiative in consideration may not be workable or the obstacles standing in the way of accomplishing the work is essential—these types breathe balance to the decision-making discussion. People who think like a lawyer, a banker, or an engineer will enhance the decision-making process as these types are apt to climb into the particulars and bring wise counsel to the rest of the team.

A Response to Two Often-Stated Facts and a Workable Option for Many Churches

Many of you are saying to yourselves, "My church will never be an elder-led church." Others of you are hearing a voice in your head declaring, "I know some huge churches that aren't elder-led." I want to give you hope, understanding, and a possible option. First, a fact that may be helpful:

the necessity is to be a church that has centralized decision-making in place. The group making those decisions needn't be elders or be called elders.

When a very large church is flourishing but doesn't have elders, the staff team has taken the authority or been given the authority to make critical decisions. The church trusts them to do that, and the church is growing because they are. They have a centralized team making critical decisions—the church staff.

Many churches have a centralized decision-making team, but they might be called the "administrative team," the "church council," or another term that defines them as a high-level decision-making body. They carry out many of the same functions as an elder body but aren't described as elders.

No matter the title, the function is what matters. With that in mind, if your church has numerically plateaued, it may be that the bottleneck is the decision-making process. If your church or denominational polity allows it, begin the process of creating a team that streamlines decision-making.

Chapter 19

The Excellence Factor

Evaluate, Elevate, Execute

And whatever you do, whether in word or deed, do it all in the name of the Lord Jesus, giving thanks to God the Father through him.

—Colossians 3:17

PGCs strive for excellence ALWAYS!

Every worship service, group gathering, event, and staff meeting has an excellence goal. While PGCs realize this isn't always possible, they are always aiming at that target.

Three Reasons to Strive for Excellence

Why would churches choose this seemingly impossible goal? Here are three reasons.

First, the church is to offer God its best lamb. Malachi 1:6–14 (NASB95) reveals a declaration from God to His priests:

"'A son honors his father, and a servant his master. Then if I am a father, where is My honor? And if I am a master, where is My respect?' says the LORD of hosts to you, O priests who despise My name. But you say, 'How have we despised Your name?' You are presenting defiled food upon My altar. But you say, 'How have we defiled You?' In that you say, 'The table of the LORD is to be despised.' But when you present the blind for sacrifice, is it not evil? And when you present the lame and sick, is it not evil? Why not offer it to your governor? Would he be pleased with you? Or would he receive you kindly?" says the LORD of hosts. "But now will you not entreat God's favor, that He may be gracious to us?

With such an offering on your part, will He receive any of you kindly?" says the LORD of hosts. "Oh that there were one among you who would shut the gates, that you might not uselessly kindle fire on My altar! I am not pleased with you," says the LORD of hosts, "nor will I accept an offering from you. For from the rising of the sun even to its setting, My name will be great among the nations, and in every place incense is going to be offered to My name, and a grain offering that is pure; for My name will be great among the nations," says the LORD of hosts. "But you are profaning it, in that you say, 'The table of the Lord is defiled, and as for its fruit, its food is to be despised.' You also say, 'My, how tiresome it is!' And you disdainfully sniff at it," says the LORD of hosts, "and you bring what was taken by robbery and what is lame or sick; so you bring the offering! Should I receive that from your hand?" says the LORD. "But cursed be the swindler who has a male in his flock and vows it, but sacrifices a blemished animal to the Lord, for I am a great King," says the LORD of hosts, "and My name is feared among the nations."

In Deuteronomy 15:21 (ESV), God strictly prohibits sacrificing a blemished animal. "But if it has any blemish, if it is lame or blind or has any serious blemish whatever, you shall not sacrifice it to the LORD your God."

Instead of offering their best to God, the priests were bringing blemished sacrifices and dishonoring God. God asked, "Where is My honor? And if I am a master, where is My respect? (v. 6). PGCs take the responsibility of bringing their best seriously to God in every setting and in every way. They strive for excellence, first and foremost, because it honors God.

Second, excellence is a magnet for people with leadership gifts. True leaders intuitively long to be part of organizations, churches, or ministries doing things with excellence. When a lay leader or a candidate staff member attends a church and the experience is accomplished with excellence, or the event is done with excellence, or the building and grounds are in excellent condition, leaders seriously consider becoming part of and serving at that church. These are the people you need to have on your team.

Third, excellence *captures* the best people. Many churches can get high-performance team members to join them, but only churches that do things with excellence will *keep* them.

Acquiring an off-the-charts elder body, staff, a group of gifted lay leaders, and lay servants is difficult. A lead pastor is likely to lose them if the church isn't striving for excellence in all things.

When a church nearby opens its doors and excellence is seen in all they are doing, the pastor's team may slowly trickle out and join the new church. Whether or not this is right or ethical makes no difference. It is a fact that cannot be ignored.

If a lead pastor wants to keep his high-performance people, every ministry must strive for excellence.

Three-Step Process

PGCs systematically strive to up their game. Many use a three-step process—evaluate, elevate, and execute.

Evaluate

Evaluation is the only way to determine what went well, what was good but could be better, what went poorly, and what should never happen again. PGCs ask or discuss these questions, or some form of them, following worship services, events, many PGC meetings, and all other experiences.

Evaluating Services, Events, and Meetings—This evaluation happens following worship services, events, or meetings. First, the church leadership celebrates wins. During this part of the meeting, the group acknowledges all that went well. If discussing a worship service, someone may speak of the number of people who started a relationship with Christ, share the number of attendees, or share a story of someone who talked to a team member, telling them of a life-changing moment they experienced in the service. The group may also celebrate a time during the service that the presence of the Holy Spirit was evident and what element in the worship service strengthened that special moment, a strategically planned transition that worked well, who performed well, or a video that moved people to celebrate what God is doing through the church and how that was effective in inspiring people to greater commitment.

Second, the team then goes into a time of bringing to the forefront those elements that were good but could be better, what went poorly, and what should never happen again. This time is not considered a time of expressing negativity or venting, but a strategic practice with the goal of offering God a better lamb in the future.

Each time a problematic moment is revealed, the group then concludes one of three things: what to do to make sure it never happens again, what to change so the element of the experience is done with excellence in the future, or what to never make part of the experience again.

Evaluating Ministries—When evaluating ongoing ministries, PGCs check attendance, ask if those leading the ministries are hitting the agreed-upon markers, and ask attendees if the ministry is hitting the target they were told it was aiming at.

Attendance tells the church if the ministry is life-giving enough to draw people to it on an ongoing basis. If the ministry is diminishing in numbers, the church asks four questions:

1. Is this still a viable ministry, or has the culture transitioned and this ministry no longer effective?
2. What must we tweak or change so that this ministry is invigorating enough to draw and keep people for the long haul?
3. Do we have the right leadership in place?
4. Is the ministry doing what it was designed to do?

Answering these questions allows a church to do one of four things, each based on the four questions asked in the prior paragraph: (1) determine whether or not to do away with the ministry. If the ministry is never going to grow, it will steal people, space, and financial resources from thriving ministries. (2) Decide what changes need to be made so that the ministry is viable. (3) Conclude if the church needs to equip its present leader further or replace the leader. (4) Determine if the ministry is carrying out the objectives the church determined it would do. For instance, if the church predetermined that the women's ministry strategy would involve four practices—connecting women through small groups, discipling women in groups of three, seeing women set free through support groups, and inspiring women through large gatherings—but the women's ministry is only hosting a once-a-month large group event, the women's ministry is not doing what it was designed to do so it will never accomplish what it was intended to accomplish. The ministry must be done away with or redirected to achieve the four goals it had at first.

Getting team members to share their honest evaluations is difficult, especially in a culture where passive-aggressive behavior is intuitive. To get people to speak openly without being perceived as negative or judgmental, it would be wise to instill two values and practices that many PGCs use: (1) say the last 10 percent. Many people are willing to speak 90 percent of what is on their minds. The 90 percent is the safe space. No one will judge a team member for verbalizing that which creates no cringe. But the last 10 percent, which is difficult to hear, is where the game-changing critique lives. Tell the team the last 10 percent is honored, and affirm each person when they give the last 10 percent. By doing this, you will create a safe place and an environment where actual evaluation occurs. (2) Ask for an umbrella of grace. When someone is uncomfortable stating a critique that needs to be brought into the open, asking for an "umbrella of grace" before making the statement will alleviate much of the fear the evaluator is feeling. For example, if someone realizes it's essential that the worship team be aware that waving to family members in the congregation is distracting, they will say, "I'm asking for an umbrella of grace. I noticed that a band member was waving at their preschooler when the pastor was welcoming the congregation. I think we need to talk about this." By asking for an umbrella of grace, the team member exhibits a spirit of humility and prepares the rest of the team for the awkward conversation to come.

Elevate

Once a team has determined what needs changing or tweaking, the next step is to elevate the responsibility. A team elevates those things that must be revisited by making them a priority. This is a vital part of the process as the whirlwind of ongoing, weekly responsibilities will overtake the added task. Because of the whirlwind, there are things that may never get accomplished.

For instance, if a worship team has decided they need to spend much time perfecting video presentations, this will easily get placed on the backburner. The weekly responsibilities that oftentimes fill the agreed-upon working hours are obligatory and part of the workers' weekly rhythm. The only way the necessary changes are accomplished is by elevating them as an essential and high priority.

Execute

PGCs go beyond evaluating and elevating, and they ultimately execute the steps necessary to complete the agreed-upon changes.

This is done by concluding together what changes need to be made and then assigning responsibilities with deadlines. Only when someone is given a task will anyone feel the burden of completing the task. Without setting a deadline, the job will get lost in the busyness of everyday responsibilities.

The team leader or the individual assigned the responsibility must determine the steps to be taken, including who needs to be notified or involved, what specific actions need to be taken, who will accomplish each task, and when each step of the process and each task must be completed. Once these four pieces of the process are concluded, the team leader graciously holds each person accountable to accomplish the assigned tasks on time. Then and only then will the work be completed by the agreed-upon deadline, and the changes leading to excellence be executed.

The excellence factor cannot be overlooked. Each time a guest attends a worship service or shows up to try out a ministry, if it is perceived to be haphazardly put together or unorganized, the guest will most likely not return. We must always remember that offering God our best lamb is an act of worship and a magnet for the unchurched.

Chapter 20

Six Essential PGC Practices

Put your outdoor work in order
and get your fields ready;
after that, build your house.

—Proverbs 24:27

I've often been asked, "Are there any essential practices churches must dive into if they're going to be on a consistent growth trajectory?" There are at least six that PGCs are consistently implementing:

1. Ask the right questions.
2. Have enough parking.
3. Do whatever it takes when worship seating reaches 80 percent capacity.
4. Have an Off-the-Charts Kids Ministry.
5. Be sure all ministries are equally effective.
6. Conquer one Wildly Important Goal (WIG) annually.

Ask the Right Questions

PGCs ask questions that lead to strategic change, such as, are we meeting the needs of our church members and are we doing what it takes to connect deeply enough with unbelievers and first-time guests? By identifying the needs of these essential groups, the church can dive into the changes necessary to meet them where they are and ultimately keep them.

The Village Church, led by Pastor Matt Chandler, has created a survey for the congregation. They are pursuing knowledge of their congregation in five areas: (1) demographics, (2) communication, (3) financial questions, (4) connection and community, and (5) spiritual growth. They wisely give their congregation time to take the survey during worship services because they receive input from a much higher percentage of church members and attenders than by sending a digital questionnaire. Taking time during the weekend worship service might feel out of place, but, in the big scheme of things it's worth it. See appendix 5 for The Village Church's survey.

Have Enough Parking

The simple principle of having enough parking cannot be ignored. If first-time guests arrive at the church and down deep are fighting the urge to drive away, not having enough parking gives them the excuse they need. Every church must have enough parking spaces.

There are two rules of thumb.

1. When parking reaches 80 percent full, it's time to add more parking spaces.
2. There should be one parking space for every two worship attendees (many churches are now using a ratio of one parking space for every 1.5 worship attendees).

The truth is this—a church will grow to the size of its parking capacity. Not having enough easy access parking is the death of church growth.

Do Whatever It Takes When Worship Seating Reaches 80 Percent Capacity

When the worship center is consistently 80 percent of its capacity, PGCs do whatever it takes to make more space. At 80 percent capacity, first-time guests and many church members don't feel comfortable. This is especially true following COVID-19. First-time guests will attend once but will not come back a second time.

When 80 percent capacity is reached, PGCs add a worship service, create an overflow room using live music with a video feed of the sermon, build to accommodate more people, or become a multisite church.

Have an Off-the-Charts Kids' Ministry

Faith-driven parents are deeply concerned about their kids' spiritual condition. They long to see their kids come to a knowledge of the gospel and respond to it. They are seeking a kids' ministry that recognizes this essential responsibility, prioritizes it, and creates a culture conducive to it. These astute parents are also seeking an environment that is so exciting to their children that their kids long to come back each week.

It is imperative that the Kids' Ministry hold to the following necessities:

1. A joyful environment. When parents drop their kids off, they will be most comfortable when the person greeting them exhibits joy, connection, and care. This is especially important when dropping a child off for the first time. The child may be hesitant to leave their parents. But, when the person taking the child into the Kids' Ministry space portrays exuberance both the child and the parent are set at ease.

2. A structured experience. Parents seeking a church will not return if they drop their child off and, from conversation with their child, conclude the experience was haphazard and without structure.

3. Bible-based teaching. Parents want to be certain their children are experiencing biblically sound teaching, not just being entertained with games, projects, and crafts.

4. An engaging space. Themed Kids' Ministry areas are very appealing to parents as well as children. Murals on walls depicting the stories of the Bible, Bible characters, nature scenes, and so on, are common.

5. A safe environment. It's imperative that the church have a check-in and check-out system.

6. An uncluttered space. Each room should be clear of stuff strewn about the room. Piles of toys, books, and materials for projects on tables, in corners of the room, and so on, sends a very negative message to church-seeking parents.

7. A clean room. After each group gathering (or at least after each day's meetings are concluded), the tables, chairs, toys, and all other things in the room should be sanitized. Floors should be kept spotless with carpeted floors being vacuumed consistently and tiled floors mopped weekly.

8. A take-home component. Almost every PGC is certain every child leaves with something to help reinforce what they've learned, something the parents can use to disciple their children, or a project idea to be done at home.

When PGCs build their Kids' Ministry, it's obvious they are focusing on two audiences: the kids and the parents. When parents are fully aware that their child is entering a joyful, structured environment and experiencing a Bible-based study in a room where the space is engaging, the environment is safe, the meeting space is clean and uncluttered, and parents receive a take-home, those parents will bring their child back again and again. And most important, the child will be begging to return.

Be Sure All Ministries Are Equally Effective

One ministry area lagging in its effectiveness will stall church growth.

Imagine a church has a thriving group ministry, student ministry, and children's ministry. Because all these ministries are flourishing the church is experiencing overall numeric growth. But, if even one of these ministries doesn't transform with the growth, and therefore continue to grow, the church's trajectory will go south.

As a church begins to grow, each ministry leader must evolve with it. The ministry leaders must change their infrastructure, the way they work, and the work they do to meet the needs of their growing ministries. If a group pastor, student pastor, children's pastor, or any key leader is unwilling or unable to change, this area of ministry will struggle.

The problem isn't always the incompetence of a staff pastor causing the lack of growth. It could be the ministry area isn't given the resources needed, there's a need for new technology, the ministry area isn't given enough space to house the growing number of people, and the list could go on and on.

No matter the cause, when one ministry area stagnates or declines, the church's numeric growth comes to a halt. The church may be gaining new members but, at the same time, the church is losing those who are discontent.

Imagine a three-legged stool. If one leg is shorter than the other legs, the entire seat falls. In the same way, if one leg of the church's ministries isn't equal to the other legs, church growth collapses. As the church grows, each leg must grow with it.

When any ministry area lags behind, the church leadership must conclude what's causing the ministry's ineffectiveness and take the necessary steps to solve the problem.

Conquer One WIG Annually

PGCs prioritize one Wildly Important Goal (WIG) annually. They ask the question, "If we're going to continue to grow, what is the one thing that must be started, shored up, built, or rebuilt in the upcoming twelve months?" The church may conclude it's essential to raise funds for a new building, revisit their group ministry strategy, rebuild the staff team, or some other goal.

Once the wildly important goal is determined, it becomes the priority for all involved. Once completed, it will make a major difference in the present season and for decades to come.

Each of these six essential practices is critical to church growth. Write them down, practice them, and you will most likely experience some level of growth in the years ahead.

Chapter 21

Uncomplicated Group Ministry

And let us consider how to stir up one another to love and good
works, not neglecting to meet together, as is the habit of some,
but encouraging one another, and all the more as you see the Day
drawing near.

—Hebrews 10:24–25 ESV

PGCs place an extraordinary amount of emphasis on and invest much in the church's group ministry. There are two reasons groups are vitally important. First, Jesus calls His church to "make disciples" (Matthew 28:19). The church's group ministry is its disciple-making strategy. Second, it is the primary way today's church captures people for the long haul. People on a quest to land in their next church may visit as first-time guests. They'll stick and stay for years when and only when they have spiritual co-journeyers who are their friends. Friends are made in small groups.

Building a potent and captivating groups ministry is a journey many churches have taken. Because there are many group systems and finding the right one for a particular church and its culture is essential, those churches have taken the groups highway only to come to a dead end. They've chosen a group system that might have been effective in another culture but not in the culture of their church. While finding the right system for each church is critical, there are some principles and practices that PGCs engage in no matter what the system; they are principles and practices that make all the difference.

Start New Groups Often

PGCs start new groups often because it's the key to getting new people to stick.

Many guests and new church members are hesitant to join a group. They are aware that a group of brothers and sisters in Christ who have met together for a year or more is a circle of relationship they may never be fully welcomed into. It doesn't take long for their concern to be confirmed. In just a few short weeks of attending, the new group members realize the longtime group has history. The group members discuss past pains they've suffered together, life accomplishments they've celebrated together, and endeavors they've engaged in together. The group may accept the newbies as part of the group, but the newcomers know they'll never be a part of the inner circle.

When new groups start, everyone starts on equal ground. The church attenders and guests are excited to join others on the same journey they are on, knowing they'll start from the same trailhead. So, they take the first step and join a startup group, a group of people who will create their own history as they do life together.

Due to life rhythms and the importance of capturing the moment, the optimal time to start new groups is best described as *the afters*— after the first of the year, after school starts, after Easter, and after special days or sermons or sermon series. It would be wise to start couples groups after Valentine's Day, men's groups after Father's Day, and women's groups after Mother's Day. If there's a sermon series or sermon on finances, create a short-term group on handling finances after a sermon on tithing. If there's a sermon series on parenting, start a short-term group on healthy parenting. If there's a sermon series on overcoming strongholds, start a healing group or support group to aid those who long to be free of their addictions.

Easy On-Ramps to Groups

PGCs make it easy to join a group by assessing what is necessary to be a life-transforming group member. It takes commitment to the group and its values and doing life as a group member. To ask anything more con-sequentially stalls the spiritual growth of individuals, the growth of the group ministry, and thus the church's growth.

Some churches have made the misstep of requiring people to attend a series of classes, complete the reading of a book, or engage in a series of devotionals before having the opportunity to become part of a small group. Before joining a Christian group, the early church didn't demand a precursory class, reading, or study, and wise churches don't do so either. Acts 2 unearths this truth.

After the pouring out of the Holy Spirit, Peter preaches and three thousand are saved. Without any introduction to group life, these brand-new believers intuitively began meeting together in small groups, "They broke bread in their homes and ate together with glad and sincere hearts, praising God and enjoying the favor of all the people. And the Lord added to their number daily those who were being saved" (Acts 2:46b–47). These young-in-the-faith believers intuitively met together, discussed Jesus and the Word of God, and did life together, and the greatest Christian movement in history swept the known world.

PGCs make it easy to join a group, and acute churches do the same. They do this by creating easy on-ramps into a group.

Kiosk in the church lobby. Before and after each weekend service, an individual standing at the small-group kiosk is there to answer questions, conclude which affinity group is right for the person or persons seeking a group, and take the necessary steps to get them to their first group meeting.

Connection Event. A connection event is a two-and-a-half- to three-hour experience. Round tables are set up around the room. Each table is outfitted with a sign describing the group's affinity. If life stages are a church's affinity markers, "Parents of Preschoolers," "Parents of Teenagers," "Empty Nesters," or "Saintly Seniors" might be on the signage. If a church was more prone to choose affinities based on hobbies, the signage might read "Golfers," "Tennis Players," "Fishermen," or "Quilters." It might be a regional church wanting groups that reach into every part of the county where the church is connecting with people. In this case, the church might use communities to describe each affinity. In the Dallas, Texas, area where I serve, the table signage might read "Mesquite," "Fate," "Royce City," and "Greenville." All of these are towns where LakePointe Church members and attenders live. As people seeking a group arrive, they seat themselves at the table describing their affinity.

The experience includes guided conversations based on predetermined questions. Saddleback Church uses the following questions as part of the day's journey.

- What is your name?
- Where do you live?
- What are some of your hobbies or interests?
- Briefly (about two minutes) tell us about your spiritual journey to this point.
- How did you start attending this church, and what do you like best about it?
- What is your previous small-group experience?
- What is one thing you hope to gain by being in a small group?
- What is one fear you have about joining a small group?[1]

At the end of the experience, those around each table determine who their group leader will be, when they will meet, where the group will meet, and, under the guidance of the church leadership, decide what their next steps are.

Special Events. If the church hosts a men's conference, women's conference, or marriage conference, by showing a captivating video testimony of a life transformed or a marriage saved because of being part of a group, many people often sign up for that group. When using this strategy, attendees must be able to sign up immediately via digital sign-ups or hard copy and group leaders must be trained and ready to lead their first group meeting.

Church-Wide Campaigns. A church-wide campaign is a six-week topical emphasis. The church may give attention to what it means to be a church member, prayer, or any other topic the church leadership believes the church needs to shore up. The church-wide campaign engages people in daily devotions, small groups discussing and studying the topic, and the pastor preaching on the topic in weekend worship services. The church asks everyone, even those not presently in a small group, to make a short-term commitment to a group throughout the six-week emphasis. PGCs leverage the short-term groups made up of those who aren't committed to an ongoing group and strategically invite them to consider staying together when the church-wide campaign concludes. A high percentage of them do.

Online Signups. Some PGCs have created an online option for finding and becoming part of a group. A group seeker inputs the "meeting day" that is best for them, the "category" of group they're seeking to become part of, their "age," and "keywords" describing themselves or the kind of group they're looking for into an online form. Then a list of groups that is right for them will be presented. The future group member then registers for the group and is contacted by the group leader.

Easy Off-Ramps for Group Members

Everyone needs and deserves to be part of a small group they enjoy spending time with, but chemistry cannot be created. It is an intangible that either exists between people or doesn't. PGCs realize this and make it known and appropriate for people to exit without judgment. Two practices are commonplace.

1. Permission to try a different group. PGCs make it part of their strategy to let people who are kicking the tires on a group know that if they don't feel a connection after four to six weeks, they have permission to leave the group and try another. Group leaders are trained to be aware of the practice and that it is acceptable for unfulfilled people to try another group. People seldom leave a group once they've attended for four weeks, but when it happens, the leader celebrates the exit because the group leader knows the why behind the decision. The leader doesn't question their ability to lead the group or the integrity of those exiting the group.

2. Semester groups. Some PGCs have a semester-based group ministry. Every semester all groups shut down, and new groups start the next semester. This gives leaders and group members an easy off-ramp. Leaders decide if they want to lead another semester, and group members decide if they want to join a group when it's time to sign up again.

Lower Group Leader Expectations

PGCs know that creating obstacles to group leadership hinders the number of available leaders, which impedes the growth of the group ministry. They strategically and purposefully make it as easy as possible for people to become group leaders.

First, PGCs are careful to use terminology that draws everyday believers in, not vocabulary that deters. I was once in a conversation with Bill Search, who was the small-group pastor at a PGC, Southeast Christian Church in Louisville, Kentucky. I had been using the term "small-group leader" over and again when training those leading groups. He asked me if I was using that term in every church I consulted. I told him I was. He warned me that I might be keeping many from crossing the line and becoming small-group leaders. He once shared this profound description of his experience with me:

> I grew up in Michigan and the first ten years of my ministry was in a growing church in west Michigan. Michigan at that time had an interesting culture deeply impacted by the unions. Unions preached "solidarity"—that we were all together. No one is better than anyone else. While there is an obvious good side to that culture, one of the downsides is that it denigrated and depreciated leadership. No one wanted to be a leader and it seemed when someone would pop up there was a game of Whac-A-Mole to put them down again. How do you raise up leaders in a collective culture? One key way was to downplay the term *leader* and call them *facilitators*.

Steve Gladen at Saddleback Church had much the same experience. He describes the changes he made in his book *Small Groups with Purpose*:

> We asked people to become H.O.S.T.s, and they agreed in amazing numbers. By now you can guess that we have the letters in H.O.S.T. each represent something that gives a snapshot of what we are asking our people to do when they start leading a group:
>
> H—Have a heart for people.
> O—Open your place (meet in a home, coffeehouse, restaurant, or workplace).
> S—Serve a snack.
> T—Turn on the video.

The very same people who said no to becoming a small group leader now agreed to be a H.O.S.T., even though the responsibilities were the same.[2]

Terminology matters, and PGCs get it.

Second, PGCs are careful not to overtrain their group leaders. Overtraining group leaders has plagued group ministries for decades. PGC group pastors are careful to train group leaders in core principles and little more. Bill Willits at North Point Community Church in Alpharetta, Georgia, writes:

> For groups to work, the systems that define them must work. That means they must be realistic. They must be designed for real people who live in the real world.
>
> For example, most leader training seemingly embraces the "more is more" approach. This view suggests that effective training is about exposing people to a lot of information—the more the better. The assumption is that the more information leaders are exposed to, the better prepared they will be to lead. But, like the conference notebook gathering dust on the shelf, it is not the acquisition of information that properly prepares a leader to lead; rather, it is the application of the right information. People need to be trained around core principles they need to know, not an endless amount of information that is nice for them to know.[3]

Group pastors often make attendance at all training sessions mandatory and host way too many mandatory sessions. Group pastors that overtrain their group leaders create an unnecessary mountain many viable group leaders are unwilling to ascend.

Finally, PGCs remove the "perfect group leader" criterion. When considering who will be an effective group leader, many churches ask questions like, How much doctrine do they know? What books have they read? Who mentored them? What groups have they been a part of, and did they attend every week? Do they practice spiritual disciplines daily? While these are all worthwhile questions, very few people can meet these too high standards.

"If you wait for perfect people to lead your small groups, you'll be waiting until Christ's return. You don't need all-star, super-trained small-group leaders to create a successful small-group ministry. All you need is people who are willing and obedient. Remember, God doesn't call the equipped; He equips the called."[4]

Eddie Mosley is Adult Groups Minister at Brentwood Baptist Church in Brentwood, Tennessee, a perpetually growing church. He has a DMin in spiritual formations from New Orleans Baptist Theological Seminary and is the author of *Connecting in Communities: Understanding the Dynamics of Small Groups*. He has served as the groups pastor at multiple perpetually growing churches and is a well-known and influential voice in small-group ministry.

I asked Eddie to tell us his story.

> *Every church has leader enlistment standards for their Small Group Bible Study leaders (some written, some "understood"). While well-intended, these expectations can act as a control mechanism, impeding the recruitment of more leaders.*
>
> *When God called me to serve a new church, I was excited to learn of the church's reputation for high-quality Bible study. Individuals with outstanding academic achievement were teaching Sunday school on campus as well as a few off-campus small groups. God was sending many new people to our church who wanted to be a part of a Bible study and caregiving group. We weren't creating enough leaders to accommodate everyone God sent our way. To create room for new leaders, we had to change our enlistment and vetting procedures.*
>
> *When I studied our vetting procedure, I noticed that it was highly rigorous, and only people with high skill levels would pass. Then I discovered more about church leadership's goal for greater academic demands and quality control early in the church's life.*
>
> *I asked the pastor about his vision for the group's ministry. He quickly declared his desire "to see a disciple-making organization in every subdivision in our city," which necessitated a different recruiting method to gather the necessary number of leaders.*
>
> *We now provide a Host Starter Kit to anyone who wishes to lead a Bible study with a group of friends. The kit includes a six-session Bible study, icebreakers, steps for Leader Training/*

Development, and our support (coaching) network, which we supply to every Host and Leader.

We were able to create a Host to Leader approach for growth while keeping control to a respectable level.

Many group pastors need to revisit group leader requirements and make it easier, as Eddie did.

Many PGCs believe that any church member willing to adhere to the directives of the church's leadership should be considered for small-group leadership. Anyone a few others will follow can most likely lead a small group.

I'm grateful to Dr. Bill Donahue for agreeing to be interviewed for this part of *The Perpetually Growing Church*. He has been a leader for the small-group movement for more than three decades. During his eighteen years at Willow Creek Community Church, he led a pace-setting small-group ministry and spearheaded training experiences for small-group pastors worldwide. He has written or coauthored more than twenty books and leadership training resources including *Leading Life-Changing Small Groups, Building a Life-Changing Small Group Ministry, Building a Church of Small Groups, Coaching Life-Changing Small Group Leaders, The Seven Deadly Sins of Small Group Ministry,* and *The Irresistible Community: An Invitation to Life Together.*

Dr. Donahue continues to be a leading voice in the small-group movement. He is Founder and President of the LeaderSync Group. He also coleads the doctor of ministry program at Trinity International University, teaching leadership, team-building, organizational communication, and group dynamics courses. He is in demand to coach leaders and work with organizations to develop leaders at every level, and he is a highly sought-after speaker.

Author: Bill, you are also a leadership expert. With your background and knowledge in mind, what characteristics have you noted are evident in group pastors who lead a perpetually growing group ministry?

Bill Donahue: First, a growth and development mindset is key. It cannot be an afterthought. There is so much to "manage" that growth might slip to a low priority. Successful group pastors set time aside to ask these questions: are people growing spiritually in groups, are potential leaders being identified and invited into apprenticing roles, and is our coaching structure growing to support the leadership growth we are expecting?

Author: When you think of the church that has had the most success in starting new groups consistently, what was that church's system for creating new groups, and why do you believe that system is so effective?

Bill Donahue: Actually, the successful churches have two things. First, a system or process that is clear, simple to follow, and accessible to the most people. Second, they do not just rely on that one system. In other words, even though they have a solid plan A, they add variety of opportunities and creative pathways to group life and to leader development. Events, gatherings, classes, newcomer and next step ministries, and serving opportunities can all be leveraged to connect people and identify potential leaders.

Author: If you were consulting a growing church with a struggling group ministry, what components of the ministry would you be putting under a microscope? Are any of them, if not working effectively, the death of the group ministry? If so, what are they?

Bill Donahue: I always look for where they are in the cycle. Are they stuck, poised for a new start, engaged but hitting barriers, exhausted, or really dying? Then—and this may sound simple—I go back to the basics. Clear strategy? Fresh vision? Modeling done by senior staff and church leaders? Creative connection strategies? Effective leader pipeline? Spiritual formation focus in groups? Appropriate measures for identifying and gauging success? If I had to pick three, I would look at clear strategy, leader pipeline and development, and clear connection pathways. But all this is fueled by a passionate and compelling vision.

Author: There has recently been much discussion and debate about group ministries using a coaching system. Does a growing group ministry need a coaching system? If so, why? If not a coaching system, then what?

Bill Donahue: Call it whatever you want but every church with at least fifteen to twenty groups needs a support structure. Leaders need nurturing, regular connection to other leaders and staff, encouragement and prayer, and someone to help them grow spiritually as followers of Jesus. The vitality of group leaders is directly proportional to the vitality of the overall ministry. Coaches are not bosses; they function to support and shepherd leaders. There are many models, but you need some structure and it will likely change over time as you grow.

Author: If a church doesn't have a coaching system, how many groups can one full-time staff member effectively oversee?

Bill Donahue: Depending on what the full-time staff member also does (any teaching, pastoral duties like weddings, baptisms, and funerals), they can handle twenty to forty, depending on the maturing and experience of leaders. If you have a lot of new leaders, then twenty to twenty-five. If half your leaders are strong and have been leading for two to five years, you can handle more. The number also depends on how much time is expected for leader mentoring and development, versus if the staff member is just checking in and sharing vision and information, and meets with groups of leaders versus some one-on-one meetings.

Author: Who are the key players in a growing group ministry, and what role do they each play?

Bill Donahue: Assuming at least fifty groups, you need a staff member whose job is at least 50 percent devoted to small-group ministry, primarily leader training and connection strategies. In larger settings (75 to 125 groups), a full-time staff member should be doing group ministry for 80 to 90 percent of their job. The next key roles are coaches. With a large system of groups, leaders, and coaches you need at least ten to fifteen hours a week of administrative support, including managing the tracking system, communication, and event planning. Unless you want to pay a lot of money for your small-group pastor to do admin work (which you do not!), then get at least a part-time admin.

Author: In growing churches, what percentage of weekend worshippers involved in a group is average?
Bill Donahue: Assuming group life is a core value and practice alongside worship, evangelism, and education, and participation is modeled by senior staff and elders/deacons, close to 60 to 70 percent. If you have lots of new people, especially if you have visiting non-Christians, your weekend attendance is likely to change. And data show attendance patterns are averaging near two times a month. So, if you have regular attendance of one thousand adults, you actually have two thousand. So, fifteen hundred in groups is more than your weekend attendance (don't count Christmas and Easter) but is about two-thirds of your overall numbers. But we hope all believers who attend are moving into group life of some form.

Author: What percentage of weekend worshippers engaged in a group is possible? Why do you say so?
Bill Donahue: It always depends on what you are measuring— percentage of all believers? Of average weekend attendance? If you are reaching people with groups, and they are not attending weekend services yet, that messes with the percentage. I think the key question is: "Is everyone who *could* be in a group presented with a clear, simple, and easy way to get connected to a group (regardless of attendance patterns)?" If you know eight hundred of your one thousand could be in a group, and you get eight hundred, that's 100 percent. Because some will never get in a group, and you have a constant flow of people in and out. And it also could be 120 percent of weekly *average* attendance because committed people attend two to three times a month. So, find a way of identifying the "get-able" people—the ones we can connect with who could be in a group. Success might be 70 percent or 90 percent or whatever. I think you will always have 20 percent who are unreachable right now for some reason (not ready, between groups, never will join, and so on).

Author: If you were consulting a church that once had a flourishing group ministry but is now floundering, what steps would you lead them through to help them become a growing group ministry again?

Bill Donahue: Going back to the first question, where are they in the cycle? Tired? Wounded? Numb? Angry? Get a clear and honest picture of reality and listen a lot! I believe in smaller, behind-the-scenes relaunch or refresh approaches. Get a fresh vision, start with a few committed leaders and begin to rebuild it somewhat organically. Grow into it, don't *go* into it. No campaigns or big splashes. Model the new direction or approach, multiply quality leaders, shepherd them, and wait until you get some momentum. If there is damage, you need time to heal wounds. What is worse than having no group ministry for a season is having a bad group ministry. So, recovery from a broken or tired system should be only as fast as the healing you see happening. Take your time. It may take two to three years to restore and rebuild a really broken effort. Take care of the members, leaders, and coaches, and you will know when it is time to go public again.

Almost all PGCs possess a flourishing group ministry. The worship service gathers people, and the group ministry keeps them. Only when people engage in intimate, ongoing relationships will they "stick." And this happens when they connect with a group of twelve or fewer people who care for one another, grow spiritually alongside one another, and do life together for a significant period of time. All these requirements happen in a small-group setting.

Chapter 22

Three Essential Systems

So Christ himself gave the apostles, the prophets, the evangelists, the pastors and teachers, to equip his people for works of service, so that the body of Christ may be built up.
—Ephesians 4:11–12

To equip their people, PGCs are laser-like focused on three essential systems: (1) assimilation, (2) volunteer engagement, and (3) leadership development. If any of the three are not managed well or are ineffective, the church will cease to grow.

Assimilation

Without an off-the-charts assimilation process, first-time guests will become back-door escapees. PGCs are passionate about connecting with first-time guests, capturing their hearts, seeing them become Christ-followers and church members, and journeying with them until they land firmly on the runway of spiritual maturity. This is the goal of assimilation.

Perpetually growing churches know that new attendees often complete five steps before they can be "assimilated" into the church culture.

1. View the church's website. This is the first act of discovering the church.
2. Watch an online service. This is the attendee's first view of the church.
3. Attend a worship service in person. This is when the attendee meets the church family.
4. Attend for a period of time. This is when they get to know the church.
5. Take part in the church's assimilation experience. This is when they become part of the church and begin to assimilate.

1. View the Church's Website

The church's website is the first touch for those in the hunt for their next church. The website must be captivating and practical. If it doesn't capture the viewer's attention instantaneously and make it possible to find the most essential information quickly, the church seeker will move on. It must also describe what a first timer will experience when attending the church and should include: (1) where guest parking is located, (2) what attire is common and acceptable, (3) where the guest center is located, (4) where the nursery is and where children and student ministries are, and (5) what to expect upon arrival and while attending the worship service.

Because people searching for their next church will view the online service before attending in person, the homepage should link directly to worship service videos and show a countdown to the next streaming service.

Pinelake Church is a multisite church with five campuses in Mississippi. It is one of the largest churches in the country, with more than eleven thousand average weekly attendance. When Reach Right Studios ranked the top 100 church websites in 2021, Pinelake was thirty-sixth on the list.

David Martin is Pinelake's web developer. When Dave was called to work in the church, he was a teenager working as the webmaster for a large online eCommerce store, one of the top stores in the country at the time. He took his experience and knowledge of the web and love for the church and combined them. In the past ten years since serving in this position, he has seen many changes in digital communications. He remembers setting up the first Pinelake Facebook page and streaming the church's services online for the first time.

I'm indebted to David for his wisdom and practical guidance. As you read his interview, ask yourself what your church needs to do to have your own PGC website.

Author: What are the elements/characteristics of an effective church website?

David Martin: Make the things our people are looking for easy to find. Surveys and Google Analytics are tools we used to help determine our top searched-for content. It is important to observe people from multiple demographics, within and outside the church, to see who is navigating your site. A simple site map is a must for us having a larger church. Another essential aspect of our website is a very clear next step and way to contact someone for more information.

Author: Is Pinelake's website a static or dynamic website? Why does the church use the option you chose?

David Martin: The Pinelake website is a dynamic website, but content is the same for every user. However, our app allows users to log in and see content that is more tailored to them. For us, a fast-loading website without hoops to jump through is very important. We want to remove any obstacles for guests visiting our website, maybe for the first time. The app is geared more to our internal audience, who seem okay with features such as a login screen and slower load times.

Author: How often does Pinelake update its website? Why do you update the website at this rate?

David Martin: We adhere to the theory, less is more. However, we try to keep the content on the site up to date—content that changes, such as meeting times, events, sermon series, and seasonal information such as Easter. We try to keep photos and videos updated to keep the site fresh. For example, pictures of people in winter clothes feel out of date if it is summer. Our ministry pages have general information about the ministries and do not get updated as often, but they should be accurate.

Author: What individuals or teams decide the website's content?

David Martin: We have five campuses, and the website, which falls under the communications team, is overseen by a central leadership team. That team determines the ministries and events that the communications team will help resource. Resourcing the campuses with a communication plan may include promotion or content that lives on the website. An example of something that may not get space on the website is a men's golf ministry at one specific campus. Years ago, we had every ministry the church had on the website, and it was overwhelming. We try to provide other platforms such as email, social media, and print pieces for campus-specific events and ministries. Our goal is to connect you to a person who can get you connected to ministries to fit your needs best.

Author: How often do those determining the website content meet, and what does the meeting look like?
David Martin: If we were building a new website or microsite, there would be meetings specifically to discuss the content and strategy for that site. For information that is part of a project or promotion plan, the website content would be discussed in those project meetings. Many times the same or similar copy, graphics, videos, and so on would be used across all communication platforms.

Author: What list of evaluation questions are you consistently asking yourself, or is your team discussing, so the website remains relevant and exhibits excellence?
David Martin: Focus groups are the best! Around once a year, we bring in two groups of diverse people, one internal group and one external group. We ask them questions such as, What is important to you when searching for a church? What is clear, and what is confusing about our website? Anything you feel is missing or hard to find? One interesting find this year was that parents said that teaching their kids truth in our current climate was their most important thing. So that changed our strategy for the students' page. Less focus on fun and more reassurance that students will be learning about the Bible. Also, always ask for feedback from those around you and your team. Never stop learning and asking the question "What is the next big thing?"

Author: What changes did you make to the website due to COVID-19? Are those changes still in place?
David Martin: Where to start. It felt like everything had to

change to reflect where our world was for a season. Pictures of people wearing masks, no in-person gatherings, services moved to online-only, events canceled. . . . So what do we talk about, and what do we encourage our people to do during this season? We shifted our focus to being the church, no matter where we are, which is still ingrained in who we are as a church and in the website. We beefed up our online campus, and many of those enhancements are still in effect. We made our next-steps process much more accessible and provided faster responses, like texting keywords for prayer and how to get involved.

Author: What is the church's budget for website design?
David Martin: For a new website from the ground up that is database-driven, we generally expect to spend anywhere from $15,000 to $35,000.

Author: Many churches have chosen to host a church Facebook page but have no website. Is this a good idea? If so, why? If not, why not?
David Martin: The best we can, we try to be where people are, such as Google and Apple maps, YouTube, Facebook, Twitter, and Instagram. If we are not in these places and someone goes to Google Maps and searches for us, they will not find us. But we would never use these platforms in place of our website. Our website is tailored to our needs and doesn't require a Facebook account to interact with it.

Author: What are three aspects of the Pinelake website that every church would be wise to emulate?
David Martin: Keep the main thing the main thing, the gospel of Jesus. Make essential things easy to find and load fast. Less content that is accurate and has clear ask or next steps.

One last thing that I don't think I should have to mention anymore, device-friendly! The numbers show that more people are visiting our site from a phone or tablet than a computer and every year that percentage increases. If your website doesn't work or look well on a phone, it's time for a new one.

2. Watch an Online Service

Bodily attending a worship service is no longer how church hunters determine if a church's service is right for them. The online service has replaced "entering the building" to check out the church's musical style, the preacher's approach to preaching, and the seating situation. If the online service isn't excellent and the production professional-grade, the possible first-time guest will never take the plunge and attend a live worship service.

Rusty Anderson has been a live video director for twenty years. He has had the privilege of serving Chris Tomlin, Louie Giglio, Passion, David Crowder, Matt Redman, Hillsong, Kari Jobe, and others. He has served on staff at Passion City Church and Passion Conferences, directing weekly gatherings and conferences in arenas and stadiums all over the world. He has also worked with churches and organizations such as Elevation, Vous, Willow Creek, Global Leadership Summit, North Point Ministries, and others across the country.

Rusty is in this space every day. Here's his description of the situation.

It's no secret that the average person is spending more and more time watching media content. Sure, the average person is watching less traditional TV, but streaming content and social media consumption are on the rise. As someone who lives in the church production world, I have to be aware of this. The people that we are trying to reach through online worship broadcasts are being bombarded with content every day, content that people spend millions of dollars to produce. Meaning, online content is generally excellent quality with lots of dollars behind it. Quality, however, can take different forms. It can mean the traditional sense of high-budget productions that look and sound great. The rise of social media content, however, is challenging this definition. Some of the most successful streaming content providers would not be considered "technically excellent." I would argue, though, that they are excellent in storytelling and engagement. YouTube and TikTok stars are seen as genuine and connect with people on a relational level, arguably more so than big-budget productions.

So, what does this mean for the church? I believe there is some level of excellence that is required when it comes to an online broadcast. Foremost, since it represents our Creator, I strongly believe it should be presented well, within the means of the individual, local church. Furthermore, since people are constantly bombarded with content and at least subconsciously know when something looks and sounds good, it is important to present something that is well made. You don't have to be a career video director like myself to know that you had a good or bad experience when you watched something online. So, we need to light things well, we need to mix audio well, and we need to use cameras and video to help tell the story of Jesus, just like the worship leader and pastor do from the stage. This means we need to allocate budget toward those disciplines, hire staff to manage them, and train them to do it well. Your online broadcast doesn't have to look and sound as good as the megachurch on the other side of town, but it does need to have someone caring about it because it's obvious to the viewer when no one does.

More important than the look and sound of your online broadcast is the message within it. Hollywood is full of big-budget productions that are total flops and failures. No quality of camera, light, or microphone can make up for a broadcast that feels inauthentic and lacks meaning. We should take a lesson from social media content creators. Connecting with people on a deeper relational level is far more important. A quick story— my church has multiple campuses from which we broadcast the online gatherings. A few months ago, a woman moved into town from across the country. She didn't really know anyone but she knew exactly where to go to church, more specifically, which campus to attend. She had been watching our church online for the past several months during the pandemic. She knew which campus she wanted to attend because she had connected to people from that particular campus though the broadcast. She didn't personally meet or talk to anyone, she just watched online from afar and decided that one particular campus felt like home to her. It's not to say the other campus is bad, but for this woman, there was an obvious relational connection. Nothing is said from the broadcast that would describe the different campuses; it just comes through the people when they are genuine. Don't present your best self on your online broadcast, just present yourself—a human who struggles with life but has found the truth and hope of Jesus wants to share it with anyone who will listen.

There are two sides to the equation. There is an allocation of funds necessary to creating a good broadcast. Equipment matters, to an extent. Expertise certainly matters. But of at least equal importance is the content and the message being broadcast. Authenticity matters. When push comes to shove, err on the side of authenticity. That's the goal of any broadcast I'm involved with.

Every church doesn't have the means, team, or technology to do a professional-grade online service. But every church should do the best online service their church is capable of making available.

3. Attend a Worship Service in Person

Once a household in the hunt for their church has viewed a service online, if they are stirred by what they see, their next step is to attend a worship service in person. At this point, the church must be hitting on all pistons. One miscue may keep the guests from showing up a second time. One enchanting moment may spark the guests to continue the journey toward church membership.

PGCs implement certain practices and characteristics with supersized dedication. Getting these things right is unarguably indispensable:

- well-groomed landscaping
- a clutter-free parking lot with clearly painted lines
- easy-access guest parking
- a welcoming, joy-filled, animated parking attendant
- clear signage in the parking lot as well as throughout the building
- a clean, uncluttered facility with up-to-date architecture and contemporary decor
- a well-staffed guest center

- a well-staffed kid's check-in center
- a safe and well-secured preschool and kids' ministry area
- seven touch points before arriving at their seat in the worship center
- not singling out guests in the worship service
- acquiring the guests' contact information and following up with them as soon as possible
- give guests one clear next step

Five exhilarating teams are essential.

- Parking Team—setting the tone by exhibiting joy and animation when guiding people to their parking spot.
- Guest Center Team
  - greeting guests joyfully
  - answering the guests' questions
  - getting the guests' contact information
  - giving guests a gift
  - directing guests with children to the kids' ministry area
  - telling guests there's a coffee bar, where it's located, and that it's free to them
- Greeter Team
  - greeting guests joyfully
  - located in the lobby and at each entrance throughout the building
  - escorting guests to any location they ask about
- Host Team
  - located at worship center doors
  - escorting guests to a seat in the worship center
- Kid's Check-In Team
  - explaining the check-in process and what is needed to pick the child up
  - giving a tour of the kids' ministry area
  - taking the child and parent to their room and introducing them to the kids' ministry worker
  - showing them the family lounge and the moms' room

Bill Buckingham has served as assimilation pastor of two perpetually growing churches, The Bridge Church in Spring Hill, Tennessee, and LakePointe Church in Rockwall, Texas. It has been my honor to work alongside him, experience his training pastors from churches of all sizes to build their assimilation process, and see him build teams that are off-the-charts. Bill's interview unearths principles and practices that will take your church's first-time guest experience to the next level and beyond!

Author: Bill, you've had the responsibility of first-time guests' services in two of the fastest-growing churches in the country. Why is the first-time guest experience so important?

Pastor Bill Buckingham: I like to approach the guest experience from a perspective of expectation and anticipation. This means that as a church, we expect there will be guests joining us and we anticipate their needs ahead of time. We plan and prepare with that in mind.

We need to also acknowledge the fact that we never know where a guest is coming from in their faith journey. Some might be far from God, others may already know Him, but ultimately the guest experience is a way for us to remove any barriers that may get in the way of someone coming to know God or take a next step in their faith. Oftentimes we only get one shot to make a great first impression with our guests. The guest experience places an emphasis on hospitality and helps ensure we create environments that reflect a gospel culture so we might effectively share Christ.

Author: How would you describe the environment that captures the heart of first-time guests?

Pastor Bill Buckingham: Some things are out of our control, but what we can control is doing our part to create an environment of hospitality where their heart is softened and receptive to what they're about to hear. A warm and welcoming environment where we reflect the heart of the Father in the story of the prodigal son and go to meet them where they are. Ultimately, people may disagree with what they heard, but they should never be able to disagree with how they were treated. We don't want this environment to reflect a posture of "where have you been?" Rather, we want it to say "welcome home!"

To create a "welcome home" environment, we must first create a healthy culture. We can have the most compelling vision, the best strategy, and the highest level of execution, but if the values we embody aren't lived out, all those things fall flat. Culture isn't what you say; it's what you do. Our desire should be for our guests to feel noticed, loved, and ultimately known. They're already noticed, loved, and known by God, and the culture we create should simply reflect that and point them to that truth. The way we display these things, and more, tells the guest a narrative about the message we are proclaiming and the God we follow.

Author: Who is responsible for exhibiting what you just described?

Pastor Bill Buckingham: In many ways, creating that kind of environment is everyone's responsibility as a part of the body of Christ. We each have our part to play. And I also believe if you are a pastor/leader in the church, this responsibility starts with you. You need to be the driver of that culture and set the pace for others to follow.

There are some people in the church who will have certain gifts, passions, and a natural affinity for creating a welcoming environment for guests. These folks should be the champions for the guest experience. Depending on your scope and scale, you may need to raise up someone on your staff to run point on the guest experience. Give them the support and resources they need, empower them, and watch the "welcome home" culture become a part of who you are as a church.

Author: How do you go about creating teams that week in and week out display that?

Pastor Bill Buckingham: For the guest experience, start by looking for the right people to build a foundation. It's important to find people who are not only gifted and embody the culture but also get the vision and strategy. Make sure they are passionate about hospitality as well. Plug them into a healthy system/process of development. Determine ahead of time what positions you need, clearly define those roles, and find the right people to fill them. Treat every position with great importance. Think as if it's the drummer of the worship band. If it's missing, your guest experience is incomplete and will suffer.

It's also crucial to craft an assimilation process for your teams. As you recruit new team members, building an onboarding and training process will ensure your teams are properly equipped and prepared to welcome guests. As your teams grow, you can then start to raise up and elevate team leaders to lead specific areas of the guest experience.

Finding the right tools to help with more of the administrative side of things is important too. Try to make things less memory dependent and automate what you can. There are great platforms like Planning Center, and most church-management platforms have helpful functions built in. Communicate clearly and create a rhythm of scheduling with your teams and be consistent with it. I personally like an "A/B rotation," but find what works in your context and plan out the schedule for your guest-experience team.

Author: Bill, you once told me that guests need seven touchpoints before the service begins. What or who are those touchpoints?
Pastor Bill Buckingham: Yes! These touchpoints are all about being strategic and intentional with the guest flow and making their experience as smooth and clear as possible. It's all about removing any potential barriers and helping guests feel at home during their experience. This isn't necessarily an exhaustive list, but I believe these seven touchpoints are core to creating a great guest experience and a lasting first impression. For many guests, the journey starts online and that's where we'll begin with our touchpoints!

1. Online Presence (live stream/website/social media)
    • Online is the new front door of your church. Make sure

you have guest-specific details clearly visible on your website. A "New Here," "Plan Your Visit," or even a "What to Expect" page will help give clarity ahead of time.

- Enlist a team to be chat hosts for your live services online. This might be the first person a guest interacts with at your church!

2. Parking Lot
   - I highly recommend having dedicated parking spots for your guests as close to the main entrance as possible. Create signage paired with a team member to make those spots impossible to miss.
   - Be strategic in placing friendly faces out here. A smile and a wave go a long way with our guests. These team members can help guide people to any reserved parking or open spaces.

3. First-Time Guest Station (outside/inside near entrance)
   - I personally like placing this station outside. This gives your guests an obvious first step as soon as they exit their cars and walk toward the entrance. Make sure it's labeled and clearly marked for first-time guests.
   - Place your most knowledgeable and friendly team members here. Pair them with the guest and have them act as their tour guide through the building. Take the guesswork out of everything for your guests!
   - While many people will park in reserved spaces and stop by a guest station, some may not self-identify just yet and that's okay. This is the reason we have more touchpoints.

4. Outside Entrance(s)
   - Nothing creates a warm environment like smiling faces paired with uplifting music. Place greeters at all your entrances. The goal of every greeting team member should be not to let any person walk by without a friendly verbal greeting. Make sure they know you're glad they are joining you!
   - Install speakers outside for music, pay attention to the care of your landscaping, and, depending on your facility and

how many entrances you have, it may also be helpful to add wayfinding signage.

5. First-Time Guest Kids' Check-In Station
    - For any first-time families with children, make sure it's obvious where they can take their children for any programming you have available. Create a station geared toward them. Make it visible with wayfinding signage, banners, and kiosks. A guest-team member can also help guide them to this station.
    - Train up team members here to serve first-time families with kids. Guide them through the check-in process, highlight programming and safety measures, and guide them to the classroom. Everything this team does should communicate safety and build trust with families.

6. Coffee Station/Cafe (lobby/foyer)
    - Offering coffee is not only a way to provide something people enjoy, but also a way to create a gathering spot where people naturally slow down. It takes a little time to prepare a coffee, and the connecting conversations that take place here can't be underestimated.
    - From the guest-experience perspective, place friendly people who are natural conversationalists here to pour and serve the coffee. Pro tip, budget ahead and offer quality coffee. Everything speaks, including the quality of our coffee. If you have a reputable coffee roaster nearby, consider purchasing from them as a member of your local community!

7. Auditorium/Worship Center
    - Once guests are ready to go and enjoy the service, this will likely be the final touchpoint until after the service concludes. Again, provide signage and make sure it's clear where the guest is supposed to go.
    - Placing greeters at the entrance to your auditorium is a great way to send people in to worship with a welcoming touch. It also is a good idea to have greeters inside the auditorium working the room and going out of their way to speak with people who may be sitting alone.

Author: When recruiting guest-team members, what traits are you looking for?

Pastor Bill Buckingham: I like to look for several things when recruiting team members for the guest experience. I start with the acronym F.A.I.T.H.

- Faithful
- Available
- Invested
- Teachable
- Humble

I also look for these key traits as well:

- Growing relationship with Jesus (if they aren't a Christian yet, I start there in their development)
- People focused
- Helper
- Positive attitude
- Solid character
- Proactive problem solver
- Natural connector
- Punctual
- Friendly disposition (a smile says it all)
- Encourages others
- Eye for details

Author: Please give us a quick list. What are the most essential things every church must *not* do to first-time guests if they want them to come back a second time?

Pastor Bill Buckingham: Don't . . .

- make them sit in the front row,
- pressure them to give,
- treat them like outsiders and ignore them as they walk around,
- have unfriendly people on the guest-experience team (you'd be surprised how often this happens),
- put them on the spot during service,
- say something and not follow through (i.e., if you meet

them and say you'll reach out, make sure you do),
- show up on their doorstep the next day,
- ask them to volunteer or join a small group, and
- use insider language or jokes in communication.

Author: Please give us a quick list. What are the most essential things every church must do for first-time guests if they want them to come back a second time?

Pastor Bill Buckingham: Do . . .
- put your friendliest people on your guest-experience team,
- provide clear signage around your facility,
- make your guest kids' check-in process clear and efficient,
- ensure their kids are safe, have fun, and learn something in kids' ministry,
- greet them and introduce yourself as the opportunity presents itself,
- tailor your communication and think with the guest in mind,
- invite them to sit with you if they are alone,
- remember their name(s),
- thank them for joining you (via text/email if they provided info),
- invite them to come back next week,
- keep your facility up to date with decor and style (especially in kids' ministry), and
- keep a clean and tidy environment (inside and outside).

I'm indebted to Bill. I hope you'll take into consideration all he's revealed. Because the information and action steps he's unearthed will make the difference in how many first-time guests become part of your church.

Hold this remarkable fact from church-growth guru Nelson Searcy in the forefront of your mind every weekend and every time your church gathers, "Everything speaks to first-time guests—everything. From the moment the guests set foot on your property, they tune in to receive the message your church is sending. And your church is always sending a message, whether you realize it or not. The condition of your building, your sign, your grass, and your parking lot all speak to guests. Gut-level judgment calls are already being made."[1]

4. Attend for a Period of Time

If first-time guests have a great experience, they will continue to attend services and may get involved in some of the church's ministries. At this point they're asking some of the following questions (each person is different but some of the questions below are running through the mind of almost anyone who has gone from first-time guest to attender).

- Are there people like me here?
- Will I be accepted just as I am here?
- Can I make friends here?
- Will my needs be met here?
- Will my kids like it here?
- What ministries does the church make available to my kids?
- Will my kids grow spiritually here?
- Are there programs, groups, or ministries that I would like to attend?
- What church ministries can I serve in?
- What mission opportunities are open to me?
- What community ministries does the church partner with, and can I serve them through the church?
- Is there a Sunday school class or small group that I will feel comfortable with?
- If I join the church, what will be expected of me?
- What is the process for becoming a member of this church?

Answers to most of these questions are discovered in one of four ways: (1) looking around, (2) taking the plunge and joining a small group, (3) finding the answers through conversation, or (4) finding the answers on the church's website.

When people ask themselves, "Are there people like me here?" "Will I be accepted just as I am here?" "Can I make friends here?" the questions they're asking are "Are there people in my age group?" "Are there people with kids the age of my kids?" or "Are there people in my economic demographic here?" These questions are answered when they simply "look around."

When those seeking their next church attend the church, it's crucial that the church has people on the parking team, guest center team, greeter's team, host team, and worship team who vary in age, stage of life, and status. The question growing churches ask is, When a guest looks around, do they see people like themselves, or are they only seeing one primary demographic represented?

Many PGCs consistently promote involvement in groups. Some will unapologetically declare that "if you want to make friends, you'll want to join a group. Groups are where friends are made and caring for one another happens." Most people on their journey to find their next church won't choose to be part of a group until they are church members, but some will. Encouraging checking groups out is an effective way for some to make the friends they are seeking.

When church hunters who are attending often need answers to their questions, they need a place to go for those answers. Most PGCs use their guest center or the church's information desk. It's very natural for guests to ask questions at the guest center. On their first visit to the church, they have been there and have already conversed with a guest center team member. Some churches have a guest center as well as an information desk.

The person at the guest center or the information desk must know the answers to the questions asked of them. If a person in the process of concluding if the church is the right fit builds up the courage to approach the desk host and the host doesn't know the answer, the answer seeker may not pursue the answer further and walk away never to return.

Most important, the host should never tell them they need to speak to so-and-so and give them that person's contact information. Suppose the guest asking the question is willing to give the guest or information desk host their contact info. In that case, the host should get their contact information, give it to the ministry leader who can answer their question, and be sure the ministry leader contacts them within forty-eight hours (twenty-four hours is much better). The host should *never* leave the person without an answer to their question or knowledge that someone will contact them with an answer to their question promptly.

Most people on their journey to gain answers to their questions are best served by going to the church's website. A description of each church ministry, what the ministry's goal is, who can serve in it and be serviced by the ministry area, how to become involved, and who to call for more information will answer the questions most people are asking.

It's essential that the kids' ministry page, student ministry page, and the group ministry page answer the questions people are asking. What is gained through these ministries is the reason most people stick. For those with children ages birth through sixth grade, if their children have a great experience when visiting, they will often beg their parents to attend again and again. When this happens, most of the time, parents will choose to make the church their church home. If their teenagers are psyched to participate in the student ministry, parents will choose the church. And, if the heads of the household are making friends and finding spiritual fulfillment in a group, they are most likely going to choose the church they've been checking out. Having basic information about the ministry easily accessible and answering guests' frequently asked questions online may remove the obstacle keeping them from trying the ministry or the church the first time.

5. Take Part in the Church's Assimilation Experience

For most church shoppers, the final assimilation step is taking part in the church's assimilation experience. The assimilation experience is either a session or series of sessions where the person, couple, or household find out what the church's vision is, the church's governance, the church's non-negotiable doctrines, the church's membership expectations, how to become a recognized part of the church body, and then are given the opportunity to join the church. For most PGCs the assimilation experience is required for membership.

A few principles and practices are consistent in PGCs:

- The functional goals of the assimilation experience are for attendees to realize and (1) learn the vision, practices, and governance of the church, (2) sign up for their place of service, (3) commit to the practices of a growing disciple, and (4) join a small group. When they understand the church and involvement in these three mentioned commitments, they are apt to stay at the church growing in Christ and making an eternal difference for many years. Not only does the church have the volunteers needed to function effectively and efficiently. More importantly, the church members experience a fulfilled life.

Pastor Chris Hodges, the pastor of Church of the Highlands, who wrote the book *What's Next?*, unearths how church members can know God, find freedom, discover their purpose, and make a difference. The foreword was written by his good friend and mentor, leadership guru John Maxwell. John writes,

I have some questions for you. Check the box that interests you right now. Would you like to
- Know God?
- Find Freedom?
- Discover Your Purpose?
- Make a Difference?

I bet you said yes to all four of those questions. I did! If you and I could discover the answers to those four questions and apply those answers to our lives, we would certainly be fulfilled.[2]

When church members are finding fulfillment, they seldom leave the church they're attending.
- Most PGCs agree that attending a worship service weekly, being in Christian community through a small group, exercising spiritual gifts by being on a ministry team, and worshipping through giving of time, talents, and finances are key elements on the journey to spiritual maturity. With that in mind, PGCs create an easily recognizable structure, a series of easy-to-remember terms, and unearth them during the assimilation experience. Each of the terms aligns with an expected practice. Church of the Highlands utilizes the following four terms and descriptions. Hundreds of churches have successfully adopted or adapted the terms used below.

Know God (Weekend Services)—God wants to know us personally. More than just practicing religion, He wants a relationship with us. Our weekend services are where we focus on that relationship.

Find Freedom (Small Groups)—One of the ways God designed for us to live in freedom is to have people in our life to help us in the journey. Connecting with others in Highlands Small Groups is a practical way to find that kind of life-changing community.

Discover Purpose (Growth Track)—We're all an important part of God's plan, and our life will never make sense until we discover our purpose. The Highlands Growth Track is designed to help us take steps in the important process of discovering our purpose, and there are opportunities to attend weekly at every Highlands location.

Make a Difference (Dream Team)—This is God's ultimate plan for our life—to make a difference in the lives of others. When we do, the Bible tells us we will experience joy. Through the Highlands Dream Team, we hope to connect every person to an opportunity live out their calling by using their gifts and talents to serve others in the church and community."[3]

A stereotypical assimilation is as follows.
- Attendees are greeted at the door and taken to their assigned seats.
- A table host is assigned to each table. During some of the sessions, there is a Q-and-A time. The table hosts answer questions at these points.
- Attendees are seated at round tables. This creates an informal environment, offers an organic opportunity for people to begin building friendships with people at the same starting point as themselves, and aids the table host in making everyone feel welcome.
- A meal is served.
- At the end of the final session, attendees are offered the opportunity to become church members.

- Churches doing multiple sessions focus on one or a few related aspects of church life at each session.

  ○ Session 1—What the Church Believes and the Church's Governance
  ○ Session 2—The Importance of Small Groups
  ○ Session 3—Finding Your Place of Service
  ○ Session 4—Becoming a Church Member

At the end of each session attendees can sign up for the next session. They will also sign up for a group and the ministry they will serve in, or they can commit to the other membership expectations.

During the first and final sessions, attendees are made aware of what it means to be a Christ-follower and how to become a Christian and are allowed to choose Christ. There is also a time for Christ-followers who have never been baptized to commit to baptism.

Volunteer Engagement

Volunteers are the engine that keeps the machine in motion and speeding forward. PGCs are unapologetically overzealous in recruiting, placing, and keeping volunteer team members. Without an effective system landing volunteers in the roles the Holy Spirit created them for, the church will be unable to grow believers spiritually and grow numerically.

There are a few essential principles that PGCs embrace:

- Vision inspires the volunteer's heart. When recruiting volunteers or encouraging volunteers already serving, the ministry's vision statement is the key. It creates a passion for the work that nothing else can.
- Volunteers *must* be led well. Volunteers need a leader who

  ○ inspires the volunteers passionately,
  ○ equips the volunteers effectively,
  ○ cares about the volunteers personally,
  ○ encourages the volunteers consistently,
  ○ holds the volunteers accountable graciously, and
  ○ answers the volunteers' questions promptly.

- Finding the right people for the right position is the key to long-term service.
  - When people serve in their gift and passion areas, serving is exhilarating.
  - When people serve outside their gift and passion areas, serving is exhausting.
- Real-life people live real-life lives. They can only do what time allows.
- Everyone, including volunteers, needs and deserves to know their roles' expectations before accepting the position they are considering.

It's undeniably factual that PGCs are constantly recruiting, placing, and doing what is necessary to keep an essential, kingdom-transforming workforce, volunteers.

Recruiting Volunteers

PGC leaders realize there are multiple types of volunteers. Some volunteers are able and willing to volunteer every week, and others are short-timers. Knowing which category of volunteer the individuals being recruited are will determine the roles they're asked to take on. It will also determine the way staff members set up their volunteer teams. If a volunteer is a one-timer, the individual is best used for special events or when a workforce is needed to prepare for an experience or clean up after an event.

If the volunteer is a long-term worker, the role to place them in is quite different.

Below is a list that describes the types of volunteers some PGCs have in their ministry rotation.

- Long-term—On the team and committed to serving each time there's an opportunity. These people are those most often called on to serve weekly.
- Short-term—On the team and committed to serving for a season.
- Substitute—On the team and is available to substitute when someone is unavailable.

- On-call—On the team but cannot commit to ongoing service. Will serve, if possible, when called on.
- One-time—Is available and willing to serve for one event.

Recruiting volunteers demands a multidimensional approach. While there may be one ideal practice, those whose teams house the necessary number of volunteers use multiple avenues to find and recruit essential volunteers.

- Assimilation Experience—The ideal system for finding and recruiting volunteers is the church's assimilation experience. During the assimilation experience (or one of the assimilation experience sessions), attendees are made aware of the ministry areas they can consider serving in and the volunteer opportunities in each ministry area. The door is thrown open for each attendee to begin the process of being cleared to take on a particular role (some roles such as children's-ministry or student-ministry volunteer require a background check) or to sign up to serve in a specific volunteer position. Ideally, every volunteer position would be filled through this process, but that isn't any church's reality.
- The Database—Some PGCs keep meticulous records of each individual's group attendance and volunteerism. When seeking workers for a specific ministry, wise staff members go into the church's database. The staff member finds those who have volunteered in an ongoing role in an area of ministry in the past. They also search for those who have volunteered for that ministry's special events. People found in the database who have served in the past may be ready to join the team.
- Conversations with Past Team Leaders—Those who have spearheaded a team in the past can often give a list of names of people who have served in the past. Many people left a volunteer position because they were overwhelmed at the time by difficult life situations, child-rearing, or burnout. Those individuals may be ready to join the team again. They are the best options as they already know the leadership, know how to accomplish the work they will be doing, and most likely found fulfillment in the work during a past era.

- Friends Inviting Friends—People enjoy working alongside their friends. Saying to a team member, "Is there someone you know who would enjoy serving on this team with you?" then asking them to invite that friend can pay enormous dividends.
- Small-Group Announcements—Gaining permission to speak with a small group or Sunday school class, telling them the ministry's vision, the available roles, the time it takes, and how to sign up is an effective recruitment approach.
- One-on-One Conversations—When a staff member sees someone in the lobby exhibiting the characteristics that suit an available role, the staff member should introduce himself. He should then tell the individual that he sees something in her that is important to the kingdom and to the ministry he is leading. Finally, he should let her know he's putting a team together, then ask the possible volunteer if she'd be open to talking about joining the team. If her response is positive, the staff member sets up a phone call or a meeting to discuss the opportunity with her.

Placing Volunteers

Volunteers serving the roles God made for them is the key to accomplishing effective ministry.

God gave each person an area of ministry passion and spiritual gifts. Ministry passion is the people group or cause that resonates with someone. When asked what brings their heart to life, they will respond by speaking of a people group in the church or a cause the church is involved in. Some people are passionate about seeing children come to Christ. Children's ministry is right for them. For others, the cause of homelessness is what keeps them awake at night. The church's homeless ministry or food pantry is their ministry passion.

Ministry passion is the first of two God-given traits that help in placing volunteers in the role that is right for them. The second is spiritual giftedness. A spiritual gift is a supernatural ability given by the Holy Spirit for service in the church. When each believer became a Christ-follower, the Holy Spirit gave them a spiritual gift or multiple spiritual gifts.

A third element that must be considered is the volunteer's schedule.

Some volunteers can give many hours a week in service while others only a few hours. Others can serve occasionally for a few hours. When a volunteer is recruited and not made aware of the time required, frustration and a quick exit will often follow. Some PGCs create a volunteer job description that reveals these crucial understandings. When recruiting a volunteer, they need to be given the following information in writing.

- What the responsibility is and what is actually to be done.
- Who will train them, how they will be trained (one-on-one mentoring, attending a class, and so on), and when they will be trained.
- Who will lead them.
- What success looks like.
- Where to find answers to the questions they have.
- What expectations are there, including how much time it will take to prepare to serve before arriving to serve.
  - Daily
  - Weekly
  - Monthly
  - Special Training Events
  - Team Retreats

When a volunteer is placed in a ministry space that aligns with their ministry passion, spiritual giftedness, and schedule, they will find fulfillment in serving and joy in the journey.

But how does a church aid volunteers in finding out their ministry passion and spiritual gifts so they are placed in the role God made them for?

Let me oversimplify the process. First, the church must work with each ministry area leader to determine what roles are to be filled. The second responsibility is for each leader to conclude or work with a team to determine what spiritual gifts best suit each role. A list is completed then turned in to the individual responsible for compiling a church-wide exhaustive list. The exhaustive list includes every ministry area's list. This list is then turned over to the person spearheading volunteer placement.

On an ongoing basis, the church offers a volunteer placement class. Part of the class experience is taking a spiritual gift assessment and an assessment that helps attendees determine their ministry passion. Suppose the individuals in the class agree to serve. In that case, their information is turned over to the aligned ministry area leader who is responsible for meeting with the future volunteers. The ministry leader points out the expectations of the roles and confirms the volunteers are willing to serve in the roles. The volunteers are then made aware of the equipping system they will be trained with and they confirm the training days.

Some PGCs help people find their ministry passion and spiritual gifts while attending the assimilation experience. During the sessions each person takes a spiritual gift and passion assessment. Individuals in attendance give permission for the team spearheading the assimilation experience to turn their contact information over to the ministry their assessments point out they should serve in. The team leaders then meet with the future volunteers to discuss volunteer positions with them.

Let me speak to those of you whose churches use a committee put together annually to fill the church's vacant positions. In these situations, a small group of people is handed a list of roles that must be filled. Without considering ministry passion, spiritual giftedness, or the candidate's schedule, the committee pursues individuals they believe are willing to fill the spot. While your church may fill the position, the individual placed haphazardly without any concern for them is most likely going to bail as quickly as possible and may never serve again.

Filling vacant positions should never be a church's goal. Placing volunteers in the fulfilling, life-giving role God created them for must be.

Keeping Volunteers

Placing volunteers in the role that God made for them is *huge*! If they are led well, honored rightly, and cared for proactively, they will serve well. But volunteers have lives outside of church life. They have full-time jobs, children to raise, homes to take care of, aging parents to care for, and many other obligations constantly pulling them in many directions. With everything tugging at volunteers, keeping them demands that the work they're doing is fun and that the team they're on is a blast to spend time with. They must also be reminded that they are making an eternal difference and that their work isn't going unnoticed.

How can a leader create this kind of environment and meet these needs?

- Have a compelling vision—When a ministry leader consistently reveals a compelling vision, people's hearts come to life, and they want to work alongside the leader to make that vision a reality. For instance, if a group pastor's vision is to see "a small group in every subdivision within a ten-mile radius of our church reaching those far from Christ with the gospel and discipling them to maturity," many team members will be so inspired they stay with that pastor for a lifetime.

- Lead an annual retreat—Turning a ministry team into a family cannot happen when the group is together for training experiences and organizational meetings only. When leading a small team, retreating together overnight or for a weekend, even if much of the time is spent strategizing and calendar planning, can create a substantial bond.

- Start with a team-building experience—Spending fifteen minutes building the team will seem like eternity to those personalities who are uncomfortable allowing people to know their hearts and for those who believe task accomplishment is the only goal. But team-building experiences will pay off in the long run.

- Host an annual church-wide volunteer recognition night—Many PGCs host a night to celebrate and honor all the church's volunteers. The experience is spearheaded, and every aspect of the event is handled by the church staff. Volunteers are welcomed at the door by church-staff team members. The church staff serves volunteers a meal and volunteers are honored as the lead pastor encourages them and thanks them for their many sacrifices (the pastor *does not* preach a sermon). Awards for serving long-term or effectively are handed out, and everyone leaves with a gift.

- Pray together—Few things bond a team more than crying out to God on behalf of the ministry or team members facing a difficult life situation.

- Meet the needs of volunteers—When a volunteer loses a family member to death or is struggling with a life issue, be the minister who reaches out with acts of compassion.

- Take volunteers out to breakfast or lunch—Do this just to get to know them better and be sure to thank them for the ministry they're doing.
- Send birthday and anniversary cards to volunteers.
- Encourage volunteers consistently through gift-giving—Throughout the year, give gifts to key volunteers and those who are excelling. When possible, give them something related to their personal interest. For instance, if a volunteer you're leading golfs, give them a three-pack of their favorite golf balls. One gift that is always a winner is a gift card to Starbucks, a local ice cream shop, or a restaurant. Tickets to sporting events are a big hit for those who follow sports.

Aldger Armstead is Central Dream Team director at Church of the Highlands and more than anything, wants to see the Church unified and growing. For more than a decade, his roles in ministry have varied from bi-vocational student minister to full-time student ministry, to campus pastor, and Dream Team (volunteer) director at a campus. He now combines his experiences and a passion for reaching people to assist Highlands campuses and other churches as they develop and build volunteer teams.

Read his interview slowly. You will not want to miss a single word.

Author: Aldger, in your estimation, how important is volunteerism to the growth of Church of the Highlands? Why do you say so?
Aldger Armstead: Great question! First, thanks for having me! To your question, it's hard for me to use the term *volunteer* as our Senior Pastor Chris Hodges and our leadership team have worked so hard to build a culture of team, purpose, and equipping people to make a difference in the lives of others. We use the term "Dream Team," so you'll hear me use the term early and often. To answer your question, "volunteerism" is central to what we do as

a church as our vision is to take people on the journey to Know God, Find Freedom, Discover Purpose, and Make a Difference. This journey culminates in making a difference by volunteerism and the journey is practically facilitated by volunteers who have found their purpose and are using their God-given giftings to help others.

Author: Why do you call the volunteers at Church of the Highlands the Dream Team?
Aldger Armstead: The term *Dream Team* has been a part of our church since before it began. The Dream Team received its name from our senior pastor while he was building a "launch team." He challenged the "launch team" to dream of what the church could be and how they could use their gifts to make it happen. As others joined our church and heard the vision for the team, others asked to join this "dream team" and the Dream Team was born.

Author: Your website says, "The Dream Team is a group of incredible people that have discovered their gifts and passions and are actively serving in them." In what setting and how do you help people discover their spiritual gifts and their ministry passion? Also, please describe the experience.
Aldger Armstead: We host a weekly Growth Track for anyone who wants to learn more about our church, themselves, or how they can take next steps. Our Growth Track is three steps on consecutive Sundays, repeating each month—Step 1 (Membership), Step 2 (Discover Purpose), and Step 3 (Join the Team). We help people discover their personality and gifts at Step 2. At every step, we offer dinner and childcare, and at Step 2, we take a brief personality assessment and spiritual gifts assessment to help people discover their God-given design. Because we believe that "design points to destiny," these assessments are great conversation starters for our Growth Track team, a group of trained volunteers who are familiar with our church, gifts, personality, and how participants can make a difference in the lives of others. They are trained and encouraged to have conversations with participants throughout

the Growth Track to help people identify and take their best next step.

Author: What curriculum or assessment tools do you use to help people find their spiritual gifts and ministry passion?

Aldger Armstead: We use a seventy-two-question assessment for spiritual gifts and a twenty-question DISC assessment for personality. Our Growth Track book contains both assessments as well as the result keys and descriptions for participants to better understand their results.

Author: Once someone has discovered their spiritual gifts and ministry passion, what steps does the church take to place them in the ministry they are designed for?

Aldger Armstead: Our third step of the Growth Track is built around helping people find their "best next step." We believe every member is a minister, every task matters, and every person is a "10" at something. Our goal is to help them find it! After Pastor Chris opens Step 3 via video, our campus pastors give localized serving details to help orient participants to possible next steps for them and then participants are able to choose an area of ministry that interests them. Upon hearing a brief vision of the ministry area from a team leader, participants have a personal conversation with a leader from their area to better understand their best fit. Before beginning to serve on a ministry team, participants are encouraged to find their best fit. And after they begin to serve, we welcome them to change teams if they feel another team is a better fit.

Author: Once someone is placed in a ministry role, who trains them and what is the church's philosophy concerning equipping volunteers (one-on-one mentoring, large group training events, and so on)?

Aldger Armstead: While step 3 acts as an orientation for teams and ministry areas, the new team members first serve is where they receive hands-on training and the "what" and "why" of each team's ministry expression. Each team has a leader who connects with people who are serving for the first time and walks them through the ins and outs of their serve area.

Author: Does Church of the Highlands create a job description for volunteers? If so, what information is listed on the job description?

Aldger Armstead: No, we don't create job descriptions per se. We create a team description for each team that includes a one- to two-sentence team vision (why the team exists and its goal), a cultural value this team lives by, a serve overview, what happens next to begin serving, and frequently asked questions like attire, arrival time, and first serve details.

Author: What characteristics are you looking for in those who lead teams?

Aldger Armstead: The first thing we look for may sound obvious but must be said; they must love God. We believe that our serve is an overflow of our love relationship with Jesus. We have four core values as a Dream Team and the first one is Love God. Love People, Pursue Excellence, and Choose Joy are the remaining three values, and we look for these values in those who lead teams. The vast majority of new leaders are currently on the team, exemplifying our core values, excelling in their serve, and leading their peers to do the same.

Author: What training is required of those who lead teams?

Aldger Armstead: Each new team leader is selected and trained by our campus staff teams. Because the majority of new team leaders are already serving, limited functional training is needed. We are more intentional to train new leaders to carry and pass on culture, how to care for their team during the week, how to prepare for their serve as the leader, and how to intentionally duplicate themselves. We use the fourth Sunday night of each month to host a community night to welcome new team members, reinforce relationships with team leaders, teach leadership, and reinforce cultural values. These nights are fun with food, childcare, and fun elements incorporated by each campus.

Author: How often does the church leadership host an event or experience to encourage and inspire all the church's volunteers? What are the elements of those experiences?

Aldger Armstead: Twice a year our church has a night focused on the Dream Team. Every February we have a Dream Team party that coincides with our church anniversary (see "launch team" reference above) to celebrate the Dream Team and all that God has done in the past year and to get excited about the year to come. We invite anyone who served in the past calendar year to attend with their spouse and we cater food, have entertainment, give awards for those who go above and beyond, hear a message from Pastor Chris, and give everyone on the Dream Team a gift. Every year it's always a blast, well-received, and adds energy and culture to the team. The second event for the entire Dream Team is in August and it's simply called Team Night. This night is a night for Pastor Chris to update the team on the coming season, to deliver fresh vision and leadership teaching, and to encourage the team. We celebrate Dream Team members who go above and beyond and include a fun element in the night.

Author: On a weekly or monthly basis, what do team leaders do to keep volunteers inspired and motivated?

Aldger Armstead: We encourage every team leader to contact every person on their team once a week via text or phone to check on them, encourage them, and offer prayer. On Sundays, every service has a "Dream Team Rally" before the team serves. Each five-minute rally has a pep rally–type environment as we celebrate "wins" from the previous week, hear a scripture and focus of the day, and pray for those coming and for God to show up in a powerful way. Each team is also encouraged to have at least a quarterly gathering with the entire team to build relationships, to welcome new team members, and to promote the small-group atmosphere that makes and keeps teams healthy.

Author: If I remember correctly, Church of the Highlands has locker rooms for volunteers. If this is true, why did the church decide to create these, and how do they aid the church in keeping volunteers motivated and serving?

Aldger Armstead: No, we don't have a locker room for the Dream Team, but we do create a space called "Dream Team Central" at every campus. This space is a meeting place for the Dream Team to connect in between services, before service for Dream Team Rally, and during serve breaks. It is hosted by a serve team that provides food, refreshments, and encouragement to the team as they serve.

Author: What does Lead Pastor Chris Hodges do to promote volunteerism?

Aldger Armstead: Where do I begin? First, Pastor Chris lives it and truly believes that we are all called to make a difference in the lives of others. I vividly remember our senior pastor leading worship, then delivering a message, then loading the Hodges family van with church equipment because we were portable at the time. Even now, at every staff meeting Pastor Chris reminds our entire staff team that we were once on the Dream Team and we still are on the Dream Team. The staff team at Highlands still serves and models our core values as we encourage others to do the same. And lastly, only to be brief, every time he speaks a message, he finds a way to encourage people to take spiritual next steps, to attend the Growth Track, and to serve and make a difference in the lives of others. Our senior pastor has truly created and bolstered a culture that encourages people to find what God has put inside of them and to use it, no matter how insignificant it may seem, to impact others.

Leadership Development

Leadership development is a church-growth prerequisite.

As a church experiences ongoing and often exponential growth, new leaders are essential. Birthing new teams is a must, and each new team requires a leader. Without a pool of exceptional leaders to place over new teams, numeric growth will decelerate at an alarming rate. Also, a church may have a quiver full of active volunteers, but if those volunteers aren't well led, they will become frustrated. Many will bail. Some of the discontents will begin the journey to discover their next church. Others will choose to remain service-less, experience a lack of fulfillment, and become apathetic. Apathy leads to indifference, indifference is the pathway to negativity, negativity is the route to disparaging conversations, disparaging conversations are the bridge to disunity, and disunity lands a church squarely in the land of an unhealthy and repellent culture.

PGCs understand the leadership principle and raise lay leaders as well as future staff leaders. Three leadership-development practices are commonplace in PGCs: (1) the leadership pipeline, (2) internships, and (3) organic leadership development.

Leadership Pipeline

A leadership pipeline is a systematic approach for preparing leaders to lead at all levels of a church's needs. Mac Lake, in his groundbreaking book *The Multiplication Effect*, unearths five levels of leadership and describes each:

> The first level is *leading self.* In the local church context, this is someone who is in the basic discipleship process. Perhaps they are simply attending church or maybe they've gotten involved in a small group or ministry team.
>
> The second level is *leading others.* Once someone has learned to lead themselves, the next step is to take on leading a small team or group of people.
>
> The third level is *leading leaders.* Now that the leader has mastered the skills of leading a team, they can begin to lead a small team of others.
>
> The fourth level is *leading a ministry area.* This means the leader is now ready to provide visionary leadership for a ministry area with oversight of those who are leading leaders.
>
> The fifth level is *leading the church.* This is an individual or a team of people who provide visionary oversight of the church as a whole.

The illustration below depicts five levels of leadership:[4]

The size of your pipeline will be determined by the size of your church. Smaller churches (30 to 250 people) usually need three to four levels in their pipeline. Larger churches (250 to 1,000 people) generally will need four to five levels in their pipeline. Churches above 1,000 in attendance will usually need five to six levels in their pipeline, and churches 5,000 in attendance may have seven levels in their pipeline.[5]

A few important principles are in play when a church develops and implements a leadership pipeline:

- A church must determine its own language for each level. Below are terms a church might create to describe the same levels described in *The Multiplication Effect*:
  - Lead Self—Team Member
  - Lead Others—Team Leader
  - Lead Leaders—Coach
  - Lead a Ministry Area—Staff Pastor
  - Lead the Church—Lead Pastor or Elder

- Every ministry area must use the same language.
- Every ministry area must conclude which category of leadership every role they oversee falls into.
- Defining what competencies are necessary to lead at each level is essential. The predetermined competencies tell a leader in training what competencies they must get a solid grip on before moving to the next level.
- The goal isn't to move everyone to the highest possible level of leadership. The goal is to move those who long to, and have what is required to, lead at the level they were created for. Five critical transition questions must be answered before moving someone to the next leadership level:
  - Calling—Do they have the calling to lead at the next level?
  - Competency—Do they understand the competencies needed to lead at the next level?
  - Commitment—Do they understand the higher level of commitment needed to lead at the next level?
  - Core Values—Can they embody the core values of the organization at a deeper level?
  - Character—Do they have the character necessary to lead at the next level?[6]

A leadership pipeline is the most systematic and effective way to place off-the-charts leaders at every leadership level. PGCs know this. Many use the system as unearthed in Mac's book or have created their version of it.

No one knows more about the leadership pipeline and the local church than Mac Lake. Mac has a driving passion for leadership development. He has planted a church, served as a leadership development pastor for a large multisite church, started a church planting network, and founded his own company, Multiply Group. He is the author of five books including *The Multiplication Effect* and *The Discipling Leaders series.*

I am grateful that Mac was willing to be interviewed. His interview below will answer the most-asked questions.

Author: How has the leadership pipeline philosophy transformed your perspective on disciple-making and leadership development?

Mac Lake: The book by Ram Charn, *The Leadership Pipeline*, had a huge effect on my thinking regarding disciple-making and leadership development. The primary influence it had on me was showing me that there is a development pathway that needs to be intentional in the local church. The church does a decent job discipling people at the basic level, but we fail to create a pathway of development for leaders in the church. We need to be discipling leaders in the church through a clear development pathway.

Author: You implemented a leadership pipeline at Seacoast Church. How did the leadership pipeline change the leadership culture there?

Mac Lake: At Seacoast Church, I began to experiment with many of these concepts. I had not fully played them out yet, but I did experiment with them there. This is where I discovered the power of Ephesians 4:11–12. We are all familiar with that verse, "So Christ himself gave the apostles, the prophets, the evangelists, the pastors and teachers, to equip his people for works of service, so that the body of Christ may be built up." My paraphrase of that verse is "He has given leaders to equip the saints to do the work of ministry." So, for the first time in my life, I began to ask the question, "What would happen if we decentralized leadership development and began to put leadership development in the hands not just of staff and paid clergy but in the hands of volunteer leaders?" So, we did that, and it was fascinating. I began to see coaches reproducing coaches, volunteer leaders reproducing leaders. Some leaders were serial reproducers. They continued to reproduce leaders one semester after another. The pipeline helped raise up an army of leadership developers.

Author: What are the signs a leader in training should move to the next level?

Mac Lake: Really there are several things you have to look for.

The first thing you look for is, do they have the calling to move to the next level. Not everybody is called to go to the next leadership level. The question that must be asked is "Is God calling them to the next leadership level?" The second thing I would look for is whether they have developed the competencies required at their current level. If they developed those competencies, then we can begin to develop them toward the next level. The third thing I look for is character. Do they have the character if we move them to that next level of leadership? Do they have or can they develop the character that will sustain greater levels of pressure against pride, power, and prestige.

Author: In your book *The Multiplication Effect*, you state that no one should ever skip a leadership level. Why is this so important?
Mac Lake: It's important because every leadership level has different competencies that have to be learned, gained, and embedded in our skills to lead well at that particular level. So, leading a small group in a church is very different from leading the entire small-group ministry of a church. It is a different skill set. So, we don't want to put somebody upper level too soon. If we advance them without them developing the previous competencies, it undermines their ability to lead well at that next level.

Author: How long should it take for the average and passionate church member to go from Lead Self to Lead a Ministry Area?
Mac Lake: This is going to differ based on every individual because every individual comes into the training experience with a different level of experience, background, and knowledge. So, for someone to go from leading self to becoming a leader is going to differ. It's probably going to take three months to learn to lead others, but then we want them to season as a leader at that level for a while. So say they stay there for a year to eighteen months, then we move them to the leading leaders level. It's going to take them maybe three months to really learn how to lead at that level and be mentored into that. Then you would want them serving there for a year at that level before leading a ministry area. Then we could develop them toward leading a ministry area. So, someone who

is passionate could probably make that journey in two and a half years in a larger church. In a smaller church, they could probably do that in eighteen months.

Author: What are the adverse outcomes when the process is rushed?

Mac Lake: When the process of development is rushed, you may have exposed leaders to the competencies they need but did not embed those competencies in them. Therefore, they lack the confidence to lead, leading to a high turnover. The adverse outcomes are high turnovers and leaders not leading well, which end up hurting groups and hurting teams.

Author: You've aided churches of all sizes to implement a leadership pipeline. Most of the pastors reading this book will pastor churches with under three hundred in weekend worship attendance. In your experience, how does the implementation of a leadership pipeline in a church of two to three hundred transform the lead pastor's ministry and life? Why does it?

Mac Lake: In churches that are smaller, pastors tend to try to do too much. They don't empower enough people. Therefore, there is a lot on their shoulders. And so, churches this size that implement the leadership pipeline end up with a group of leaders who can carry the weight and share the load that the pastor is burdened down with. It doesn't take very long to build a culture of leadership development in a church like that where leaders are fully equipped and empowered in carrying out the ministry. So, it is essential as you develop people and empower people to realize the level of ownership of ministry goes up and the level of ownership goes up. When you do this, people tend to make decisions on their own without relying on and running to the pastor to make those decisions. So, it can be a huge benefit to that pastor because they know that all decisions are not being made through them, and they are no longer the decision-making bottleneck.

Author: Is there a time in a church's life when you would advise a church to wait before beginning the process of building a

leadership pipeline? If so, what is that, and why do you say so?
Mac Lake: We are talking about discipling leaders, but there are times when churches have a major emphasis that they are focused on or major conflict they are going through. Whenever you decide to design your leadership pipeline and transition to a culture of leadership development, it has to be a major priority. The other times I discourage or advise a church not to participate is if the senior leader is not bought in. They don't have to lead it. Still, if they aren't championing it and not modeling leadership development, they will never build a culture of leadership development. So, it has to be modeled from the executive level. A lot of pastors want it done, but they don't want to participate in the development of leaders themselves.

Author: What would you say to the pastors reading this book in churches running less than 150. They don't know that they have time to implement a leadership pipeline. They are overwhelmed by the weekly whirlwind of work that must get done and can't see how they can find time to build a leadership pipeline.
Mac Lake: What we have to recognize is that even in Jesus's ministry, after meeting his disciples and hanging out with them, it was about a year and a half in that he appointed twelve and began to spend a disproportionate amount of time with those few to impact the many. He spent the rest of his public ministry doing leadership development with those twelve, intensified development. So, when pastors or staff members say that they don't have time to do leadership development, I share with them that those who say they are too busy are actually prime candidates to do leadership development. If you're too busy, caught up in the whirlwind, then it means you are probably working more than forty hours a week, which gives people more than forty units of opportunity to watch you do something. If you have so many things on your task lists, then that means there are some things you can give away. Those you're raising up to lead can follow you and watch you do those things. So, actually saying I'm too busy is not a good excuse because it means you are the prime candidate for someone to learn from you. I recognize the whirlwind is a

reality, so I coach church leaders to carve out just 20 percent of their week to begin to build out the leadership pipeline because once it's built then you're operating it and executing it. Building it does take time, but the question I ask is, What pain do you want to live with? You get to choose your pain. Do I want to choose the pain of my existing reality of not having a leadership development strategy, or do I want to choose the pain of doing the hard work over a few months and knocking it out and getting it done so that we have an intentional leadership development strategy executed to move forward with?

Author: How many months or years will it take the average church to prepare and launch a leadership pipeline?
Mac Lake: It's a lot less than it used to be because over the years I have refined the process, refined the tools, refined the samples, and refined some of the system. Today, I can get a church up and running within about four months. They can be in the implementation phase of the leadership pipeline and begin to experience reproduction within six months. So that has been really exciting, but it's just because I have had the opportunity to develop more tools and resources around this.

Author: When a lead pastor longs to start a leadership pipeline, but his staff isn't on board, what should the lead pastor do?
Mac Lake: He should take his staff and begin to do leadership development with them. If the staff is unwilling to do leadership development, it tells me that they do not have the conviction that leadership development works. This means they never had an experience where leadership development has benefited them. Because they have never experienced leadership development that benefited them, they have never had a conversation about the fact that leadership development is important and works. Once you have a conversation about something that works and benefits you, you become an evangelist of that thing. It's like my story. A pastor did leadership development with me that had such a transformational effect on my life that I decided I had to do this with other people. So, the fact that he developed me, gave me a

deep conviction that leadership development works. Anytime I run into staff members who do not do leadership development or resist it, it simply tells me that no one has ever developed them in an effective way. Because of this they lack the conviction that leadership development really does work. Verbally they will tell you yes it works, but behaviorally, they do not.

Author: If you were a lead pastor and you realized the game-changing outcomes of creating a leadership pipeline for the very first time, what would your first steps be?

Mac Lake: I would get two to three influential leaders around me, and I would begin to disciple them as leaders, taking them through the steps in my book *Leading Others*. I would take them through that book over a period of two or three months, ask those experienced leaders to begin to disciple new leaders, and then find two more people and lead them through the steps in my *Leading Leaders* book, and I would just begin to live it. I tell churches all the time you do not want to build a leadership pipeline and announce it to your church because the day you announce it to your church is the day it becomes a program, and that's the day you put a death nail in your leadership pipeline. You want to build an intentional leadership development strategy that you execute organically because leadership development is not a program in the church; it is a lifestyle of your leaders. If a church can get that, that's game changing.

Internships

Internships are a common practice of PGCs. An internship is a short-term preparation for ministry experience. While interning, interns have the opportunity to work alongside seasoned church leaders and gain the knowledge and skills the long-term practitioner and their team has acquired.

The specifics of ministry internships vary from church to church, but some of the most influential PGC practices and opportunities are described below.

Life.Church, Edmond, Oklahoma (Life.Church central internship)

Internships at Life.Church have set start dates in January, May, and September and are three months long. Interns work up to forty hours per week to develop spiritually, personally, and professionally through development calls, staff training events, and other ministry opportunities. Each intern can choose from a wide range of areas they're interested in, can earn $13 per hour, and are considered temporary employees of Life.Church.[7]

The Summit Church, Raleigh-Durham, North Carolina

At Summit, interns are anyone over the age of a college senior and are expected to attend weekly sessions for development. Interns are expected to integrate themselves into the Summit culture and are treated as an integral part of the ministry. Internships go August through May and require twenty hours per week of the intern's time. Although there is no compensation for interns at Summit, each intern is assisted in raising financial support. There is also up to six credit hours available via Southeastern Baptist Theological Seminary or Liberty University's Rawling's School of Divinity.[8]

Elevation Church, Charlotte, North Carolina

Elevation Church designates 70 percent of their interns' time in their department and 30 percent of their time in an intern program where they participate in various weekly activities and assignments within the intern program to encourage teamwork and camaraderie. They pay their interns a weekly stipend of $150 to offset living expenses and offer school credit if they are interested.

They also offer free housing for anyone who lives outside the Charlotte area but requires a reliable form of transportation. The Elevation Intern Program is open to young adults ages ten to twenty-five, and even to people outside the US (visa is required). They ask that applicants don't work other jobs while in the program as the internship often requires late hours and last-minute requests.[9]

North Point Community Church, Alpharetta, Georgia (intern expectations and understandings)

North Point Community Church's intern program offers twenty hours a week for eleven months of the year at a rate of $8.00 per hour. They also provide a laptop when you complete the program. They encourage interns to pick the campus and ministry focus they most feel suited to.[10]

Saddleback Valley Community Church, Lake Forest, California

Saddleback Church offers full-time internships. Interns commit to serving between six months to one year and typically serve full-time hours. The church also offers part-time internships. Interns commit to a minimum of fifteen to twenty hours per week for a semester (spring, summer, or fall).

The primary goal of internships in PGCs is to prepare exceptional church leaders to send around the globe. An extraordinary outcome and an added bonus is hiring the best of the best. When PGCs realize they have interns who have off-the-chart leadership gifts, outrageous people skills, chemistry with the team they're on, have wholeheartedly embraced and live the church's culture, and are capable of a continuing trajectory of personal growth, PGCs are quick to make these interns full-time pastors or employees.

As you can see, internships vary in payment (or lack thereof), length of the internship, opportunities offered, benefits, and expectations. Churches of all sizes are capable of hosting internships. Smaller churches make internships available in areas of ministry they are practicing and offer the interns under their tutelage what they are capable of making available.

Organic Leadership Development

Great leaders draw great leaders. When a lead pastor and the lead pastor's staff team are exceptional leaders, leaders choose to become part of their church. Most PGCs are led by lead pastors, executive pastors, and staff pastors who are extraordinary leaders. Because this is true, the church is a magnet for people with the leadership gift.

When laypersons with the God-given gift of leadership become part of the church body, serve in a lay leadership position, are noticed as standout leaders, are then brought into the church's high-level leadership circle, and begin to understand church leadership, oftentimes those individuals are prime candidates to join the church staff team.

While no one purposefully took the lay leaders under their wing or systematically guided them through a leadership process, they are ready to lead at high levels and most often make outrageously productive staff members.

Why wouldn't they? They love the church, believe in its vision, respect the church's pastors, and have proven themselves in real time.

Great PGC pastors are constantly watching those with the leadership gift to see if they are ready for greater leadership and willing to sacrifice much to join the church's staff team.

This chapter was very purposefully titled "Three Essential Systems." Without each of these systems in motion, effective, and ongoing, a church will lose ground and will never become a PGC. But, it is important to realize that scalability is key. Small to midsize churches would be unwise to do everything revealed. For instance, small to midsize churches don't need to create an intern program, but the lead pastor and other full-time ministers would make the right choice if they took someone under their wing to mentor.

A church that ignores building and maintaining each of these systems may see some growth, but it will be fleeting.

Chapter 23

Multisite Church

When they came to Jerusalem, they were welcomed by the church and the apostles and elders, to whom they reported everything God had done through them.

—Acts 15:4

Multisite churches grow.

Multisite church is "short for multiple-site church, or one church with multiple locations. A church is considered multi-site if it has more than one worship venue, more than one campus, or a combination of both."[1]

Multisite churches create a high probability of exponential growth. Each year *Outreach* magazine unearths the "Largest Churches in America." Of the top twelve fastest-growing churches listed in 2022, all but one is a multisite church. While the number of campuses and the size of each campus varies, the largest churches in the country use multiple campuses to reach those far from Christ with the gospel.[2]

Church	Lead Pastor	Location	Number of Campuses
Life.Church	Craig Groeschel	Edmond, OK	45
Church of the Highlands	Chris Hodges	Birmingham, AL	25
Lakewood Church	Joel Osteen	Houston, TX	1
Crossroads Church	Brian Tome	Cincinnati, OH	10

Church	Lead Pastor	Location	Number of Campuses
Christ's Church of the Valley	Ashley Wooldridge	Peoria, AZ	13
Saddleback Church	Rick Warren	Lake Forest, CA	18
Elevation Church	Steven Furtick	Matthews, NC	21
Southeast Christian Church	Kyle Idleman	Louisville, KY	13
Christ Fellowship Church	Todd Mullins	Palm Beach Gardens, FL	16
North Point Ministries	Andy Stanley	Alpharetta, GA	8
Fellowship Church	Ed Young	Grapevine, TX	7
Central Church	Jud Wilhite	Henderson, NV	7

Why Go Multisite?

Pastors often ask if the outcomes of multisite are worth the strain on the church leadership and the financial investment. Warren Bird's research concluded that

- multisite churches reach more people than single-site churches,
- multisite tends to spread healthy churches to more diverse communities,
- multisite churches have more volunteers in service as a percentage than single site,
- multisite churches baptize more people than single site, and
- multisite churches tend to activate more people into ministry than single site.[3]

If a church's goal is to reach more people with the gospel, engage more people in serving, and place healthy churches within reach of the masses, then multisite is a huge win!

Three Multisite Models

While terminology varies, there are three primary multisite models: (1) franchise model, (2) modified franchise model, and (3) co-operative model. No matter the model, each multisite location is part of the one church.

Below is a list describing how each model functions. Keep in mind that the titles for each model and the practices of each model vary from movement to movement and church to church. My goal is to give you the best possible overview of each model.

The Franchise Model—One church cloned in multiple locations

- One elder team has oversight of all church matters.
- Worship attendees at each location receive the same sermon via streaming technology.
- Worship services are a mirror image on all campuses, including songs, service flow, video content, transitions, and so on.
- Campus pastors on each campus oversee the staff team, care for and guide the staff team, administer the sacraments, handle on-site matters, but do not preach or make church-wide decisions.
- A central team is responsible for making the content the same across all campuses. While a central team may be assigned to speak into other aspects of church life, there is also a central team for each of the church's ministries. The central team calls the plays, and the ministry leaders on every campus run the plays. For instance, the student ministry central team may decide that every student ministry will host a weekend discipleship retreat. Every student ministry on every campus will host a discipleship retreat on the designated weekend. When a play is called, central teams also resource each campus with the step-by-step procedures and the necessary materials.

The work of central teams makes it possible for campus staff pastors to focus on building teams, leading volunteers, and shepherding people.

The Modified Franchise Model—One church contextualized in multiple locations

- In some situations, each location has its own elder team. This is unusual.
- Worship attendees at each location receive the same sermon content. The local campus pastor sometimes does the preaching. The campus pastor will preach six to twelve times a year in many settings.
- Worship services will differ on each campus, with their own feel based on the demographic the church is reaching or striving to reach. But each campus must stay within the boundaries that keep the experience aligned with the church's vision.
- Campus pastors on each campus have more autonomy to lead the staff and congregation and are continuing to be supported by the larger church leadership body.
- There is a top-down feel, and a centralized team is still making most of the decisions, but some freedom is given to church leaders.

The Co-Operative Model—One church made up of numerous somewhat-independent churches

- Oversight, resources, and branding connect these sites.
- Each location has its own elder team in many situations, but each campus is still connected to the larger church body and answers to elders overseeing all campuses.
- Worship attendees receive the same sermon content at each location, but the local campus pastor does the preaching. In many settings, the campus pastor works with a team of campus pastors and the church's lead pastor to determine the year's preaching calendar. The group also gathers weekly to work on the weekend sermon.

- Worship services differ on each campus based on the demographic the church is reaching or is striving to reach.
- Campus pastors and staff members on each campus have much autonomy in decision-making and are supported by the larger church leadership body.

Two Essential Awarenesses

Pastor Larry Osborne, who was instrumental in the growth of multisite church North Coast Church in Vista, California, alerts pastors to two often-overlooked facts.

The first is an *Attendance Ceiling*. Few video campuses ever break through the one-thousand-people barrier. Almost all are midsize or smaller. Ten years into the multisite movement, no one has come close to breaking the code for planting multiple large-attendance video campuses. And the handful that have planted one all feature very expensive facilities *and* a nearby celebrity pastor with an enormous regional following.

The second is a built-in *Geographical Limitation*. The farther from the mothership one gets, the harder it is for a video-driven campus to succeed. Most (not all, but almost all) of the video-venue success stories are found within the same geographical region as the main campus. Those that do succeed at the outer edges seldom grow beyond the mid-hundreds.[4]

Decision-Making and the Multisite Church

The question is often asked, "What decisions are made by the leaders with oversight of all the campuses and what decisions are made by the local campus pastor and their team?" North Point Community Church, Alpharetta, Georgia, has concisely stated its decision-making strategy. The following diagram specifies which of these critical teams is given authority for decision-making in four areas—Personnel, Programming, Facilities, and Volunteers.

Keep in mind that this is North Point's conclusion based on their multisite church model.

Multi-Campus	Campus

PERSONNEL
• Vetting and prequalifying new staff
• Role development
• Job descriptions with lead pastor
• Staff assessments
  1. Directors
	PERSONNEL
	• Recruiting and hiring
	• Personal development
	• Job descriptions with M/C Director
	• Staff assessments
	  1. Directors
	  2. Ministry staff

PROGRAMMING
• Core branding
  1. Logo
  2. Programming elements
  3. Ministry look and feel
• New initiatives
  1. M/C (Lead)
  2. Campus (Support)
• Curriculum content (Lead)
	PROGRAMMING
	• Creative/local expression
	  1. Specific campus implementation
	  2. Ministry R&D/Betas
	• New initiatives
	  1. Campus (Lead)
	  2. M/C (Influence)
	• Curriculum content (Influence)

• Program assessment (Lead) • Budget (Influence)	• Program assessment (Influence) • Budget (Lead)
FACILITIES • Physical environment • Guidelines, oversight, and compliance	FACILITIES • Physical environment (Local look and feel) • Modification and enhancements • Space usage/calendar

VOLUNTEERS
• Training/development strategy
  1. Philosophy
  2. Plan
  3. Frequency
• All-campus events
	VOLUNTEERS
	• Recruiting and training implementation
	• Campus-specific events

I'm so honored that one of the leading voices in multisite church ministry was willing to be interviewed for this book. Geoff Surratt has almost forty years of pastoral experience and was a pioneer in the multisite movement. He developed and oversaw Seacoast Church's fourteen locations and led Saddleback Church's eight campuses as well as their church-planting initiative. Geoff has coauthored several books including *The Multisite Church Revolution* and *The Multisite Church Road Trip*. He is executive director of Rethink Leadership.

Author: In your experience, what are the reasons churches choose to go multisite? Which of those reasons is a poor reason to try the multisite model?

Pastor Geoff: Early on in the multisite movement, the primary reason for churches to go multisite was rapid growth. When I was at Seacoast Church in Charleston, South Carolina, we had no idea that multisite would be a popular form of church growth; we just couldn't come up with another idea. We were filling five identical services a weekend, and the city would not let us build a bigger building. Multiple locations seemed like the least bad idea at the time.

Soon churches were going multisite to be able to impact other communities. Maybe there was a community that seemed to be underserved by similar churches. Or sometimes there were communities where other churches were moving out.

Another healthy reason for going multisite was in support of a leader the local church believed in. He or she might not have been a church planter but had a vision and the gifts to start something new similar to the sending church.

Unfortunately multisite soon became popular. Eventually almost all the largest and fastest-growing churches in America had multiple locations, and going multisite became a church-growth strategy. I've always said that if you are not growing in one location, it is unlikely you will grow in two.

Author: At what point should a church consider adding its first multisite campus?

Pastor Geoff: I think it is good stewardship to maximize your current facility. If you are in one service, add a second service. If you have two services, can you add a third? In most cases I recommend not trying to add another location until you are filling at least two services at your primary location.

Another factor is financial, can the sending congregation support the new site? Planting a new location is like having a child; it will cost more and make life more complicated than you imagine. It is important to count the cost before reproducing.

Author: What staff positions should be in play from day one?
Pastor Geoff: The biggest key is the site leader or pastor. I encourage churches to not move forward with plans to launch a new campus until they know who the leader will be. And with the first site it is very important to use a leader who has the DNA of the sending congregation. Not someone who seems to fit in, but someone who is integral to the church. It is almost always a mistake to hire a first offsite leader from outside the local church.

After the site leader the key positions are a children's ministry director, worship director, administrative assistant, groups leader, host team leader, and set-up-and-tear-down coordinator if the location will be move-in/move-out. These can be paid or volunteer staff depending on the projected size and budget of the new site.

Author: What is the pay scale for non-broadcast-campus campus pastors and staff members? If it's not the same as the broadcast campus, how do the two compare?
Pastor Geoff: Unfortunately I only have anecdotal data on this question. In my experience there is a wide range of pay for campus pastors, from $50,000 to more than $100,000, depending on the size of the location and the church budget. I don't always see a gap between the pay at the broadcast campus and offsite locations.

Author: Considering the fact that a campus pastor needs to exercise the gift of leadership but is led by the lead pastor over all campuses, what characteristics best describe an effective campus pastor?

Pastor Geoff: The primary role for a campus pastor in most environments is to identify, develop, and deploy leaders. If a candidate has a track record of building into volunteers who eventually take on significant leadership responsibilities, he or she will likely be an effective campus pastor.

The second characteristic is the ability to lead within the confines of a larger organization. While there is an entrepreneurial element to leading campuses, a leader who wants to craft the church's own story should probably plant a church. Regardless, the culture of the sending church comes with restraints.

A third important characteristic is to be an effective communicator. There is a fallacy that communication skill isn't that important in a video-driven teaching environment. The reality is that whether the campus pastor preaches on the weekend or simply hosts the service, the campus pastor's communication skills will often drive the health of the campus.

Author: On average, what does it cost to launch a campus?
Pastor Geoff: This reminds me of the question, How much does it cost to buy a car? Are you looking for a Porsche 911 or a Ford Escort? I've seen campuses launched for as little as $5,000 and as much as $2 million. Cost factors include:

- Are you going to rent a room on Sundays, lease a storefront, or build a building?
- Are you going to use existing equipment or buy all-new gear?
- Will you offer a full slate of children's ministry at every service?
- Will you use existing staff or hire new leaders?
- Is your new location in a decaying part of town with low rent, or are you moving into a fast-growing suburb?

Author: Are non-broadcast campuses financially self-sustaining? If not, should that be a goal? Why do you say so?
Pastor Geoff: There are two overarching financial models in multisite churches. The first is similar to socialism; from each according to their ability, to each according to their need. In this

model, campus budgets are built not on income but on need. As long as the overall church is in the black, not a lot of attention is paid to the bottom line of each site.

The second model is more like capitalism; you eat what you kill. Each campus budget is built on the income of that campus. In this model, each campus is expected to be financially self-sustaining.

Both models can be effective. It depends on the vision, mission, and culture of the sending-to church as to which model to choose.

Author: To be successful, how many church members must commit to leaving the broadcast campus and becoming part of a startup campus prior to launch? Why is this number of people necessary?
Pastor Geoff: This depends on the context of the site. In a neighborhood church or a rural context fifty people could be a healthy starting core. In suburban environments, it is often best to start with two hundred or more people.

It is important to consider whether the sending congregation can sustain the loss of the people who help start the new location. The biggest factor is whether the leaders who leave can be replaced quickly. It is unproductive to launch a new site but leave the sending congregation in an unhealthy state.

Author: What steps must be taken before launching a new campus?
Pastor Geoff: The barebones steps I recommend include:
- selecting a campus pastor
- selecting the new location (community and building)
- identifying core leaders (kids, worship, groups, hosts, setup/tear down)
- building core teams around core leaders
- purchasing equipment
- inviting people in the sending church to become a part of the new congregation
- marketing through social media, flyers, signs, and emails

- to the new community
- conducting practice services
- launching

Author: On average, how long does it take to complete all the steps?

Pastor Geoff: I think the ideal time line from the selection of the campus pastor to the launch of the campus is six to twelve months.

Author: What question or questions did I fail to ask that need to be answered before considering becoming a multisite church?

Pastor Geoff: Before taking any steps to becoming a multisite church, it is important to have a clear *why.* Often the *why* is stated as "We want to reach more people for Jesus." We all want to reach more people for Jesus, but few of us need to launch a new campus to do that. Why is launching a new site the most effective and prudent step toward fulfilling God's vision for your church? Until the leaders can answer that question in a clear and concise way that the average person can understand and get onboard with, it's not time to launch a new location.

Chapter 24

Exploiting Social Media

He said to them, "Go into all the world and preach the gospel to all creation."

—Mark 16:15

PGCs reach the masses through social media.

Social media platforms are essential outreach tools for PGCs. Many are deep into Facebook, Snapchat, Instagram, YouTube, Pinterest, Twitter, and Nextdoor. Not only are these online marketing tools easily accessible but also they are the cheapest way to make the church known, connect with those seemingly unreachable, continually make content available to the church membership and beyond, and target specific audiences.

Pew Research's 2021 study made today's church vividly aware of the need to use social media. "[Seventy-two percent] of Americans say they ever use social media sites."[1] Today's church can theoretically reach 72 percent of the adult population through social media!

A church can determine which platforms to leverage based on usage. "YouTube and Facebook continue to dominate the online landscape, with 81% and 69%, respectively, reporting ever using these sites."[2] "When it comes to the other platforms in the survey, 40% of adults say they ever use Instagram and about three in ten report using Pinterest or LinkedIn. One quarter say they use Snapchat, and similar shares report being users of Twitter and WhatsApp. TikTok—an app for sharing short videos—is used by 21% of Americans while 13% say they use neighborhood-focused platform Nextdoor."[3]

Also, a church can decide which platform to give the most attention to based on the church's primary demographic or target audience.

Majorities of 18- to 29-year-olds say they use Instagram or Snapchat and about half say they use TikTok, with those on the younger end of this cohort—ages 18 to 24—being especially likely to report using Instagram (76%), Snapchat (75%) or TikTok (55%). These shares stand in stark contrast to those in older age groups. For instance, while 65% of adults ages 18 to 29 say they use Snapchat, just 2% of those 65 and older report using the app—a difference of 63 percentage points.[4]

Twitter users vary.

> As of April 2021, Twitter global audience was composed of 38.5 percent of users aged between 25 and 34 years old. The second-largest age group demographic on the platform was represented by users aged between 35 and 49 years old, with a share of almost 21 percent. Users aged less than 24 years old were almost the 24 percent worldwide, while users aged 50 or above accounted for roughly 17 percent.[5]

PGCs are reaching out to various audiences using the platform that is most effective in reaching their target audience.

- Facebook—All age groups
- Instagram—Teens and those under twenty-four
- Snapchat—Twenty-four years of age and under
- Pinterest—Women of all age groups
- YouTube—Ages eighteen to forty-nine
- Twitter—All age groups

With specific accomplishments in mind, wise church leaders:

1. build a social ministry team,
2. set goals (i.e., reach 45 percent of the congregation on the Facebook site by next January, one hundred first-time viewers watching online worship weekly, and so on),
3. choose the platforms and the demographic each platform is to reach,
4. schedule daily, weekly, monthly, quarterly, and annual responsibilities. They give special attention to special services

such as Easter and Christmas Eve, the annual vision-casting service, and so on, and

5. collect data and make changes based on the received data and feedback from viewers.

Carlos Erazo is passionate about seeing people changed by God's transforming love. After spending more than a decade as a YouTube creator, content creator, and multinational bilingual speaker, he now serves as pastor of Church Online and Social Media at LakePointe Church for both its English and Spanish online congregations. Alongside his wife, Brooke, they've created more than five hundred videos on social media with biblical messages, accumulating more than ten million views.

Author: Why is social media an **essential** tool for churches today?
Carlos: In one sense, social media is no longer just a thing people use; it's also a place people are present in. Currently over 4.6 billion people use social media regularly. In the US, 80 percent of our nation's population is active on social media. That's eight out of ten people. That's a great opportunity for the church to be present in these digital spaces, to reach and engage with people in need of the gospel.

From a spiritual formation perspective, we host a one-hour weekend service in person (and online) every week. Social media is a great way to stay connected, interact, pray for, and continue to engage with our people the other 167 hours in the week as we seek to pastor them and encourage them to deepen their discipleship through relationships.

Author: What should be the stated goal of a social media ministry team?
Carlos: Our social media team has two goals; one comes from a marketing perspective while the other one comes from a pastoral perspective, and they're both important. First, increase the church's reach through marketing strategies on as many social media platforms as possible. Second, pastor and engage people

there through content shared, descriptions of posts, comment replies, private inbox communication, and more.

Author: What social media platforms do you utilize at LakePointe Church, and why do you choose to use each of them?
Carlos:

- YouTube—Currently the world's second-largest search engine (after Google). We stream our church online services weekly here.
- Facebook—Even though it's not the trendiest, it's still very popular worldwide. Many of our people still use it widely. Great with ages thirty and up.
- Instagram—Increasingly popular with our people.
- Twitter—Although this is the one we used the least, a smaller portion of our people still use it.

Author: Carlos, many of those reading this book know how to write effective articles, even blog posts. When posting on social media platforms like the ones mentioned in this chapter, how must the content differ from an article or blog post?
Carlos: Each social media platform is built differently so it's necessary to contextualize your message to the nature of each platform.

For example: YouTube, on the one hand, is primarily a longer-form video social platform so we work really hard to create high-quality longer-form video content for that platform. Instagram, on the other hand, is not a platform for longer-form video, but for quicker thirty- to sixty-second video content. Our team, therefore, will trim video excerpts from weekend sermons to create quick clips that people can easily consume while on Instagram. Facebook can handle video, graphics, and text so we diversify our posts and we keep track of what our people respond to most, for us to continue to engage with them effectively.

Author: Would you share the church's social media schedule with us? That is, how often do you post on each social media platform?
Carlos: Our team's Facebook/Instagram weekly schedule:

Sunday—two posts: a post to promote the weekend + sermon quote
Monday—one post: weekend recap post
Tuesday—one post: miscellaneous post
Wednesday—one post: promote upcoming events or ministries
Thursday—one post: sermon excerpt video
Friday—one post: encouragement graphic
Saturday—one post: a post promoting the weekend

A minimum of eight times per week on each main external social platform, plus additional content on stories, plus two to three times per week in our Facebook groups pages.

Author: What is the role of the lead pastor and other staff members in the church's social media ministry?
Carlos: Our lead pastor is very active on social media. He models engaging with our people from a loving, pastoral perspective. We encourage our church's staff to be active on social media, especially when re-sharing all posts from our church.

Ultimately, we're attempting to build community on our social media platforms and strengthen our current church community. Therefore, our staff is intentional in how we all use social media knowing that there will be many people outside our church who will first interact with us through these platforms before they step into any one of our buildings.

Author: Can a volunteer or a team of volunteers do social media ministry effectively? If so, what might that team look like? If not, what paid staff is necessary?
Carlos: Yes! We have the following social media volunteer teams:
- Engagers: We believe comments on social media are not just comments, but people whom we can pastor, minister to, and engage with. This team is scheduled to do "social media checks" regularly throughout the week to respond to comments, engage with people, and answer any questions from posts.

- Social Media Photography Team: In addition to our church online community from more than one hundred countries, we have seven physical locations in two countries. In order for us to cover all our photography needs, we're building our photography team of volunteers to equip them, train them, and empower them to help our church meet all photography needs for social media, our websites, and other communication projects.
- Social Media Designer Team: Social media is all about content, which includes video, photo, and graphic design. This team works on multiple creative projects that involve digital design elements to offer biblical encouragement, invitations for people to stay connected to our church, and so on.

Author: What technology and software are necessary and effective when starting a social media ministry?

Carlos: As long as you have social media accounts, you should be good to go! Having said that, there are some software programs that could be helpful when scheduling, posting, and managing multiple social media accounts. Some examples of these software programs include Hootsuite and Trello.

Author: What is your annual social media budget, and what line items compose a social media budget?

Carlos: Our team's annual social media budget last year was around $38,000. This helps cover expenses for the multiple platforms that our church manages and creates content for, such as LakePointe Church, LakePointe en Español, Student Ministry, LakePointe School of Ministry, LakePointe Worship, and so on. This accounts for social media software, content-creation libraries, video and DSLR camera gear, lighting equipment, special content-creation projects, and other things.

Author: What questions did I fail to ask that needed to be discussed? Please list them and respond to them.

Carlos: In the same way there's a lot of positive about social media, there's also a lot of negative implications about social media use, if not used with wisdom and intentionality, such as addiction, distraction, toxic content, and mental health issues. How does your team handle those things as a social media team?

According to research, people start experiencing mental health issues when using social media primarily for content consumption and to compare their lives with others, instead of for facilitating connections and building community. Our team is intentional in pursuing that goal of building community for our church. Having said that, we find Jesus models a rhythm of ministry of engaging and disengaging constantly. We work with our team to do the same when it comes to social media. There is a time to engage on social media (be active and connected) and there's also a time to disengage on social media (disconnect). We're always striving to keep each other accountable in finding the right rhythm for the right season.

Church leader, you don't want to ignore the availability, cost, or effectiveness of social media. For the first time in human history someone else has built platforms through which you can make the gospel and your church known. Use the platforms to tell the stories of changed lives, to announce upcoming opportunities the community will consider attending, to advertise a sermon series that is widely relatable, and to announce what your kids' and student ministries are offering.

Social media is a gift that, when used wisely, will connect your church with thousands of people instantly and often.

Chapter 25

Data Diving

After the plague the Lord said to Moses and Eleazar son of Aaron, the priest, "Take a census of the whole Israelite community by families—all those twenty years old or more who are able to serve in the army of Israel." So on the plains of Moab by the Jordan across from Jericho, Moses and Eleazar the priest spoke with them and said, "Take a census of the men twenty years old or more, as the Lord commanded Moses."

—Numbers 26:1–4a

PGCs peer into the data microscope to discover trends and patterns. They strategically gather, analyze, and act on data.

For each learned reality, an action is required. Something may be done away with, started, tweaked, prioritized, or continue to be evaluated. For instance, if it is determined that there is a congregation-wide need, the church leadership will strategize to respond to that need. If a pain point is revealed, the church will do what is necessary to alleviate the problem. Suppose through data gathering it is obvious a ministry is no longer relevant. In that case, the church can do away with the ministry and give attention and resources to that which the present constituency is responding to or will respond to. If, after gathering data, an assumption concerning a ministry is believed to be accurate but demands more understanding, the church will continue to collect data and come to a conclusion later.

Face-to-Face Data Points

PGCs collect many data points. The face-to-face data points most often sought after are (1) worship service attendance, (2) group attendance, (3) volunteerism, (4) the number of first-time guests, and (5) the number of guest repeats.

Worship Service and Group Attendance

When analyzing worship attendance and group attendance, a church may go about this two ways. First, the church may count how many people attend the worship service and/or each group gathering. Second (which is much more difficult), the church may ask attendees to sign in each time they meet personally. The second option reveals each *individual's* attendance patterns.

By knowing the month-by-month trends in overall attendance, the church can easily see what month or seasons the number of attendees is down and do something to gain numeric momentum. For instance, by gathering worship attendance data, multiple PGCs realized their July numbers were low. The following July, some of those churches experimented with a worship strategy called "At the Movies." "At the Movies" is a sermon series based on themes from popular films. The church decorates the lobby based on the theme of that week's film, and snippets from films are shown as sermon illustrations. Some churches even offer popcorn and soft drinks. In many instances, the church's attendance shot through the roof compared to prior years. Data drove the churches to discover a creative way to make the gospel known to more people.

By gathering individual attendance data, a small-group leader can see what members are coming and when. This may lead to asking individuals why they come during some seasons but not others. The group leader may find out that a topic was personally cringe-worthy due to a past painful experience, opening the door to minister to the group member's needs. It may reveal that group members have teenagers involved in travel sports teams. The leader can remind them that they are still loved and cared for by the group and that the group will be praying for them as they continue to make Christ known as they travel each weekend. The group leaders may realize through follow-up conversations that there's tension between group members and disciple the group members through their differences.

Volunteerism

Every church is constantly on the hunt for more volunteers. Each time there's a need for work accomplished, church leaders dig deep for volunteers. Knowing the number of volunteers who serve once and never again, the number of volunteers who bail on the team they're serving on and why, why volunteers return to serve again, and what team leaders retain volunteers will unearth what motivational factors are important to the church's volunteers.

PGCs create and administer a survey volunteers take after a project, while serving on a team or when leaving a team. The gathered information aids in learning how to more effectively recruit, retain, and honor volunteers and leaders of volunteers.

The Number of First-Time Guests

First-time guests attending worship is the key to leading a growing church. First-time guests become second-time attendees who become growing disciples and involved church members.

Knowing how and when the optimal time is to invite and enamor them is crucial. By counting the number of first-time guests each week, accumulating that data, and analyzing it, a church can see what season and what type of sermon series is magnetic.

PGC church leaders ask themselves three crucial questions related to first-time guests and preaching: (1) Is there a season when first-time guests are apt to try the church? (2) Are there sermon series topics that are more appealing to first-time guests? (3) If there is a season that guests are apt to try the church and if there are series topics that appeal most to first-time guests, then what is the suitable series to preach and in what season should it be preached?

Gathering first-time guest data also allows church leaders to determine if other factors are keeping the first-time guest numbers from being consistent. If there's a plunge in first-time guest attendance, it may be that the church's reputation in the community needs rebuilding, the demographic in the community has changed, the worship style needs to be revisited, or the church members need to be reminded of their role in inviting others and passionately welcoming guests.

The Number of Guest Repeats

PGCs know that growing a church depends on getting first-time guests back a second time. If the percentage is low, the church knows they must review their first-time guest hospitality practices. In each assimilation experience, it's essential to ask attendees to put in writing why they returned a second time. By getting this information, a church can determine how to make those things available to every first-time guest.

Digital Data

Today's church shoppers and today's church members are digital people. Most guests find out about a church through digital means. The church membership continues a relationship with the church through online means. Growing churches are using online engagement to connect. Blog posts, social media, church websites, and streaming views are keys to continuing to experience a church on an upward trajectory. And data is easily retrievable when people are clicking in.

Blog Posts

By discovering what a blog post engagement is, a church can determine if the time given to the blog is worth the effort. When a blog is experiencing significant hits, gather data on where the visits originated. Did they originate from social media posts, search engines, or somewhere else? Blogs are easily optimized by analyzing this data. Also, by analyzing the data a church will begin to realize what kind of topics the blog readers are connecting with. The church can then create more blog posts related to those themes or topics.

Social Media

Social media networks come with analytic tools, which are used to collect data. Using the retrieved data, a church can determine which post type users interacted with the most, which posts get the most comments, and which posts were often shared. These data are priceless. By determining what social media practices are most effective, the church can focus on those things.

Church Websites

The church website is the most critical content and the church's most important delivery system. Those seeking their next church dive into the church's website long before attending a worship service. To continually improve the website, measure the website's bounce rate and website visits.

Streaming Views

Streaming an engaging and captivating worship service is essential to growing a church. Since first-time guests watch the service online before attending face-to-face, it's critical that the church continually up their online service production. By measuring how long each viewer stays connected and how many reactions and comments the live stream receives, the church can analyze the experience and continue to tweak it.

Individual Data

Some PGCs work diligently to gather data for each individual. Data gathering begins with an individual's first-time visit and continues throughout the person's history with the church. These data allow the church leadership to understand better each individual's history with the church, family status, stage of life, attendance practices, preferred types of special events, areas of service they are passionate about, and giving.

Getting this information also greatly aids in understanding the spiritual growth or lack of spiritual growth occurring in an individual's life. Suppose the church's disciple-making strategy includes ongoing connection to and attendance in a small group, serving consistently in a ministry area, giving sacrificially, and attending worship weekly. The church knows what responsibilities need to be encouraged by reviewing the accumulated data. If an individual isn't in a small group, the church can be sure he or she is invited to one. If someone isn't on a serving team, the church can graciously make him or her aware of service opportunities.

PGCs gather the following individual data primarily:

- first visit date
- baptism date
- date membership was established
- marital status

- family members
- stage of life
- giving record
- training attended
- digital training completed
- groups involved in
- group roles (i.e., teacher, small-group leader, missions coordinator, etc.)
- group attendance
- ministries involved in
- volunteer involvement (one-time or short-term opportunities)
- events registered for
- events served at
- events attended
- mission trip involvement
- mission giving (special offerings)
- capital campaign giving

To get these data, for almost every experience, individuals must sign up before involvement (events and one-time or short-term ministry opportunities) or be in a group or on a ministry team list (groups and ongoing ministry or service teams). Each person must also register upon arrival (events and one-time or short-term ministry opportunities), or a roll is taken each time the group or ministry team gathers or serves together. The data must then be input into the church's database system.

All the above data are not available to all church leaders. Giving records and other predetermined information is available only to a few select people.

PGCs utilize data to conclude weaknesses and strengths then make the necessary adjustments.

Chapter 26

Foresighted Succession Plan

Elijah took his cloak, rolled it up and struck the water with it. The water divided to the right and to the left, and the two of them crossed over on dry ground.

When they had crossed, Elijah said to Elisha, "Tell me, what can I do for you before I am taken from you?"

"Let me inherit a double portion of your spirit," Elisha replied.

"You have asked a difficult thing," Elijah said, "yet if you see me when I am taken from you, it will be yours—otherwise, it will not."

As they were walking along and talking together, suddenly a chariot of fire and horses of fire appeared and separated the two of them, and Elijah went up to heaven in a whirlwind. Elisha saw this and cried out, "My father! My father! The chariots and horsemen of Israel!" And Elisha saw him no more. Then he took hold of his garment and tore it in two.

Elisha then picked up Elijah's cloak that had fallen from him and went back and stood on the bank of the Jordan. He took the cloak that had fallen from Elijah and struck the water with it. "Where now is the Lord, the God of Elijah?" he asked. When he struck the water, it divided to the right and to the left, and he crossed over.

—2 Kings 2:8–14

PGCs are fully aware that growth often comes to a screeching halt when a long-term pastor with a track record of casting vision passionately, preaching with excellence, and leading extraordinarily resigns or retires. Few things are more devastating to a congregation, having made a monumental difference in the lives of individuals and the community, than to lose its transformational potency.

To prevent this unnecessary outcome, PGCs are proactive in choosing the lead pastor's successor and preparing that person for the role. No church has done this more effectively than Southeast Christian Church in Louisville, Kentucky.

Pastor Bob Russell started his pastorate at Southeast in 1966 and exited forty years later. In 2006, at the time of Pastor Bob's retirement, the church was one of the country's largest and most influential churches. It remains so today.

Many said the church would be doomed when Bob Russell stepped aside. He wrote about a conversation one of his members had with a skeptic.

> One of our deacons, Don Whitley, a gentle, soft-spoken man, had a conversation some time ago with a man who obviously didn't think too highly of our church. The man said, "When that man dies, that church is going down the tubes."
>
> Don quietly answered, "That man died two thousand years ago and came back from the grave. You need to know that there is no man who runs the church. Its foundation is Jesus Christ."[1]

While Jesus is the foundation and Great Shepherd of every church, PGCs are diligent and wise when they painstakingly seek God when mining for the church's next undershepherd.

Before Pastor Bob exited, he and the elders created a systematic succession plan that has seen two generations of lead pastors placed successfully. When Pastor Bob stepped aside, Pastor Dave Stone took the helm. When Pastor Dave moved on, Pastor Kyle Idleman took the reins.

The church didn't miss a beat and continues a pattern of steady growth. As of 2019, Southeast Christian Church was the fourth-largest church in the United States with an attendance of nearly twenty-six thousand.

In his book *When God Builds a Church*, Pastor Bob Russell reveals the wise succession plan his elders approved. Part of it reads:

> Dave Stone will become the senior minister at my retirement, sometime between my ages sixty-three and sixty-five. Dave is a man of integrity, intelligence, and extreme giftedness who over the past ten years has become familiar with our church's culture

and has gained the respect of the congregation. He is an excellent communicator and an outstanding husband and father. He loves Southeast, and his heart and future plans are here. Dave is preaching one additional weekend each year. In the year 2000 he will preach twenty times, and I'll preach thirty. In 2001, he'll preach twenty-one times, and I'll preach twenty-nine, and so on for the next eight years or so.[2]

But the opportunities Pastor Bob afforded Pastor Dave went beyond preaching. When interviewed, Pastor Dave described why the succession plan worked and how Pastor Bob prepared him to take on the role of megachurch pastor.

> I think the reason it's worked well in this setting is because of Bob's humility and his willingness to share the spotlight. He's given me more and more leadership responsibilities. We've had a couple of coaches here in football at University of Louisville who would put the backup quarterback in the second quarter, let them run some plays and take a drive and see if they could take them down for a touchdown. And I felt like that's what Bob did for the first ten years of my being here. I got to play quarterback as a backup behind an All-American.
>
> Yet rather than him run the score up all the time, he was looking toward the future and letting me get some snaps and letting me get some experience, which isn't always the case with a dynamic preacher and visionary leader like Bob. His humility and his integrity have paved the way for me. I told somebody the other day, if things don't go well in the next few years, it's not because of Bob Russell. He has laid the foundation and has really done everything he possibly can to ensure continued growth and success for Southeast.[3]

Pastor Dave Stone served at Southeast Christian Church a full twenty-nine years. Long before becoming the church's lead pastor, he served seventeen years as a teaching pastor. So there was much time for him to learn the culture, know the leadership, and engage with the people.

When passing the baton, the successor and the longtime lead pastor do have overlapping periods of service in most situations. The amount of time varies from church to church.

Pastor Bob Russell has been a wise, humble, gracious, giving pastor and extraordinarily gifted leader his entire adult life. The pastor emeritus of Southeast Christian Church in Louisville, Kentucky, gifted us with this revealing interview. I suggest you read it slowly and take to heart the wisdom of this historic church leader.

Author: Did you independently choose your successor? If so, why? If not, who else or what other teams were involved, and what role did they each play?
Pastor Bob: After serving the same church for thirty-five years, I read Joel Gregory's candid book *Too Great a Temptation*. It documented the botched transition at First Baptist Church, Dallas, Texas. That failure was a tragedy and embarrassment that nearly split that great church. Gregory's book sobered me. I thought, "We can't allow that to happen at Southeast Christian." God has been doing such a good work here we can't give Satan a foothold in the future.

I shared my concerns with our elders and asked them to read the book. That stimulated their concerns as well. They suggested I come back from my next study break with a tentative long-range transition plan for the future.

So, in answer to your question, I chose my successor in that I recommended him to the elders for their approval. We did not appoint a pulpit committee and search for the best available candidate. I was convinced that Dave Stone, who had been on staff for more than a decade and who already was a frequent preacher in our pulpit, was very capable and the best choice. The congregation already knew him and responded well to his preaching. If he were bypassed for an outsider, it could be a potentially divisive course of action and make it extremely difficult for another successor to rally the congregation behind him.

Initially, several elders had some reservations about Dave Stone being the senior pastor. All liked him, but he was young. He was an effective college minister, but would older people respond well to him? Dave was often very humorous, and some wondered if the congregation would take him seriously. Our leadership team has generally operated on consensus—believing if the Holy Spirit guides us, the elders should be united. Since we weren't in a rush to endorse the transition proposal, we decided to pray about it some more and seek God's wisdom. After six months, all the elders agreed Dave Stone should be the next preacher, but several insisted Dave take an in-depth secular leadership course to enhance his leadership skills. Once that was arranged and completed, all the elders were on the same page. And there was no looking back. All the elders were on the same page.

Author: What process did you use to find your successor?
Pastor Bob: We decided first to determine if my successor was on staff. It wouldn't be fair nor unifying to do a nationwide search and put outsiders in the same pool with insiders. That could breed hurt feelings and division. So, once we decided Dave Stone was the logical and best candidate, we announced him to the congregation as the designated successor. It was an elder decision that the congregation accepted with very little questioning.

An important piece of my recommendation to the elders was hiring a third, younger pastor to serve on the teaching team with Dave. To preach every Sunday in a megachurch was too much of a burden for one man. Since Dave's favorite preaching style is inspirational and topical, I felt it would be healthy for the congregation for Dave to team up with a pastor who was strong in teaching gifts and more expository in preaching style. Dave and the elders agreed and assigned Dave and me to search for and then recommend the third man.

We did a casual search for two years without success. Often in elders' meetings, we would be asked, "Have you found a third preacher yet?" We would respond negatively and be reminded of the importance of that assignment. While attending a convention in Columbus, Ohio, I heard an outstanding sermon by a twenty-six-year-old California preacher named Kyle Idleman. His sermon was so dynamic and thought-provoking that halfway through, my wife whispered to me, "I think that should be your third preacher." Kyle had served a year-long internship with us several years before, but I did not realize he had become such an engaging preacher. However, I heard his new church plant in California had grown to a thousand people in about four years.

I contacted Kyle and said, "I'm going to be in California in a few weeks—could we talk?" Our breakfast meeting went so well I came away convinced it was God's will for Kyle to be our third man and split the preaching responsibilities with Dave upon my departure. Kyle seemed very open to the idea as well, especially since he had spent a year with us as an intern. Dave was totally on board.

When Kyle told me he was scheduled to be in Louisville in several weeks, I said, "We have an elders' meeting that week. How about letting me introduce you to them on Tuesday night, and we'll get the wheels turning?" It seemed to me the Lord was paving the way. At the elders' meeting, I said, "You've encouraged us to find a third man. We've finally got someone to recommend to you, and it just so happens he's in town this evening, and we'd like for you to have an opportunity to meet him."

I was shocked at the response. You would have thought my plan was from the pit of hell! Several elders had strong objections for some strange reason, and not one was nearly as excited as Dave and me. They said, "We're not ready to hire a third man tonight!" I said, "I'm not asking you to hire him; I'm just asking you to meet the guy who is our recommendation." They said, "We need to appoint a committee and go hear him preach and gather information about him." I responded, "I thought Dave and I were the committee!" "No, this is such an important hire we need more time and research."

The discussion went on for a half-hour and all the while Kyle was in the next room, waiting to meet the elders. I managed to restrain my anger and begged the guys, "Will you at least meet the guy? He's in the next room!" Finally, they relented, "Okay, but this is not an official interview. We're not hiring anyone tonight." So, we brought Kyle into the room.

Kyle Idleman was so poised and impressive they couldn't help but like him immediately. There were a few introductory questions, and someone brusquely asked, "You're a very young man. What experience do you have with suffering that would equip you to relate to hurting people?" Kyle's answer disarmed them. He said, "To be honest, my life has been pretty much free from major pain. I've lived a pretty comfortable life. I'm sure something will come down the road to deepen me in that regard, but I'm not looking forward to it or asking for it. But all I can do at this juncture of my life is teach what the Scripture says about suffering and point them to Jesus, who certainly understands what they're going through."

I could sense the temperature in the room warm up to Kyle. His honesty and humility had softened the hearts of those who were skeptical. The more questions were asked, the more impressive he was. Forty-five minutes later, he left. There was prolonged silence, and one by one, there were supportive comments. "Certainly, an impressive young man." "I can see why you were so excited about him." "Where did you say he was preaching now?"

Then one of the elders said, "If he gets back to California and his church gets word that we've talked with him, they may put pressure on him to stay. Maybe we should make an offer tonight. It seems like he would be a perfect fit for our congregation." Another suggested, "Let's send a delegation over to his hotel and tell him how impressed we are and make an offer to him tonight."

The elder chairman appointed two guys to go to his hotel and call Kyle down to the lobby. In the meantime, Kyle was in his room saying to his wife, "I think the meeting went fairly well, but I wish I had some confirmation from the Lord that this is the right move." Just then, the phone rang, and he was asked, "Can you meet us in the lobby?" The rest is history.

Author: What characteristics were you looking for in the person who would succeed you?
Pastor Bob: The primary reason our plan worked well is Dave Stone is such a quality person. He and I are quite different. He's an extrovert. I'm somewhat of an introvert. He's young, and I'm older. He's more of an evangelist. I'm more of a teacher. I'm not

out to clone me. He will be his own man, but there must be several qualities for a transition to work.

1. Character matters—a lot. It's of prime importance. We're tempted to choose talent over integrity in hopes the person will grow into the role. That's almost always a huge mistake. Just about every time we hedge on character it comes back to bite us.
2. Doctrine matters—a lot. There must be a common set of core convictions.

I have a friend who developed a friendship with a young local pastor from another denomination. They enjoyed each other's company, and doctrinal differences didn't seem to matter much. They were seldom discussed.

When it came time for my friend to retire, he recommended this young friend as his successor. The elders agreed since he had already been a guest preacher on occasion.

Within a few months, my friend began to hear some things from the pulpit that concerned him. He discovered the direction of the church was much more Pentecostal and Calvinistic than he had anticipated. The elders and the preacher were soon at odds over doctrine. In two years, the church with four hundred in average attendance dwindled to around one hundred and eventually merged with another congregation of similar size.

Dave Stone and I share the same doctrine. We believe the same thing about the inspiration of the Bible and the deity of Christ and the purpose of the church. The apostle Paul instructed his understudy, "Watch your life and your doctrine closely. Persevere in them, because if you do you will save both yourself and your hearers" (1 Timothy 4:16). And "the things you have heard me say in the presence of many witnesses entrust to reliable men who will also be qualified to teach others" (2 Timothy 2:2).
3. Loyalty matters. Your successor should be loyal to you.

Dave Stone was my designated successor for five years. In most instances, I wouldn't suggest that long a runway; two years should be plenty of time. Dave was loyal to me, praised me in public, and stood up for me behind my back the entire time. He would say, "He's the quarterback, it's his call."

4. Patience matters. You want your successor to be a zealous visionary and lead the church forward. But if he's overly eager beforehand and jumps the gun, it creates tension, and the congregation senses it. During the transition period, the church can be divided into camps.

He creates unrest if he's too quick to introduce significant changes when he becomes senior minister. Fred Craddock once suggested, "You don't rearrange the furniture in a room of a disoriented person." A change of pastors in and of itself, in a sense, disorients the church. If a successor implements his new ideas too fast, it will create instability in the congregation already trying to adjust to new leadership.

5. Talent matters. The successor should be very gifted. In fact, he should be more talented than you because you want him to take the church to the next level and beyond. Initially, he's not going to have your experience or your deep relationships with people. But he should have the potential to preach better than you and lead better than you because you want him to take the congregation to the next level. If there is a significant decline in the quality of preaching, the congregation will be unsettled and easily agitated.

Dave Stone is more talented than I in many ways. He remembers thousands of names. He's more comfortable circulating in a crowd of strangers. I need to read over a sermon six times before delivering it. Dave has it after a once-over.

Since I left, I've had hundreds of people say to me, "Bob, we really miss you, but Dave and Kyle are doing a really good job." That's what you will hear if you choose your successor wisely.

Author: Were you purposefully looking for someone whose leadership style or preaching style was different from yours? If so, why? If not, why not?

Pastor Bob: I'm probably not going to be much help on this question, although I've thought about it a lot. I knew Dave's preaching style was significantly different from mine. Because we had often shared the pulpit, it seemed the change of pace was good for the congregation when we were team-teaching. We complemented each other.

But I had concerns about whether the congregation would be satisfied with Dave's topical, somewhat lighthearted approach as a steady diet. That's why I recommended we hire a third man (eventually Kyle Idleman) to complement Dave. That really served its purpose and worked well. But I would hasten to add that the congregation quickly noted that Dave's preaching deepened once he stepped into the senior pastor's role and my concerns were unfounded.

It's my observation that the preaching style doesn't have to be the same for a transition to be effective, but it does have to be equal in quality and consistency for a transition to work well. If there is a decline in preaching quality, the congregation will soon begin to murmur, and an unhealthy atmosphere will be created.

Author: How many years before your successor became the senior pastor did you bring him on board? Why did you bring him onto the team at that time?

Pastor Bob: Dave Stone had been on board for almost a decade before he was selected to be my successor. He was officially announced as the heir apparent about five years before it actually took place. It worked for us because Dave was humble and patient, but I wouldn't recommend that lengthy of a runway in most circumstances. Two years seems plenty of time for the successor to become acquainted with the congregation and vice versa.

Author: What roles and responsibilities did your successor have other than preaching before becoming the senior pastor?

Pastor Bob: Before being called to serve as an associate minister at Southeast, Dave had served as a recruiting coordinator at Cincinnati Christian College. He had also been a popular speaker at youth conferences.

We hired him to be college minister and fill the pulpit in the minister's absence. He proved to be a very influential member of the staff and was given additional leadership roles as time went on.

Author: Throughout the transition, what role did your successor play in relationship to the staff team?

Pastor Bob: Dave was a very effective and inspirational team leader. He has a terrific sense of humor and became a natural in leading staff parties and get-togethers. The staff loved him and responded well to the funny in-house Christmas videos he prepared every year. He planned and coordinated much of our annual leadership conferences, which were attended by nearly a thousand church leaders from across the country.

As time wore on, I asked him to lead staff meetings in my absence. Or take a moment to present an award or encourage other staff members publicly since he did that so well.

Two years before the baton was officially passed, Dave was asked to chair a committee on future leadership development. We realized our method of nominating and choosing elders and deacons needed improvement, and term limits needed to be imposed. Since those decisions would significantly effect Dave's future ministry, it seemed wise to allow him to head up the committee that would recommend those changes. He did an excellent job, and the recommendations from that committee have had positive results to this day.

Author: Throughout the transition, what role did your successor play in relationship to the elders? Was he an elder? If so, why? If not, why not?

Pastor Bob: Southeast Christian's by-laws state the preacher is to be considered a paid elder. First Timothy 5:17–18 states, "The elders who direct the affairs of the church well are worthy of double honor, especially those whose work is preaching and teaching. For Scripture says, 'Do not muzzle an ox while it is treading out the grain,' and 'The worker deserves his wages.'" There is to be a plurality of elders. But there is one elder whose primary assignment is preaching and teaching. That seemed to best define the role of the preaching pastor for us. He's not a "hireling" nor the CEO; he is a member of a leadership team of elders.

However, the elders decided that associate ministers should

not be considered part of the elder team. Too many paid staff members on the primary leadership team lead to a conflict of interest when determining salaries and benefits. It also presents an awkward structure when staff members, who are accountable to the preaching pastor, also serve as part of the elder board to whom he is accountable.

When Dave Stone was designated as my successor, about two years before the actual transition, the elder board made him an elder. They determined that would give him additional credibility early and make the transition easier. That decision proved to be a good one. When I left, Kyle Idleman, the third teaching team member, was also made an elder.

Author: Did you personally mentor your successor? If so, in practice, what did that look like? If not, what was his leadership training pathway?

Pastor Bob: I originally thought that mentoring someone meant getting together at a scheduled time each week and attempting to teach that person what I knew. I heard guys talk about "pouring their lives into another." I tried that, and it didn't work. I felt uncomfortable and discovered after fifteen minutes I had told them everything I knew!

Mentoring is usually more effective when we just spend time together and share insider information. I would ask, "Want to ride with me to this speaking engagement?" Or say, "Let's go to lunch." Or, "Sit in on this meeting and keep quiet—ask questions later." It seems like much more is learned by observation than instruction.

Dave Stone and Kyle Idleman disagreed with me about my dress policy. I insisted anyone preaching at Southeast had to wear a coat and tie. Kyle argued that he didn't feel comfortable in a coat and tie. He felt like a hypocrite and didn't think he was relating to his generation. I responded, "We're meeting Almighty God! Don't you think if you were going to visit the president of the United States, you'd wear a coat and tie?" He answered, "Probably not if the president were my dad!" I couldn't think of an answer!

At this point, I realized the dress code would dramatically

change when I left in a year and a half. I also realized that while a dress code is a matter of opinion, changing it after I left would create more of a stir than they imagined. So, it would be wiser to change the dress code while I was still the senior pastor. But since wearing a suit when preaching had been such a long-standing tradition, it would be prudent of me to inform (ask?) the elders about our decision.

When I brought the dress code issue up to the elders, it was surprising how important it was with several men. It was almost like I was denying the Trinity or something! We could spend 2 million dollars in five minutes, but it took almost a half-hour to approve letting guys preach without a coat and tie! Several of the comments were overly emotional and irrational. I sat quietly and waited, and finally, everyone settled down, and the change in dress code was approved.

Dave Stone walked out of the meeting with me a little agitated. He said, "Wow! That was genius. If I had been in your shoes, I would have responded in anger or at least inappropriate sarcasm. But you just remained calm, and eventually the right decision was made, and you still have a good relationship with all the elders. That taught me a lot!"

Dave gave me more credit than I deserved, but the mentoring took place in an actual meeting under some degree of stress. Just talking about friendship with the elders or gentleness toward those with whom we disagree wouldn't have had nearly the impact. Mentoring is more caught than taught.

Author: After your successor had taken the lead position, what aspects of church life did you continue to speak into? Why did you choose to continue to leverage your influence in this way?
Pastor Bob: About eight months prior to my stepping down, I realized I was quickly becoming a lame duck. Some people, especially staff personnel, were waiting until I left; others were probably eager for it to happen. Rather than leave the church in limbo and experience a leadership void, I made a recommendation to the elders that six months before I left, Dave Stone would become the senior pastor. I'd be a staff member for the remainder

of the year. The congregation would see little difference. I would still preach on the designated weekends, but the staff could now turn to Dave Stone for guidance and decisions. (And all critical letters and emails were to go to Dave!) That proved to be a good decision for the church's welfare, but admittedly a difficult decision for me.

When Easter Sunday rolled around, Dave decided, with the leadership team's approval, to have six different services. Instead of packing people into the ordinary three services, he thought the church would be best served to double the number of services so visitors would not feel crammed into the sanctuary and not be delayed for long periods in the parking lot. I loved seeing big crowds on Easter Sunday and felt that made the experience a special day for everyone else. Besides, I was scheduled to preach on Easter since it was my last Resurrection Sunday, and I didn't relish the idea of preaching once on Friday, twice on Saturday, and three times on Sunday.

I registered my concerns and anticipated a change of plans. My concerns were heard and respected but not followed. There were six services on Easter—and they went well. I learned fast that your influence is not nearly as significant as you once thought when you retire.

I pledged that I would not return to worship service for a year once I left. That proved to be a wise decision. Dave didn't have to worry about me looking over his shoulder and second-guessing any changes that were taking place. For the most part, I tried not to influence the direction of the church. It's similar to the treatment of your kids once they get married. The wisest thing is to keep your mouth shut unless it is to encourage them. I've done all the damage I can do, it's their turn now.

Author: If you were doing it all over again, what would you do differently?
Pastor Bob: We did a lot of things right in passing the baton, but our plan wasn't perfect. There are basically four things I would do differently.

1. I would have been much more aware of how retirement would affect my wife. She also worked at church as the bookstore manager. She loved what she did and hated to leave. She was uncertain what our lives would look like once I retired. I'd be out speaking, and she would go to church alone. Today she loves retirement and wouldn't have it any other way. But I should have been more sensitive to her feelings and taken more time to discuss our future with her thoroughly.

2. I would have scheduled a monthly meeting with Dave after I left. We went separate ways and didn't see each other very often. That made it awkward for me when church members would ask me about recent decisions or the church's future direction. I could have been more supportive and encouraging had we met monthly.

3. I would have taken more time to explain the reason behind certain policies that had been in place for years. For example, I almost insisted we sing at least one hymn or familiar chorus every Sunday. That tradition seemed archaic to my successors, and as soon as I left, the church ceased singing hymns almost totally. The result was many older people, whose antennae were up, felt they were being disrespected and their desires bypassed. I think I could have saved some criticism that hurt Dave if I had done a more thorough job of explaining why that policy was important at the time.

4. We should have been more careful in evaluating the term-limit schedule for elders. The church has a policy that an elder has to roll off the board for at least a year after six years. It just so happened that two or three of the older, more experienced elders rolled off about the same time I retired, and younger, less experienced men surrounded Dave. The newer guys actually did a good job directing the affairs of the church, but the perception on the part of some older members was "There are no adults in the room!" and "The older guys are being pushed out." We could easily have averted that criticism by tweaking the system of rolling off after six years.

Author: Pastor Bob, I've listened to many of your sermons. One of your great gifts is the use of analogy. Is there an analogy that relates to turning over the reins of the church to someone else?
Pastor Bob: There are six essentials in a track meet, all parallel to successfully handing off the ministry to one's successor.

1. The runner carrying the baton must keep going full speed during the transition. He can't let up although he's tired, and his phase of the race is nearly over. He is entering the most crucial phase.
2. The person receiving must begin running prior to the arrival of the one approaching. If he waits until the runner passing the baton is even with him, he'll be bypassed. He must start running before he receives the baton.
3. The two of them must stay in the same lane. A transition will not be effective if the mentor and mentee aren't heading in the same direction.
4. There must be a timely release and reception. The approaching runner yells "Go!" when it's time for the next runner to take off. He then places the baton in the hand extended behind the runner in front of him. When it's in hand the back man yells "Take!" and the transition occurs. One has to release and the other receive at full speed.
5. If that transition is made smoothly, there actually should be a step gained in the race because one is reaching back to receive, the other forward to give.Rick Pitino turned the reins of the University of Kentucky basketball team over to a former assistant, Tubby Smith. The first year Tubby won the national championship. It's great when a step is gained in a transition.
6. Then, the one who passed the baton gets out of the way and roots for the one running. The one who has just passed it doesn't keep running alongside the fresh athlete to coach him or criticize him. He proceeds to the finish line and cheers for the end result. He waits at the end to celebrate victory as a team. Nothing messes up a mentoring friendship or a successful transition like a mentor second-guessing or criticizing.

Pastor Bob captures the essence of leading a succession plan. A few takeaways you don't want to miss are: (1) Bring the authoritative lay church leaders into the decision-making process. Pastor Bob involved his elders. (2) Choose your successor carefully, take as long as necessary to find the right person, and conclude a set of criteria to determine the type of person you're looking for. By having a list of criteria, when questioned, you and your elder team can reveal to concerned congregants that the person you chose exhibited the sought-after characteristics. (3) For a period of time, run the race with the pastor succeeding you. This allows the church to see that the exiting lead pastor is on board with the transition and allows them to still be seen as authoritative as they answer questions of concerned congregants.

Conclusion

I'm writing the conclusion to *The Perpetually Growing Church* on a flight from Detroit, Michigan, to Syracuse, New York. Glancing around me, I see people of all races, ages, genders, and classes. Two rows ahead, a young husband and wife are frantically working to keep their one-and-a-half-year-old from screaming raucously. To my left is a twentysomething cackling loudly while viewing the antics of Will Ferrell on his laptop (headphones keep him from realizing the decibel level of his laughter!). A few rows behind me is a thirtysomething, obviously in the process of transitioning from their God-given gender. Surprisingly, in view is a seventy-something deep into Richard Dawkins's *God Delusion*. And before boarding the plane, I was fascinated by a fellow waiting to board. It was apparent he was dealing with some mental issues. He fidgeted uncontrollably, looked suspicious when I spoke to him (without making eye contact or responding), and spent time pacing back and forth, mumbling while waiting for the on-time flight to board. And finally, a well-dressed Midwestern family of four boarded just before me.

These few represent hundreds aboard this Delta Airlines flight. The hundreds on this flight represent the makeup of the city we'll be landing in. The city we land in represents the state of New York. The state of New York represents the nation. And the nation represents the world.

Every person on planet earth needs the power of the gospel. Sadly, many, maybe most people will never hear the eternally transforming gospel message. They won't be exposed to the most potent story ever told, the story of Jesus's life, death, and resurrection, because the churches nearest them are hesitant to or unwilling to put church-growth practices into play or are ignorant of these practices. Internal pressures override the needs of lost people with hell as their future eternal address.

A pastor longs to make the necessary changes to reach the next generation, but fear of a few influential, aging church members overrides his heart's desire. A church needs to invest in more staff, but a vision-less chairperson dominates the lay-led finance team. A lead pastor is exhausted, depressed, and ready to leave the ministry. He needs to recruit a secondary teaching pastor, but when approaching the elders, he is told, "That's your job. Trust God. He'll give you the energy you need." A worship center desperately needs renovation, but the majority of the church membership will vote against the motion because a charter member's donated pulpit will be removed. A worship service uses worship songs from the 1970s, '80s, and '90s, and hymns from the 1800s and 1900s exclusively, accompanied by a piano and organ. The congregation is made up of believers in their sixties, seventies, and eighties. They are content to "sing the old songs" with no sense of responsibility to make changes to reach the next generation. And the list could go on and on.

Pastor, lay church leader, the eternal destiny of the masses must take precedence over the likes, dislikes, and preferences of the already convinced. Too often, status-quo church members view church-growth principles and practices as ways to make life easier for the church's staff team, opportunities for the lead pastor to grow "his audience," or as gimmicks that diminish the gospel.

Nothing could be further from the truth! When in play and coming from a church leader passionate to see people experience the power of the gospel, church-growth principles and practices are the avenues to creating a church that ensures the power of the cross is declared to the unconvinced masses. Do a deep dive into perpetually growing churches, as I have done. You'll find that perpetually growing churches are reaching and baptizing a nearly unprecedented number of far-from-Christ people.

Some congregations will wince at the thought of putting church-growth ideas into play. If that's your church, I pray you will lead them to embrace a mantra iterated by some of the pastors quoted or interviewed for this book, "We will do anything short of sin to reach people for Christ."

Appendix 1

Employee Application Form

North Point Ministries, Inc.

Date Submitted: _____

Date Available: _____

Name: _____
FIRST   MIDDLE   LAST

PERSONAL DATA

Home Address: _____
STREET   CITY   STATE   ZIP

Telephone:_____
HOME   CELL

Email:_____

Are you 18 years or older? ___ YES ___ NO

Position or type of work desired: _____

Availability: _____ Full-Time _____ Part-Time _____

Temporary Date: _____

Have you been employed by North Point Ministries, Inc., before?

_____ YES _____ NO

Current Church Affiliation: _____

Positions of service or leadership held in that church: _____

_____

Are you ordained or commissioned _____ YES _____ NO

If so, by whom?_____

If employed will you be able to produce evidence that you are eligible for employment in the United States? _____ YES _____ NO

Will you now or in the future require sponsorship for employment visa status? _____ YES _____ NO

Have you ever been convicted of a crime other than a minor traffic violation? _____ YES _____ NO

If yes, please explain:_____

EDUCATIONAL EXPERIENCE

School	Location	Dates Attended	Graduated	Course of Study

List any additional training or experience you have that qualifies you for the position you are seeking, including professional licenses or certifications.

_____
_____

EMPLOYMENT HISTORY

List your last three employers, assignments, or volunteer activities, including any military experience, starting with the most recent:

1. Employer: _____ Address: _____
Position: _____ Supervisor & Title: _____ Phone: _____
Dates Employed: _____ Starting Salary: _____ Ending Salary: _____
Reason for leaving: _____
Summary of responsibilities: _____

2. Employer: _____ Address: _____
Position: _____ Supervisor & Title: _____ Phone: _____
Dates Employed: _____ Starting Salary: _____ Ending Salary: _____
Reason for leaving: _____
Summary of responsibilities: _____

3. Employer: ———————————— Address: ————————————
Position: ——————— Supervisor & Title: ——————— Phone: ———————
Dates Employed: _____ Starting Salary: _____ Ending Salary: _____
Reason for leaving: ————————————————————————
Summary of responsibilities: ————————————————————

PERSONAL REFERENCES
(Not relatives and preferably at least one member from this church)

1. Name: ——————————— 2. Name: ————————————
Address: ——————————— Address: ————————————
——————————————— ————————————————
Telephone: ——————————— Telephone: ————————————

APPLICATION STATEMENT

I understand and agree that any misrepresentation by me in this application will be grounds for immediate termination if I have been employed. I give North Point Ministries, Inc., the right to investigate all references and to secure additional information about me, if job related. I hereby release from liability North Point Ministries, Inc., and its representatives for seeking such information and all other persons, corporations, or organizations for furnishing such information. I understand that a criminal background check will be conducted on me as part of the application process and I consent to any such check. I also understand that I may be required to have a physical examination, including drug screen.

Should employment result from this, I understand that I will be required to provide documentation to establish identity and employment eligibility. I understand that just as I am free to resign at any time, North Point Ministries, Inc., reserves the right to terminate my employment at any time, with or without cause and without prior notice. I understand that no representative of North Point Ministries, Inc., has the authority to make any assurances to the contrary. Furthermore, I agree to abide by the ministry guidelines and requirements of North Point Ministries, Inc., and to refrain from any unscriptural conduct in the performance of my services on behalf of the church. I hereby attest that I am of good moral character.

Signature of Applicant:_____ Date: _____

Appendix 2

Acceptance of Terms

North Point Ministries, Inc.

I, _____, agree to abide by the policies and provisions set forth in North Point Ministries, Inc., Personnel Policy Manual. I understand that modifications may be made in the future and that the most current copy is available to me anytime at www.npmstaff.org.

_____ Employee's Signature

_____ Date

Appendix 3

Job Classification Worksheet

North Point Ministries, Inc.

for the position of

_____

Influence

(250 points maximum)

Non-managerial Staff	0–50	Staff Leadership Team	200	
Department Director	100	Pastor	250	
Division Coordinator	150			Number of Points: _____

Responsibility for funds & property

(100 points maximum)

Dollar Amount	Points	Dollar Amount	Points	
$0–100,000	10	$500,001–600,000	60	
$100,001–200,000	20	$600,001–700,000	70	

$200,001–300,000	30	$700,001–800,000	80	
$300,001–400,000	40	$800,001–900,000	90	
$400,001–500,000	50	$900,001–1,000,000	100	Number of Points: _____

Professional considerations

(100 points maximum)

> Job-related skills or market considerations unique to this position
> Number of Points: _____

Number of divisions managed

(100 points maximum)

> 25 points per division managed directly
> Number of Points: _____

Number of departments managed

(100 points maximum)

> 20 points per department managed directly
> Number of Points: _____

Number of employees managed

(100 points maximum)

> 15 points per employee managed directly
> Number of Points: _____

Number of volunteers involved

(100 points maximum)

> 0.5 point per volunteer involved in ministry area
> Number of Points: _____

Education

(100 points maximum)

High school graduate	20	College graduate (mandatory)	60	
Some college courses	40	Master's degree	80	
Doctoral degree	100			Number of Points: _____

Experience

(100 points maximum)

No experience	0	Five to eight years	60	
Zero to two years	20	Eight to twelve years	80	
Two to five years	40	More than twelve years	100	Number of Points: _____

Special considerations

(100 points maximum)

Special Abilities   0-50   Number of Points: _____
(Music, Drama, Speaking/
Teaching, Technical)

Total points for this position   Number of Points: _____

Job Grade   _____

Appendix 4

Hiring Statement

North Point Ministries, Inc.

(To be completed by Hiring Manager)

Department _____ Hire Date _____

Employee's Full Name _____

Address _____

City _____ State _____ Zip Code _____

Social Security # _____ Date of Birth _____

Cell Phone _____ Home Phone _____

Gender _____ Email Address _____

Job Title _____

Status (full-time or part-time) _____

Number of hours per week _____

To be paid hourly or salary? _____

College Graduate? _____

Commissioned or Ordained Approved by HR? _____

Annual salary or hourly rate _____

Vacation, if different from policy _____

Name of Supervisor _____

References checked? _____ Interviewed by _____

Approved by: _____
(NPM Leadership or Lead Pastor signature)

Please complete and return to HR Assistant

Gross Pay per Period _____
Filing Status: <u>Single or Married</u>
Federal Exemptions: _____ State Exemptions _____ A, B, C, or D Medical _____ Dental _____ Vision _____ LTD _____ FSA _____ Vol. Life _____ Labor Distribution % at BBC _____ BC _____ DCC _____ GC _____ NPCC _____
NPM _____ NPR _____ WC _____
Paycom File #: _____

Appendix 5

The Village Church's Survey

Survey Introduction

In the last five years, The Village Church has navigated numerous changes. We rolled off our five campuses as autonomous churches and embraced a mission and vision as one church body in one location. We journeyed together through a global pandemic, pivoting aspects of our ministry philosophy to reach both the live and digital audiences. We've said "gospel goodbyes" to longtime members as the Lord called them elsewhere, and we've given a warm welcome to over twelve hundred new members and countless visitors.

As we look to the future together, we want to take a pulse to understand more about those who call The Village Church their home—that's you! We want to know where you are finding community and spiritual formation within TVC's ministries, how you're using your gifts for kingdom impact, and how we might serve you better.

It is a joy to serve you and to serve *with* you in this ministry work.

Every day, in all spaces, through each season of life, we are building beyond ourselves, living the greater story together, and creating a kingdom legacy for generations to come.

—TVC 2030 Vision

Survey Questions

Demographics

1. Age

    ___ 16–19
    ___ 20–24
    ___ 25–29
    ___ 30–34
    ___ 35–39
    ___ 40–44
    ___ 45–49
    ___ 50–54
    ___ 55–59
    ___ 60–64
    ___ 65–69
    ___ 70–74
    ___ 75–79
    ___ 80–84
    ___ 85 or over

2. Gender

    ___ Male
    ___ Female

3. Full Address: _____

4. What is your ethnicity?

    ___ White
    ___ Hispanic or Latino / Latina
    ___ Black or African American
    ___ Native American or American Indian
    ___ Asian / Pacific Islander
    ___ Indian
    ___ Other
    ___ I'd prefer not to answer this question.

5. Which of the following best describes your current occupation?

  ___ Community and Social Services

  ___ Business and Financial Operations

  ___ Education, Training, and Library

  ___ Architecture and Engineering

  ___ Construction and Extraction

  ___ Office and Administrative Support

  ___ Installation, Maintenance, and Repair

  ___ Protective Services

  ___ Food Preparation and Serving

  ___ Healthcare Practitioners

  ___ Sales and Marketing

  ___ Management

  ___ Computer and Mathematical

  ___ Life, Physical, and Social Sciences

  ___ Legal

  ___ Building and Grounds Cleaning and Maintenance

  ___ Farming, Fishing, and Forestry

  ___ Arts, Design, Entertainment, Sports, and Media

  ___ Personal Care and Service

  ___ Production

  ___ Transportation and Materials Moving

  ___ Non-Profit/Ministry

  ___ Stay at home

  ___ Unemployed

  ___ Other

6. What is your marital status?

  ___ Single (never married)

  ___ Engaged

  ___ Married

  ___ Remarried (after being widowed or divorced)

  ___ Widowed

  ___ Divorced

  ___ Separated

7. If you have children, please choose their age ranges and if they do or do not participate in the church ministry for their specific age range. (Mark all that apply.)

    ___ Birth–Kindergarten (Little Village)

        ___ Yes, he or she participates.

        ___ No, he or she does not participate.

    ___ 1st–5th grade (Kids Village)

        ___ Yes, he or she participates.

        ___ No, he or she does not participate.

    ___ 6th–8th grade (Middle School Ministry)

        ___ Yes, he or she participates.

        ___ No, he or she does not participate.

    ___ 9th–12th grade (High School Ministry)

        ___ Yes, he or she participates.

        ___ No, he or she does not participate.

    ___ Young Adult Ministry (post–high school, early adulthood)

        ___ Yes, he or she participates.

        ___ No, he or she does not participate.

    ___ I do not have children in these age ranges.

8. How long have you been attending The Village Church?

    ___ Less than 6 months

    ___ 6 months–1 year

    ___ 1–3 years

    ___ 3–5 years

    ___ 5–7 years

    ___ 7–10 years

    ___ 10+ years

9. How often do you attend The Village Church?

    ___ Every Sunday

    ___ 2–3 times a month

    ___ Once a month

    ___ Once a quarter

    ___ 2–3 times a year

10. If married, does your spouse attend The Village Church with you?

     ___ Yes, almost every time I attend

     ___ Yes, but only half the times I attend (or less)

     ___ No

     ___ I am not married.

11. What is the primary way you attend services at The Village Church?

     ___ In person

     ___ Streaming online

     ___ Evenly between online and in person

12. Are you a follower of Jesus Christ?

     ___ Yes

     ___ No

     ___ Not sure

13. Are you a member of The Village Church?

     ___ Yes

     ___ No

     ___ Not sure

Communication

14. How often do you visit The Village Church website (thevillagechurch.net)?

     ___ Daily

     ___ Weekly

     ___ Monthly

     ___ Rarely

     ___ Never

15. Are you receiving The Village News emails?

     ___ Yes, and I read them regularly.

     ___ Yes, and I occasionally read them.

     ___ Yes, but I don't read them.

     ___ I didn't know TVC sends out a newsletter.

     ___ No

16. What is your level of engagement with The Village Church on the following social media channels?

Facebook

___ Daily

___ Weekly

___ Monthly

___ Rarely

___ Never

Instagram

___ Daily

___ Weekly

___ Monthly

___ Rarely

___ Never

17. How often do you use The Village Church mobile app?

___ Daily

___ Weekly

___ Monthly

___ Rarely

___ Never

18. If you are a member, how often do you join our virtual Member Meeting (usually once per month)?

___ A majority of the time

___ Occasionally

___ Rarely

___ Never

___ I am not a member.

19. How often do you use resources provided by The Village Church, such as podcasts, guides, forum recordings, or past sermons or studies?

___ Weekly

___ 2–3 times a month

___ Once a month

___ Once a quarter

___ 2–3 times a year

___ Never

___ I didn't know you provided resources.

Financial Questions

20. Do you give financially to The Village Church?
    ___ Yes
    ___ No

21. How often do you give?
    ___ Every week
    ___ Twice a month
    ___ Once a month
    ___ Once a quarter
    ___ Whenever I can

22. Do you give financially to other ministries or nonprofits?
    ___ Yes
    ___ No

Connection & Community

23. In the past year, I have **participated** in the following (check all that apply):
    ___ The Art of Care
    ___ Baptism Class
    ___ Business as Mission Class
    ___ Domain
    ___ Encounter
    ___ Family Discipleship Milestones (Milestone Blessings, ID Retreats, Family Retreat, etc.)
    ___ Family Retreat
    ___ First Steps
    ___ Go Trip (Short-Term Mission Trip)
    ___ Goer Missional Community
    ___ Home Groups
    ___ LifePlan Retreat
    ___ Marriage Retreat
    ___ Membership Class
    ___ Women's Praxis Group
    ___ The Mission of God Class
    ___ Outreach Training

___ Preschool Storytime
___ Recovery Groups
___ Senior Adults Live Well Lunch
___ Steps Class
___ Student Ministry (for student-aged survey participants only)
___ Transformational Leadership Community
___ TVC Institute Bible Study or Core Class
___ TVC Institute Residency Program
___ TVC Institute Training Program
___ VBS
___ Young Adult events (Hangs, Practice Group, Summer Nights, Talks)
___ None of these

24. Have you found it easy or difficult to **participate** in a ministry at The Village Church?
___ Extremely easy
___ Relatively easy
___ Relatively difficult
___ Extremely difficult
___ Depends on the ministry
___ Describe your answer: _____

25. In the past year, I have **volunteered** in the following ministries at The Village Church (check all that apply):
___ Care/Recovery
___ Communications
___ Connections (Greeters, Ushers, Communion, Shuttles, Parking, Classes, Translation, etc.)
___ Family Ministry
    ___ Young Adults
    ___ Marriage
    ___ Senior Adults
___ Facilities
___ Home Groups
___ Next Gen
    ___ Little Village (Birth–Kindergarten)
    ___ Kids Village (1st–5th grade)

___ Middle School (6th–8th grade)

___ High School (9th–12th grade)

___ Production

___ Security/Safety

___ Sending

    ___ Church Planting

    ___ Global Missions

    ___ Local Missions

___ TVC Institute (Training Program, Men's or Women's Bible Studies, Core Classes)

___ TVC Leadership (TLC, Domain Workshop, Prayer)

___ TVC ministry partner or affiliation (YoungLives, Communities in Schools, Embrace Grace, Blue Haven Ranch, etc.)

___ Worship

___ None of these

26. Have you found it easy or difficult to get plugged in as a **volunteer** within a ministry at The Village Church?

    ___ Extremely easy

    ___ Relatively easy

    ___ Relatively difficult

    ___ Extremely difficult

    ___ Depends on the ministry

    ___ Describe your answer: _____

27. On a scale of 1–5, how well connected do you feel with others from The Village Church?

    ___ 1—little to no sense of connection

    ___ 2—little sense of connection

    ___ 3—a moderate sense of connection

    ___ 4—a moderate to deep sense of connection

    ___ 5—a deep sense of connection

28. Have you found it easy or difficult to connect with *(to access or receive a response from or follow up from)* ministry leadership or staff within the ministry in which you serve or participate?

___ Extremely easy

___ Relatively easy

___ Relatively difficult

___ Extremely difficult

___ Depends on the ministry

___ Describe your answer: _____

Spiritual Growth

29. In the past year, on a scale of 1–5, how much spiritual growth have you experienced through the ministries of The Village Church?

___ 1—little to no growth

___ 2—little to moderate growth

___ 3—moderate growth

___ 4—moderate to extreme growth

___ 5—an exponential amount of growth

30. In the past year, on a scale of 1–5, how much growth have you experienced in your ability to understand the Bible?

___ 1—little to no growth

___ 2—little to moderate growth

___ 3—moderate growth

___ 4—moderate to extreme growth

___ 5—an exponential amount of growth

31. In the past year, on a scale of 1–5, how much growth have you experienced in your ability to understand Christian belief (faith, doctrine, theology)?

___ 1—little to no growth

___ 2—little to moderate growth

___ 3—moderate growth

___ 4—moderate to extreme growth

___ 5—an exponential amount of growth

32. What are the top three avenues that have contributed most to your spiritual growth this past year? (Select up to three.)

___ Involvement within community at The Village Church (such as Home Groups, Men's or Women's Bible Study, ministry small groups, roundtable events, forums, etc.).

___ Involvement within care environments at The Village Church (such as Recovery Groups, The Art of Care, Encounter, mentorship and advocacy, etc.).

___ Consistent Bible study

___ Consistent prayer

___ Short-term mission trip

___ Serving

___ Sunday worship services

___ Personal relationships

___ Other forms of participation within The Village Church

33. If your children attend regularly in our Next Generation ministries (preschool through high school), how helpful has that experience been in aiding their spiritual growth over the last year?

___ 1—Not helpful

___ 2—Somewhat helpful

___ 3—Helpful

___ 4—Very helpful

___ 5—Extremely helpful

___ 6—My children do not attend Next Gen ministries.

34. In the past year, has someone talked to you about your spiritual growth at The Village Church?

___ Yes

___ No

35. How confident are you when sharing the gospel?

___ 1—I don't know the gospel.

___ 2—I know the gospel, but I don't know how to share the gospel with others.

___ 3—I know the gospel, but I am too nervous to share the gospel with others.

___ 4—I share the gospel occasionally.

___ 5—I actively share the gospel in my sphere of influence (e.g., school, workplace, etc.).

36. How often do you spend time reading the Bible?
    ___ Daily
    ___ Weekly
    ___ Occasionally
    ___ Rarely

37. How often do you spend time in prayer?
    ___ Daily
    ___ Weekly
    ___ Occasionally
    ___ Rarely

38. What are your primary spiritual gifts? (Choose up to three.)
    ___ Administration—Bringing order to organize and make some sense out of guiding ministries of the church.
    ___ Apostleship—Apostle is a designation of the original twelve apostles; a gift of apostleship is not an office in the church but is now most often "one who is sent" to deliver the gospel in a particularly difficult area that has never heard or is historically resistant to the good news of Jesus.
    ___ Discernment—Those with the gift of discerning spirits have the ability to sense the deceptive work of the Enemy and his followers.
    ___ Discipling—Admonishing that leads people to become all they are meant to become in Christ.
    ___ Encouragement—Admonishing that leads people to become all they are meant to become in Christ.
    ___ Evangelism—The ability to proclaim the gospel and lead more people to Christ than is normal.
    ___ Faith—Supernatural confidence in God through prayer and understanding.
    ___ Giving—Sacrificially giving of time, talents, and money to build up the church.
    ___ Healing—Divine health interventions, which are inexplicable if left to natural causes.
    ___ Hospitality—Often the first to volunteer, those with gifts of hospitality or help are empowered to be happier giving in effective service rather than receiving.
    ___ Knowledge—Ability to relate the Scriptures, and particularly the Gospel of Jesus Christ, to all aspects of life in this world.

___ Leadership—The ability to create unity, good decisions, and clarity of mission and direction.

___ Mercy—Showing supernatural compassion to the disenfranchised and marginalized.

___ Prophecy—Receiving a revelatory message from the Lord and communicating it.

___ Service—Supernaturally empowered by the Spirit that makes a way for people to hear and receive gospel ministry.

___ Shepherding—Protect the flock, guide, provide a stellar example of Christlikeness, and exhort the flock by communicating sound biblical truth in action.

___ Teaching—Communicating biblical truth and sound doctrine in a way that is comprehended and bears fruit in the lives of hearers.

___ Tongues (Speaker)—Spoken speech either in languages never studied by the speaker in order to declare the gospel (Acts 2:11) or in coded messages that speak to God or reveal mysteries by the Spirit (1 Corinthians 14:2).

___ Tongues (Interpreter)—Enabled by the Spirit to decode the message given through a tongue or tongues speech, be it in a human language never studied by them or in a coded heavenly language no one could understand apart from interpretation.

___ Wisdom—Not only to impart the truth and understanding to believers, but to invoke a response of holiness and worship lived out in the world and among God's people.

___ Unknown, but I am interested in learning more.

39. Do you have a clear understanding and pathway for how you can use your spiritual gifts at The Village Church?

___ Yes, I am currently using my spiritual gifts within The Village Church.

___ Yes, but I am not currently using my spiritual gifts within The Village Church.

___ No, I do not know how I can use my spiritual gifts within The Village Church.

___ No, I am currently unaware of my spiritual gifts.

40. If there is anything you wish to add or any responses you wish to expand upon, please add your comments here.

Notes

2. A Diverse People

1. Rightnowmedia, Bob Russell, accessed December 10, 2021. Accessed August 23, 2023, from the Internet Archive, https://web.archive.org/web/20210226222259 /https://www.rightnowmedia.org/Content/Speaker/999914.

3. Visionary

1. Rick Warren, *The Purpose Driven Church* (Grand Rapids, MI: Zondervan, 1995), 43.
2. Warren, *Purpose Driven Church*, 43.

4. Leader

1. John Maxwell, *Developing the Leader Within You* (Nashville: Thomas Nelson, 1993), viii.

5. Clarity Producer

1. Will Mancini, "Craig Groeschel Rearticulates the Core Values for LifeChurch. tv," *Will Mancini, Clarity Changes Everything* (blog), April 15, 2010, https:// www.willmancini.com/blog/craig-groeschel-rearticulates-the-core-values-for -lifechurch-tv.

6. Culture Creator

1. *Merriam-Webster Online*, s.v. "culture," https://www.merriam-webster.com /dictionary/culture.
2. The Bridge Church, "Our Culture," accessed October 9, 2021. Accessed August 23, 2023, from the Internet Archive, https://web.archive.org/web/20210725064459 /https://bridge.tv/our-culture/.
3. The Bridge Church, "Our Culture."
4. Eric Geiger, "Six Important and Impactful Quotes from Leaders," *Eric Geiger* (blog), https://ericgeiger.com/2018/03/6-important-and-impactful-quotes-from -leaders/.

9. Strategic Risk-Taker

1. "How the Best Leaders Think, Part 3, Think Investment No Spending," *Craig Groeschel Leadership Podcast*, episode 91, https://api-assets.life.church/uploads

/message/1829/podcast_show_notes/part-three-think-investment-not-spending
.pdf.

10. Team Builder

1. "Principles of Higher Hiring, Part 1, Episode Notes," *Craig Groeschel Leadership Podcast*, episode 19, https://api-assets.life.church/uploads/message/658/podcast _show_notes/principles-of-higher-hiring-part-1.pdf.
2. Rick Howerton, *Lead to Revitalize* (Abbotsford, WI: Aneko, 2020), 61.
3. Ministry Insights, accessed October 30, 2021, https://www.ministryinsights.com /about-us/ministry-insights/.
4. Clifton Strengths, accessed October 30, 2021, https://www.gallup.com /cliftonstrengths/en/253715/34-cliftonstrengths-themes.aspx.
5. RightPath Resources, accessed October 30, 2021, https://www.rightpath.com /path4-path6/.
6. unremot, Culture Index Survey, accessed November 14, 2021, https://unremot .com/blog/culture-index-survey/#What_is_the_culture_index.

11. Team Keeper

1. If you want to learn more about Gary Chapman's five love languages, see https://5lovelanguages.com/.
2. Larry Osborn, *Sticky Teams* (Grand Rapids, MI: Zondervan, 2010), 186.
3. Osborn, *Sticky Teams*, 186.
4. Osborn, *Sticky Teams*, 188.
5. Gary L. McIntosh and Charles Arn, *What Every Pastor Should Know* (Grand Rapids, MI: Baker Books, 2013), 164.
6. 4Sight Group, Discover Your Pathway to Success, https://www.get4sight.com/.

12. Evolving Role-Player

1. Dr. Tim Keller, *Leadership and Church Size Dynamics* (redeemercitytocity.com, March 2, 2010), 6.
2. Keller, *Leadership and Church Size Dynamics*, 7.
3. Keller, *Leadership and Church Size Dynamics*, 9.
4. Keller, *Leadership and Church Size Dynamics*, 10.
5. Keller, *Leadership and Church Size Dynamics*, 13–14.

13. Culturally Captivating Communicator

1. Dave Stone, *Refining Your Style* (Loveland, CO: Group, 2004), 8.
2. Stone, *Refining Your Style*, 8.

3. Baptist and Reflector, "David Landrith Dies After Bout with Cancer," November 18, 2014, https://baptistandreflector.org/david-landrith-dies-after-bout-with-cancer/.

14. Fund-Raiser

1. Aubrey Malphurs and Steve Stroope, *Money Matters in Church* (Grand Rapids, MI: Baker Books, 2007), 13.
2. Malphurs and Stroope, *Money Matters in Church*, 29–30.
3. Lifeway.generosity, accessed October 23, 2021, https://lifewaygenerosity.com/.
4. Malphurs and Stroope, *Money Matters in Church*, 40.

15. Virtuous Undershepherd

1. Rick Warren, "10 Commandments to Help Church Maintain Moral Integrity," Pastors.com, April 25, 2017.

16. Long-Timer

1. Rick Warren, *The Purpose Driven Church* (Grand Rapids, MI: Zondervan, 1995), 31–32.

Section 2: Principles and Practices of Perpetually Growing Churches

1. Larry Osborne, *Sticky Church* (Grand Rapids, MI: Zondervan, 2008), 17–18.

17. Revolutionary Relevance

1. Thom Schultz, "The Church's Frightful Kodak Moment," HolySoup.com, January 15, 2014, https://holysoup.com/the-churchs-frightful-kodak-moment/.
2. Tim Keller, *Preaching* (New York: Penguin Random House, 2015), 18–19.
3. *Merriam-Webster Online*, s.v. "branding," accessed December 7, 2021, https://www.merriam-webster.com/dictionary/branding.
4. "100 Fastest-Growing Churches, 2022," *Outreach 100*, https://outreach100.com/fastest-growing-churches-in-america/2022.
5. Catherine Marshall, *A Man Called Peter* (Wheaton, IL: Evergreen Farm, 2013), 161.

18. Centralized Decision-Making

1. Wayne Grudem, *Systematic Theology* (Grand Rapids, MI: Zondervan, 1994), 935.

21. Uncomplicated Group Ministry

1. Steve Gladen, *Small Groups with Purpose* (Grand Rapids, MI: Baker Books, 2011), 210.

2. Gladen, *Small Groups with Purpose*, 160.

3. Andy Stanley and Bill Willits, *Creating Community* (Colorado Springs: Multnomah, 2004), 152–53.

4. Gladen, *Small Groups with Purpose*, 30–31.

22. Three Essential Systems

1. Nelson Searcy, *Fusion* (Grand Rapids, MI: Baker Books, 2017), 55.

2. Chris Hodges, *What's Next?* (Nashville: Nelson Books, 2019), ix–x.

3. Church of the Highlands, About, https://www.churchofthehighlands.com/about.

4. Mac Lake, *The Multiplication Effect* (Nashville: Thomas Nelson, 2020), 66–67.

5. Lake, *Multiplication Effect*, 70.

6. Lake, *Multiplication Effect*, 79.

7. Life.Church, Life.Church Central Internship, accessed November 28, 2021, https://www.life.church/careers/internships/.

8. Summit Institute, Internships, accessed November 28, 2021, https://summitrduinstitute.com/internships/.

9. Elevation Church, Details, accessed November 28, 2021, https://elevationchurch.org/internships/details/.

10. N/P, North Point Intern Experience, accessed November 28, 2021, https://npleadershipexperience.com/internship.

23. Multisite Church

1. Geoff Surratt, Greg Ligon, and Warren Bird, *The Multi-Site Church Revolution* (Grand Rapids, MI: Zondervan, 2006), 28.

2. "2023 Largest Participating Churches," *Outreach 100*, accessed January 26, 2023, https://outreach100.com/largest-churches-in-america.

3. Ed Stetzer, "Trends in Big Church Buildings," *Church Leaders*, accessed November 30, 2021, https://churchleaders.com/pastors/pastor-blogs/170363-trends-in-big-church-buildings.html.

4. Larry Osborne, "Multisite Churches: Two Things Nobody Seems to Have Noticed," *Larry Osborne* (blog), accessed December 5, 2021, https://larryosborne.com/multisite-churches-two-things-no-one-seems-to-have-noticed/.

24. Exploiting Social Media

1. "Social Media Use in 2021," Pew Research Center, April 7, 2021, accessed December 22, 2021, https://www.pewresearch.org/internet/2021/04/07/social-media-use-in-2021/.

2. "Social Media Use in 2021."

3. "Social Media Use in 2021."

4. "Social Media Use in 2021."

5. "Distribution of Twitter users worldwide as of April 2021, by age group," *Statista*, accessed December 22, 2021, https://www.statista.com/statistics/283119/age -distribution-of-global-twitter-users/.

26. Foresighted Succession Plan

1. Bob Russell, *When God Builds a Church* (West Monroe, LA: Howard, 2000), 91.

2. Russell, *When God Builds a Church*, 89.

3. Michael Duduit, "Passing the Baton: An Interview with Bob Russell and Dave Stone," *Preaching*, accessed December 13, 2021, https://www.preaching.com /articles/passing-the-baton-an-interview-with-bob-russell-and-dave-stone/.

Perpetually Growing Consulting and Coaching

At Perpetually Growing Consulting and Coaching, our heartfelt mission is to help your church or Christian camp bring its vision to life. PGCC provides the following opportunities:

Consulting—We collaborate closely with you to craft a personalized consulting experience tailored to your specific needs and the needs of your leadership team. Our consulting approach comprises regular scheduled calls with the flexibility to incorporate on-site visits as required.

Coaching—We offer monthly coaching sessions, which can be conducted either online or in person, for church ministry leaders and Christian camp employees. The duration and frequency of these sessions are tailored to the specific requirements and objectives of those being coached.

Cohorts—We facilitate regional and online cohorts to equip pastors, church staff members, camp directors and camp staff, and lay volunteers to accomplish their ministry with understanding and excellence.

Trainings—We are available to facilitate training sessions for pastors, church staff members, Christian camp staff, and volunteers, offering a flexible range of half-day to three-day immersive training experiences.

Rick Howerton is the cofounder of Perpetually Growing Consulting and Coaching. For more than thirty years, Rick has consulted churches, coached church leaders, trained teams, and authored resources and books. He planted The Bridge Church in Spring Hill, Tennessee, and served as a church consultant for LifeWay Church Resources, NavPress publishing, and the Kentucky Baptist Convention. Rick is presently the Global Groups Pastor for LakePointe Church in Rockwall, Texas, a church of seven campuses in two countries, with a weekend attendance of more than twenty-two thousand.

A few of the books Rick has authored or coauthored include

The Perpetually Growing Church

Lead to Revitalize! 15 Practices of a Church Revitalization Leader

A Different Kind of Tribe: Embracing the New Small Group Dynamic

Destination Community: Small Group Ministry Manual

The Deacon Ministry Handbook: A Practical Guide for Servant Leadership

Rick has dedicated his life to aiding churches in discipling the membership, creating off-the-chart leaders, coaching pastors, and building and using effective systems.

Rick believes every church can be a perpetually growing church.

Lance Howerton is the cofounder of Perpetually Growing Consulting and Coaching. With more than thirty years of leadership experience in camps, events, and Christian publishing, Lance has demonstrated exceptional expertise in managing large teams and budgets. His track record includes overseeing more than sixty full-time employees and a $40 million budget, as well as managing twenty-four summer camps across the United States and Europe. With a strong background in business, marketing, and leadership, Lance played a pivotal role in the remarkable growth of LifeWay camps, increasing the number of students from thirty-seven thousand to more than eighty-seven thousand. He also oversaw the development of The Gospel Project for Kids and Bible Studies for Life curricula and provided leadership to national events. Additionally, Lance served on the Executive Leadership Team of LifeWay's Church Resource Division. He currently serves as the president of Crossings Ministries. Under Lance's leadership, Crossings has seen a 47-percent growth.

To contact Perpetually Growing Consulting and Coaching, email:

Rick Howerton at rick.pgcc@gmail.com

Lance Howerton at lance.pgcc@gmail.com

Bible
Experiences
Tours

A few years back, Rick Howerton made a transformative journey to Israel. He passionately believes that every believer, given the opportunity to tread in the footsteps of Jesus and where the church found its roots, would be profoundly inspired in their faith by making a journey of this nature themselves. Whether you're a pastor eager to lead your church membership or an individual intrigued by the idea of this remarkable trip, reach out to Rick at Rick@AdventureBibleTours.com to explore the possibilities.

Milton Keynes UK
Ingram Content Group UK Ltd.
UKHW050811010724
444982UK00015B/1181

9 781563 096785